HUMPHREY JENNINGS

HUMPHREY JENNINGS—

More Than a Maker of Films

ANTHONY W. HODGKINSON
and RODNEY E. SHERATSKY

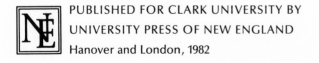

PUBLISHED FOR CLARK UNIVERSITY BY
UNIVERSITY PRESS OF NEW ENGLAND
Hanover and London, 1982

UNIVERSITY PRESS OF NEW ENGLAND

BRANDEIS UNIVERSITY   UNIVERSITY OF NEW HAMPSHIRE

BROWN UNIVERSITY   UNIVERSITY OF RHODE ISLAND

CLARK UNIVERSITY   TUFTS UNIVERSITY

DARTMOUTH COLLEGE   UNIVERSITY OF VERMONT

The publisher gratefully acknowledges the support of the Andrew W. Mellon Foundation in the publication of this book.

Stills from *The First Days*, *London Can Take It*, and *Spare Time* are copyright The British Post Office and reproduced by their kind permission. Still from *The Cumberland Story*, *A Diary for Timothy*, *Dim Little Island*, *The Eighty Days*, *A Family Portrait*, *Heart of Britain*, *Listen to Britain*, *The Silent Village*, and *Words for Battle* are reproduced by permission of David Ellender, Central Office of Information, London. "Humphrey Jennings" by Paul Eluard copyright Editions Gallimard 1939 is reprinted by permission of the publisher. "I See London," "The Plough," "The Procession," and "War and Childhood," are copyright Mary-Lou Jennings and appear by her kind permission. Stills from *The Birth of the Robot* are reproduced by the kind permission of Shell U.K. Limited. Jennings's *The House in the Woods* reproduced by permission of The Tate Gallery, London.

Printed in the United States of America

LIBRARY OF CONGRESS CATALOGING IN PUBLICATION DATA

Hodgkinson, Anthony W., 1916–
   Humphrey Jennings—more than a maker of films

   Filmography: p.
   Bibliography: p.
   Includes index.
   1. Jennings, Humphrey. I. Sheratsky, Rodney E. II. Title.
PN1998.A3J463   1982   791.43'023'0924   81-69942
ISBN 0-87451-226-3

TO PHYLLIS,
the most cheerful and supportive Anglo-American we'll
ever know

HUMPHREY JENNINGS
—Paul Eluard

Sous un ciel noir des maisons noires des tisons éteints
Et toi ta tête dure
La Bouche fléchissante
La Chevelure humide
Des roses fortes dans le sang
Désespérant d'un jour infini blond et brun
Tu brises les couleurs gelées
Tu troubles le sillage du diamant

Une barque d'ambre à trois rames
Creuse la mare du désert
Le vent s'étale sur la mousse
Un soir entier soutient l'aurore
Le mouvement a des racines
L'immobile croît et fleurit.

(1938)

Under a black sky there are black houses and extinguished
   logs
And you with that determined look
That melancholy mouth
That mane of wet hair
Those red, red roses in your blood
Greatly hoping to capture some bright infinity
You have broken solid forms
You have altered a diamond's pattern

An amber-colored boat with three oars
Plows the pool of the desert
The wind spreads out over the foam
One whole evening sustains the dawn
Movement has roots
That which is immobile grows and blooms.

(trans. James A. Chiara)

WALBERSWICK

—*Humphrey Jennings*

The lavender in pewter jugs,
Upon the window-sill,
The heather in the stoneware mugs,
We gathered on the hill;
The tall and laughing hollyhocks
I see them, smell them, still.

For it is always in that place;
For me, September days
When every flower has a face
Parcht
Torn and yet smiling, pollenless
Along the garden ways.

And the summer, yes, the summer
Is coming once again . . .
Let summer pass, then I'll go back
To garden, lane and fen;
I'll live among the hollyhocks,
And throw away the pen,
It's then I'll go to Walberswick
When Autumn's here again.

1924

CONTENTS

An illustration insert follows page 76.

FOREWORD

The work of one of Britain's finest, most sensitive, and individual filmmakers, Humphrey Jennings, is little known in America. There are, perhaps, a number of good reasons for this delayed recognition. His work lay entirely in the field known as documentary, and documentary (even exceptional documentary, such as Jennings's work represents) travels between countries rarely, compared with the feature film. His best work, too, was confined to the years of the Second World War and the period immediately following, making their subject matter even more specialized for modern American audiences, except for viewers who have some direct interest in those years, either artistic or sociological. Moreover, he died young, accidentally, while at work on location in 1950, and the postwar films to which we looked forward so eagerly in Britain were scarcely begun.

Yet I would assert he remains a great, though relatively unrecognized, filmmaker whose work, once viewed, excites immediate fascination. He can in fact be readily appreciated outside his own language and culture; when, in 1971, John Gillett of the British Film Institute and I took a selection of his films, entirely unsubtitled, to screen during a British film week in Sorrento, Italy, we were inundated with inquiries about Jennings, and he received press recognition as a newly discovered talent of cinema on the strength alone of the poetic, vivid portraiture of the British people of the 1940s that the films represented to responsive Italian film critics.

In America, with no such language barrier to leap, his films, once seen, are acknowledged immediately for their sensitivity. They have been the subject of published monographs by Evan Cameron and by one of the authors of this book, Rodney E. Sheratsky, as well as of a notable weekend celebration and succession of screenings at Boston's Museum of Fine Arts in 1976, through the enthusiasm of the museum's film officer, Deac Rossell. They have been praised in the pages of books on international documentary. And they have been regularly screened over the years by Professor Anthony W. Hodgkinson for students of film at Clark University and by myself at Boston University.

During the period 1940 to mid-1945, I was responsible in wartime Britain for the organization of a hundred or more screenings a week of Ministry of Information films, first (1940–43) in the southwest region of Britain and later (1943–45) in the northwest region. This amounted in all to some 25,000 showings, and in a high proportion of these I would always include, one by one, a film by Jennings as soon as they became individually available.

The films reached us in both 16-mm and 35-mm as soon as they were released—*The First Days* (1939), *London Can Take It* (1940), *Spring Offensive* (1940), *Welfare of the Workers* (1940), *Heart of Britain* (1941), *Words for Battle* (1941), *Listen to Britain* (1942), *Fires Were Started* (1943, of short feature length), *The Silent Village* (1943), *The Eighty Days* (1944), *The True Story of Lilli Marlene* (1944), *V.1* (1944), *A Diary for Timothy* (1944–45). Except for *Fires Were Started* (also known as *I Was a Fireman*) these films were all shorts of varying length. The public screenings lasted normally from half an hour (two or three shorts), screened by our mobile projectionists in factories during meal breaks, to ninety minutes or more (five or six shorts) for afternoon or evening shows designed for general audiences (women's institutes or guilds, for example) with halls available (however small) in town or village. Special screenings were given (often on Sundays) in local theaters when not in use for normal exhibitions. Such screenings permitted longer films to be shown, such as *Fires Were Started*, which otherwise were shown in regular cinema programs.

The reason for including one of Jennings's films in virtually all my general screenings was the poetic and emotional lift they gave to the programs as a whole. I do not exaggerate when I say that members of audiences under the emotional stress of war (especially during the earlier, more immediately alarming, years) frequently wept as a result of Jennings's direct appeal to the rich cultural heritage of Britain going back (as in *Words for Battle* and *Listen to Britain*) to Shakespeare and the Elizabethans, to Purcell and to Handel. People found themselves being brought suddenly and movingly into touch with what was at stake if indeed the Nazi forces (a bare thirty to one hundred or so miles away across the Channel) invaded and took over the conduct of their lives. Jennings made these southern English folks aware—farm workers and their families, workers in the war plants, housewives whose husbands, if still alive, were far distant, civil defense workers (as so many of us were), firefighters, teachers, and those who manned the essential services of town and countryside—what exactly a successful invasion by Germany could mean in a country that had not been invaded for close to a thousand years.

Few of the hundreds of wartime films made between 1940 and 1944 achieved this. Closest to Jennings's were, perhaps, the beautiful films of life in the English countryside made by Ralph Keene, who, like Jennings, was to die prematurely. The rest were fighting films—films about the war fronts, our Allies, the armed services, or the immediate needs and achievements in war production and food production, the sacrifices being made by our merchant navy in supplying a beleaguered island, the much-needed economies at home and the saving of every useful scrap of raw material, or the powerful dialectics of Paul Rotha's *World of Plenty*, one of the few films that attempted to look forward to a better international scene once the war was over. Into programs made up mostly of such barbed content, Jennings's films came like a breath of art and poetry that could not fail to move audiences of every background.

I remember arranging for an officer in the Free Czech forces a screening of The Silent Village, in which the people of the Welsh mining village of Cwmgiedd under Jennings's direction re-enacted the martyrdom of the Czechoslovak mining community of Lidice. He was deeply moved. Whether or not the film is regarded now as one of Jennings's major works, it had a powerful effect at the time, when the massacre was fresh in all our minds. Every foot, every sound, of Fires Were Started was meaningful if you had experienced (as we had done in both Bristol and Plymouth) the heart of your city destroyed overnight by firebombs and high explosives, or had watched in the skies above your streets the dogfights between the fighters of the Royal Air Force and the Luftwaffe, or had been on night duty during the more intense raids, wondering at each detonation what devastation the bombers had wrought and how many had died or lay injured under the rubble. Fires Were Started conveys the sights and sounds of a citizens' war, but everytime I see it I smell the aftermath, the stench of water soaking into acres of burnt debris.

Jennings's films made meaningful what civilians in particular endured in wartime Britain during the successive phases of bombing from aircraft and destruction by flying bombs and finally by the rocket bombs aimed at London in 1944. And, above all perhaps, he portrayed the great gains we experienced in cultural, communal values—the lunchtime orchestral concerts in London and the provinces, the service of war artists who celebrated the everyday and everynight sights of community endurance, entertainment provided by popular artists and concert hall singers alike to enliven the break in the shift-workers' routine in war factories, the ceaseless service of the BBC in providing music, drama, light entertainment, and intelligent talk, and the work of actors and actresses not called to the armed forces who kept the drama alive in those theaters that remained undamaged. Jennings recognized and absorbed it all into the grand, multifaceted tradition of British culture, old and new, and invigorated the imagination of our audiences, large and small.

In this first major work to be published on Humphrey Jennings,* the authors are concerned to recognize his achievements in other fields than film, as poet, painter, and sociologist, and to see him as a unique interpreter during the 1930s and 1940s of British cultural tradition and of life in England during those troubled prewar and wartime years. This book becomes, therefore, as much a study of the English scene as it is of Jennings himself; the two are inseparable. Anthony Hodgkinson, a Londoner born in 1916, who was later to serve in the British Army, understands very well the background to Jennings's thought and inspiration, particularly in light of his own contributions to Jennings's prewar organization, Mass-Observation. In this attempt to interpret Jennings's work for American readers, he has collaborated with Rodney E. Sheratsky, who represents an entirely postwar American standpoint in evaluating Jennings's various achievements. Having been myself closely involved throughout the war years as a film officer attached to the Ministry of Information, for which Jennings made his finest films, and having seen at first hand the use to which I and my colleagues put them at the time, I want to say how much I appreciate this book, which has revived for me so much of what I myself experienced during the period 1940 to 1945.

April 1980   Roger Manvell
                                                               Boston University

*Since this foreword was written, Jennings's elder daughter, Mary-Lou, has edited a volume of essays and extracts from her father's work. See Bibliography herein. —A.W.H.

ACKNOWLEDGMENTS

During the ten years or so that constitute this book's gestatory period, we have incurred debts of gratitude to a very large number of kind people and institutions who have given us their time, trouble, and labor. We feel the least invidious manner of thanking them is to list them here in alphabetical order.

Leonard Amey
Edgar Anstey
Ruth Arnon
Dennis Arundell
Bayerischer Rundfunk, Munich
Jeremy Boulton
Stanley Bowler
British Broadcasting Corporation
British Film Institute
Elaine Burrows
Shirley Byers
Cambridge University Library
Ken Cameron
Stuart Campbell
Tom Caslon
James A. Chiara

Clark University
Brian Coe
Emma Cohn
Sir William Coldstream
Merith Cole
Les Cooke
Bernard Coulson
Clive Coultrass
Eric Cross
Ian Dalrymple
Mrs. C. H. Dand
Brenda Davies and her staff
Adrian de Potier
Howard Ferguson
John Ferguson
Ann Fleming

Geoffrey Foot

Denis Forman

Fred Gamage

Mr. and Mrs. David Gascoyne

Marius Goring

Granada Television Ltd.

The late Hugh Gray

The late Tom Harrisson

The late Sir Norman Hartnell,
K.C.V.C.

Mark Haworth-Booth

Jim Hillier

Barbara Hogan

Frank Holland

Roger Holman

Spike Hughes

John Huntley

W. S. Hutton

Imperial War Museum, London

Pat Jackson

Mary-Lou Jennings

Jonathan Kannair

Gerald Karaska

Peter King

Silvia Koller

Barbara and Maurice Landergan

Laurie Lee

Nora Lee

Stuart Legg

London Symphony Orchestra

Rachael Low

Mr. and Mrs. E. C. Lowe

The late Len Lye

Charles Madge

Roger Manvell

James Mason

Bill Megarry

The Mellon Foundation

David Mellor

Joe Mendoza

James D. Merralls

Pat Miles

John Mitchell

Lilian Morrisson

Peter Mouncey

Museum of Modern Art, New
York

National Film Archive, England

New York Public Library

Nicky North

Northern Valley Regional High
School, Demarest, N.J.

Gerald F. Noxon

Diana Pine

David Pocock

W. B. Pollard

Kathleen Raine

Stanley Reed

Deac Rossell

William Sloan

Jack Smith

Tony Sweatman

The Tate Gallery, London
David Thomson
Julian Trevelyan
Clive Truman
Victoria and Albert Museum,
    London
Connie Waits
Rex Warner

Rex Warner
R. I. C. H. Warren
Westdeutscher Rundfunk,
    Cologne
Sheila Whitaker
Angelika Wittlich
Basil Wright

There is, however, one person for whom we feel we should suspend this alphabetical rule. Peggy Kenas has been more than a helpful friend and consultant: she has contributed time, research, and writing to the manuscript (notably Chapters 3 and 7) and—most valuable of all—she has "midwifed" this book into existence. Without her, we believe, it would never have seen the light of day.

We thank you, Peggy.

A.W.H.
R.E.S.

February 1982

INTRODUCTION

In a short span of seventeen years as a maker of films, Humphrey Jennings also wrote a substantial collection of poems, painted many well-regarded paintings, continued his unfinished life's work on an ambitious anthology/collage of quotations from English literature, and generally found himself near the center of the European social and artistic revolution spun into motion in the 1920s. Without necessarily intending it, he nearly became the impossible: a latter-day "Renaissance man."

What he intended to be was famous. Not just any kind of famous, however. From the very beginning, it seems, his future lay in the direction of visual art. His mother had once been a student of painting; his father drew and assembled architectural structures. When Jennings first began to demonstrate his own talent, as a schoolboy at the Perse School and later at Cambridge, his aptitude took the forms of theatrical set design, musical choreography, and the more private but no less visible architecture of poetry.

It was at Cambridge, in the late 1920s and early 1930s, that the world opened up to him. Into the moral vacuum created by World War I thronged the unorthodoxies of surrealism, psychoanalysis, and socialism. Jennings responded to each of these modernisms as though they were entirely compatible among themselves. The conservative desire to imagine the splintered modern world as whole once more, international and comprehensive, was in fact characteristic of Jennings's circle of Cambridge friends, which included William Empson, Charles Madge, Kathleen Raine, and Julian Trevelyan.

Events in the 1930s drew Jennings into the tug and pull of public life. The abdication of King Edward VIII for the sake of romance, followed by the coronation of George VI, made a bizarre contrast to the economic decline of the British as a consequence of worldwide depression. Prompted by correspondence received by British newspapers on the subject of these events and incongruities, Jennings and Madge decided to form an organization devoted to studying all forms of contemporary popular culture. Named Mass-Observation in honor of the technique that would hopefully yield a "science of the masses," the organization was founded in 1936 with the assertion that an ethnography of British customs, habits, "mass wishes," and artistic traditions was long overdue. Anthropology as a discipline (one of Cambridge's strengths) had tended to concentrate on overseas, "native" populations. What about one's own backyard?

Jennings happened to be in a particularly good position to begin such a project. Forced to find employment in the early 1930s to support a growing family, he temporarily shelved his aspirations as a painter and as a poet to work in a film unit commissioned by the British government. His schoolboy experience as a set designer and choreographer stood him in good stead. Very quickly Jennings was directing short documentary films himself.

In the beginning these films tended to be in the nature of advertisements for government services. But the passionate belief of the unit's chief, John Grierson, that modern communications should serve a democracy by informing and educating its citizens, created a new kind of film—what Grierson called a documentary. (In the same decade, John Reith established the unique BBC radio system with a similar rationale.) Jennings began making films that called up the long survival of British traditions: the appeal of rural landscape, for instance; the gregariousness of rural and village life; the tenacity of the laboring class in factories; the heritage of British song, folklore, and literature.

Like his friend Empson, Jennings saw the traditional life of England through an urban artist's eyes—with a genuine attraction to its pastoral possibilities but also with a sophisticated man's awareness of the fragilities behind the strengths. Moreover, there is in Jennings's films, despite their public context and government sponsorship, a repetitive, almost obsessional, imagery that reveals their intensely personal nature.

That imagery—horses, both zoological and mechanical, groups singing, smoking chimneys, catastrophic fires—tells us a good deal about Jennings's private and social commitments and especially about the nature of his achievement in film. Although his subject matter was by necessity public, it was also by choice. His working processes and the style of the finished product show great experimental energy in a new medium of communication. As subsequent chapters will demonstrate, Jennings's forays into surrealistic technique (including the use of accident, automatism, and violent juxtaposition) altered the rhythm of the British documentary film drastically. So did his experiments with sound overlapping. His willingness to restage recent events meticulously, as though they were happening for the first time, may not in theory seem compatible with his insistence on using real-life persons to play themselves. But somewhere between Jennings's belief in art and his commitment to the world of daily life lies the central, inclusive truth of his achievement.

In the end, prior to his accidental death in 1950, Jennings began to mistrust that achievement. He wished aloud that he could devote more of his energy to painting. Nevertheless, it is indisputable that Humphrey Jennings had already given himself completely to art in general, not to any one genre or medium exclusively. More than with most filmmakers, with Jennings we can say that his films were the result of what he learned from painting, from writing, and from his life-long fascination with music. If finally he felt he suffered from a lack of concentration, he also proved more responsive to the world than most. He closed himself to nothing, a private man in a public sphere.

Therefore, to read about this film or that film made by Jennings, about this phase or that of his career, this poem or that canvas, is to be constantly in touch with a striking phenomenon: here is a man whose ambitions and contributions synthesized, in as full a way as any individual can today, the possibilities of his age.

March 1982   Paul Jenkins

HUMPHREY JENNINGS

He should not be forgotten; he was far
more than just a maker of films.
                    —David Gascoyne, 1978

1 EARLY DAYS AND EARLY VENTURES: 1907–1932

I can imagine this letter being found in an old drawer—a hundred years hence—being certified by you or your descendents to be in my handwriting and to be presented to a museum as the earliest known literary opinions of Jennings, the famous critic and designer! I know I am born to be famous.

—Humphrey Jennings, c. 1926[1]

The picturesque fishing village of Walberswick, Suffolk, lies on the eastern edge of England, a coast washed and eroded by the North Sea. The drowned port of Dunwich, once the center of East Anglian trade with the Continent, lies just to the south. Behind, westward, stretch the Fens, swept by a cold east wind, which the locals say blows uninterruptedly from the Urals. The land is rich, with fertile black soil in which grows most of England's grain. Since World War II, East Anglia has been the main British base of the U.S. Air Force. Its roads, lined with ancient twisted red cedars, run straight as arrows, betraying their Roman origin. The road to Walberswick (*wald*, a wood, *berige*, a hiding place, *Wyc*, a winding river) leads nowhere else. There is no bridge or ferry across the mouth of the river Blyth to Southwold, and southward lies the vast protected area of Mindsmere Bird Sanctuary.

It was in this remote spot in 1906 that architect Frank Jennings and his wife came to live. On August 19 of the following year, his son, Humphrey, was born in a house called The Gazebo. Frank Jennings, according to local tales, would wander the region, purchase the bricks and beams of dilapidated farms and barns, then create designs incorporating these materials. These he would sometimes sell to builders at a nice profit.[2] Humphrey's mother, Mildred, who was an art student when she married, opened a pottery shop in the village.[3] The shop, now known as The Potter's Wheel, is still there. As part of its interior decoration, and marked "Not To Be Sold," are three or four Breton dishes, almost certainly part of the stock-in-trade that Mildred Jennings used to bring back from her frequent trips to Brittany. Except for the 1914–18 war period, Humphrey accompanied her each year and thereby acquired a fluent knowledge of French.[4]

Frank Jennings and his wife were gentle "progressives," with great enthusiasm for folk art and guild socialism. As a boy, Humphrey was allowed freedoms unusual for the period: freedom of dress—his was light and loose; freedom of movement—he would wander at will around the piers and seashore; and freedom of diet—black coffee and wine were commonplace. The Jenningses were influenced in their progressiveness by A. R. Orage's weekly, *The New Age*. It was Orage's championship of W. H. D. Rouse, the brilliant scholar-headmaster of Cambridge's famous Perse School, which persuaded them to send their son there.[5] The initial fees were probably met by his grandmother,[6] but he was soon winning scholarships for himself, and was later to secure several more during his years at Pembroke College, Cambridge.

His friend and fellow Persean, the actor Marius Goring, wrote: "He was brilliant in brain and exuberant in body; I had watched him win the Senior Quarter Mile . . . and thought, 'No hope: he belongs to a superior race.' There was nothing, it seemed, he could not do: he was original, and he conformed; his Classics were first-rate, he understood . . . Mathematics; his English was astonishing; . . . his wit in the School journals and concerts was unsurpassed."[7]

A major influence on the schoolboy Jennings was Perse's brilliant English teacher, Caldwell Cook. His philosophy of teaching—"The Play Way"—was set out by him in a book of that name, which is described by Perse's historian John Mitchell as "one of the most important and remarkable books on education ever produced."[8] Especially today, Cook's general approach, which relied heavily on dramatic work and choral chanting, and which might perhaps be summarized as "learning through pleasurable doing," has earned a respected place in current educational philosophy. Recent psychological studies have confirmed the importance in education of the release of creative energy and of play.

Cook's teaching area, which he named The Mummery, was a favorite haunt of Jennings. It was a place where he learned about drama, poetry, literature, and design through direct doing—writing, acting, painting and building, dancing, and declaiming. He was for a time a coeditor of *The Player Magazine—The Unofficial Organ of the School House Players* (these latter a creation of Cook's), did drawings, and wrote several poems and pieces for it.

Most of Jennings's juvenilia illustrate the wide range of interests that he developed during his Perse days, interests that remained with him throughout his life, guiding his experiments with all the arts. During his years at Pembroke, Jennings took a special interest in Elizabethan poetry and drama. An exceptional honors student (he took a Double First in English literature), he received a Charles Oldham Scholarship to prepare a revised text of Shakespeare's *Venus and Adonis*, based on the quarto of 1593. "Everything is retained from the Quarto of 1593 that might possibly contribute to the pleasure of the intelligent reader . . . and as little as possible beyond that."[9]

Among Jennings's fellow students and friends at Cambridge were Jacob Bronowski, Kathleen Raine, William Empson, and Charles Madge, the last of whom was to be cofounder with Jennings of

Mass-Observation. Many were involved in the Cambridge Film Guild, and at semiclandestine screenings in such places as Basil Wright's rooms, Jennings and his friends encountered the French, German, and Russian films that were beginning to challenge the minds of a generation: Clair's *An Italian Straw Hat*, Murnau's *Faust*, Eisenstein's *Potemkin*, and Pudovkin's *Mother*.

According to letters he wrote to his friend Leonard Amey between 1926 and 1928, Jennings studied Ruskin, Plato, Aristotle, Milton ("the greatest English poet"), Bernard Shaw ("the greatest dramatist—on St. Joan alone, if need be"), Ben Jonson, eighteenth-century novels, English porcelain, eighteenth-century Spanish art, tapestry, Tudor fireplaces, Greek tragedy, the influence of Captain John Smith's voyages on seventeenth-century design, eighteenth-century theater, modern line drawings, Trollope, Thomas Hardy, John Stuart Mill, Charles Dickens, and Oscar Wilde. ("I remember ten days ago reading *De Profundis* from cover to cover on top of a bus and in the National Gallery much to the amazement of the officials.") With such diversity of reading, it is not surprising that Jennings confessed to his friend, "As to my progress in art, I am as usual torn among painting, literature, and the theatre. I love each infinitely in turn and I feel that I get on well in each—but where it will all end—in which, I don't know."[10]

Up at Cambridge, says Amey, Jennings continued the interests of his Perse days:

He deplored the whole mechanization of modern life and sketched the idea of a masque whose climax should be the entry of the Devil on a reaping machine. Masques seem to have fascinated him at this time. He had a scheme for taking over a school end-of-term concert and ending it with a masque of Coe Fen, involving a policewoman as the tutelary genius and featuring the new Fen Causeway bridge, whose design he liked. He was continually drawing costume designs for masques and theatrical productions, a good many of which came to nothing. There was, for instance, a series for Hamlet in full Elizabethan style.[11]

As Marius Goring puts it: "His fireworks were fast becoming illuminations . . . and he achieved it without finding the new merely for
the sake of novelty. Contradiction had become creative."[12]

Between 1926 and 1931, Jennings's stage designs were chiefly for
productions by Dennis Arundell, later to become famous as actor,
opera director, and writer. Arundell was then a fellow of St. John's,
composing, conducting, acting, singing, and directing shows during
the ten years he spent at Cambridge.[13] Arundell claims that Jennings
and he both benefited from the expertise of Frank Birch, who was a
don at King's but had been on the professional stage. In 1926 Jennings helped design, then acted and danced in, Birch's production
of *The Christmas Revue (With Nothing at All about Christmas in It)*
for the Amateur Dramatic Club. The ADC is England's oldest and
most famous amateur theatrical group, and its productions were so
good that they always attracted the top drama critics. One London
critic, in fact, said of the revue—the only one ever given by the
ADC—that there was enough wit in it for two London revues.

In 1928 Arundell directed and Jennings designed a notable production of Purcell's spectacular *King Arthur* at the large New Theatre
in Cambridge, which won highly laudatory notices for both of them.
Here are a few extracts from contemporary reviews of *King Arthur*
contained in Arundell's book of press cuttings. (Unhappily, most of
them are without attribution of newspaper and date, owing to the
error of a professional compiler, who cut them off.)

> It is evident [they] have been guided by two principles: first, that of
> dressing the characters in the costumes of the time when the opera
> was first produced; and secondly, of avoiding any suggestion of real-
> ism in staging a work of the purest fantasy, in which enchanters evil and
> beneficent, spirits and witchcraft run riot. At first glance, it shocks one
> to see King Arthur in a full-bottomed wig of the William and Mary pe-
> riod, but in the extravagances of the concoction one is soon prepared
> to accept anything! Though it may be presumed that the post-impres-
> sionist scenery carries us, in its primitive convention, a good deal fur-
> ther back than the seventeenth century, it is not too startling in a work
> which avoids all sense of realism.

> Humphrey Jennings is a discovery. He has a quality all of his own, be-
> longing neither to the Bakst nor the Lovatt Fraser school, while his
> sense of colour is as delicate as his sense of line.

> Particular mention must be made of the scenery and dresses of Mr.
> Humphrey Jennings, because they seem to me to show a touch of
> something very like genius.

> The scenery and dresses . . . would have done honour to any opera
> house in Europe or the United States. It would be a pity if the talents of
> these two gentlemen [Arundell and Jennings] were not some day given
> the fullest scope in a large theatre.
>
> (A. Kalisch, *Musical Times*)

> . . . a very young undergraduate of absolute genius, Mr. Humphrey
> Jennings . . .   (*Sheffield Daily Telegraph*)

Arundell and Jennings each wrote careful accounts of their work on
King Arthur for *The Cambridge Review*.

Later that year, at the ADC, they were director and designer of
another rarity—the first public performance in England of Stravinsky's *The Tale of a Soldier*, with the famous ballerina Lydia Lopokova
and the undergraduate Michael Redgrave. The set involved a small
inner stage, above and around the proscenium of which was grouped
a small orchestra, the drummer on top. Jennings designed the costumes and the scenery for the inner stage, earning the following
comment from *The Cambridge Daily News*:

> Humphrey Jennings' decorations are uneven, his set for the first scene
> being extremely good, but the palace set, while not being obtrusive,
> seemed hardly in the spirit of the music at this point. His design for
> the Devil's costume in his various metamorphoses was incredibly
> ingenious.

In the Cambridge Guildhall, a very challenging locale for a stage
designer, Arundell and Jennings mounted another rare production
in 1929, Honegger's *King David*, an adaptation of Rene Morax's play
complete with incidental music, conducted at the second performance by the composer. *The Times* review described Jennings as
"extraordinarily successful in designing a framework . . . which was

at once appropriate to the play and did not clash with the undisguised walls of the Guildhall and the gilded organ-pipes which rose above it at the back. His costumes, though less consistently good than those for *King Arthur*, produced an excellent general effect." And Douglas Furber, who was writing scripts for MGM at this time, said in an interview for *The Stage* that *King David* was "the best effort I have seen in years in imaginative spectacle. . . . This seemed to me to be better done and have more invention in it than any so-called spectacular things seen in the West End since I came back from Hollywood." Young Michael Redgrave, writing in *The Cambridge Review*, had mixed feelings:

> He is old before his time. His colours, eschewing the East, were cold. . . . The whole effect was extremely beautiful, in no sense suitable to the tedium of the pageant, which asked for blood and was given a stone. . . . Saul's and David's clothes were excellent. It is vulgar of me, but I wish it had been less intellectual, and would have given all the echo-harmony in the world for a good old coat of many colours. A very notable piece of theatre design, however.

The Arundell/Jennings partnership in 1930 produced, for an all-professional London Opera Festival of seven operas from Monteverdi to Weber, *Cupid and Death* by Locke and Gibbons, Purcell's *Dido and Aeneas*, and Weber's *Freischütz*, the only box-office success because Sir Thomas Beecham was conducting. Jennings's decor in the first two operas drew favorable notices, especially for the Purcell, of the device of dressing it in "contemporary" style: "The costumes effectively viewed both the Greek and the supernatural characters through 17th-century eyes. Aeneas and his followers wore full-bottomed wigs; the witches were country folk of a sinister aspect, and the lighting and grouping of these figures made a series of vivid pictures" (*The Times*).

Back in Cambridge, at the New Theatre, seven performances of Euripides' *The Bacchae* were given in Greek, with music adapted from Handel's operas by Arundell and with Jennings's decor. This drew mixed reviews, since Jennings avoided the traditional vine leaves and leopard skins for "short purple tunics, long striped skirts, and a curiously Mongolian make-up" (*The Morning Post*).

In February of the following year, the last association with Arundell was an appearance by Jennings in Purcell's *Fairy Queen*, an opera based on *A Midsummer Night's Dream*. Jennings played Bottom ("sensibly droll" and with "slender alacrity," said the reviews), and the undergraduate James Mason was Oberon. Arundell produced, but Jennings did not design this time.

Dennis Arundell is at pains to point out that 1926–30 were not merely "years of jolly amateur fun," and that both Jennings and he had begun to be recognized as real professionals in the theater.

Among all his other activities, Jennings founded in 1928, with Bronowski, Empson, Gerald Noxon, and Hugh Sykes-Davies, a literary magazine, *Experiment*. The original resident contributors to *Experiment* included Basil Wright, Richard Eberhart, Henri Cartier-Bresson, and Julian Trevelyan. Outside contributors included Conrad Aiken, James Joyce, Mayakowski, Boris Pasternak, and Paul Eluard.[14]

After graduation, Jennings considered other possible activities, one of which was the then fashionable journey to Spain to fight Franco. Goring claims he talked him out of this—or persuaded him to talk himself out of it.[15] He finally decided to turn down proffered fellowships that might have taken him out of the country and to stay on in Cambridge in a small apartment with his wife, Cicely, whom he had wed in 1929 while still a student at Pembroke. Goring recalls that "their marriage bed was too big to go up the stairs of their flat; I helped him cut it in half and reassemble it inside."[16] Downstairs, they opened the Experiment Gallery, in conjunction with Noxon and Trevelyan. Inspired by contemporary painters such as Picasso, Braque, Léger, Masson, Max Ernst, and Magritte, they decided it was time to give Cambridge access to modern art.[17]

Jennings had, among his many passions, such a passion for contemporary art that he would complain to his friend Trevelyan: "That picture of yours hasn't got 1931-ness." Years later, Trevelyan would recall: "The least one could say of his own work was that it always had *that*. His enthusiasm was immense; I remember his waking me up at eight in the morning to show me a picture he had painted in the night. At his best his work had the purity that one associates with Ben Nicholson but without the dehydrating good taste. But his output was erratic: he had, so to speak, to talk himself into a picture."[18]

2   FIRST FILMS: 1933–1938

Gerald Noxon has entertainingly described Humphrey Jennings's initial venture into filmmaking, as he recalls it. After spending the summer of 1932 with Noxon at St. Tropez and the subsequent year in London on the remains of a small legacy, devoting all his time to painting, Jennings turned to his old Cambridge acquaintances for help in eking out a living. The addition to his family of the first of two daughters made employment suddenly necessary. In 1934, after a year with John Grierson's new General Post Office unit, which had succeeded the old Empire Marketing Board Film Unit, Noxon himself was working in the film department of an advertising agency. He involved Jennings in the making of a film for Socony-Vacuum (now Mobil), to be used in their display at London's annual Motor Show.[1]

No trace has been found of this film, although the full-scale cutaway automobile engine which Noxon says fascinated and intrigued Jennings ("His reaction . . . was almost ecstatic") is described in detail in a technical report of the 1934 Motor Show. It begins: "A trained staff is busy giving practical demonstrations of lubricants which make a very strong appeal. In fact, it is hard at times to get near this stand."[2] According to Noxon, Jennings threw himself with even greater enthusiasm into the creation of a mythical substance called SLUM, whose buildup threatened the life of any car engine which did not use Mobiloil:

"SLUM," he said, "is not a real substance. It is an idea, and what is more it is essentially an emotional idea. Therefore its nature must be demonstrated in a way which will produce a direct emotional response from the audience. There's no thinking needed here, boys." So saying, he plunged both hands and arms right up to the elbows into the ghastly mess and began to play with it like a child making mud pies.[3]

At about the same time, Stuart Legg, another Cambridge friend, introduced Jennings to Grierson. Jennings's early work for Grierson's GPO Film Unit involved an extension of his Cambridge interests—art direction and acting. To these were added editing and, possibly, camera direction. Pat Jackson recalls that his first encounter with Jennings was when Jennings was painting scenery for Cavalcanti's *Pett and Pott* (1934), in which he also played a lively vignette role as a grocer.[4] *Pett and Pott*, a tale of two suburban families, one of which prospers through installing a Post Office telephone, the other encountering predictable disaster, was one of the unit's experiments with a new sound studio, under Cavalcanti's tutelage. Basil Wright remembers:

> Cavalcanti said, "Let's record all the sound first . . . and then put the picture on afterwards." The pictures turned out to be a whole series of studio scenes—it's nothing to do with documentary. So here was Humphrey, with his considerable stage experience . . . turned on to doing the sets. As we were a tiny studio . . . he was very constricted, so he started to use false perspective in . . . a very ingenious manner.[5]

A second acting role, in Cavalcanti's *The Glorious Sixth of June* (1934), gave Jennings even more scope. He played Albert Goodbody, an intrepid young Post Office telegraph boy who brings news of reduced telegraph charges to Parliament against all odds. Black-bearded villains (one played, astonishingly, by Basil Wright) seek to foil his mission, going so far as to tie him to a tree and blow him up.

These films, as can be imagined, are little more than undergraduate romps—clever young men having fun, with very little pretension to professionalism. But Rachael Low, who has been responsible for the monumental histories of British film, has agreed that Jennings may have directed some of the shooting itself on Caval-canti's historic experiment, *Coalface* (1935). It seems to her reasonable to guess that the opening and closing shots of pitheads and smoke, and a striking evening silhouette pan right to left from pithead to trees bowed by the prevailing wind, may very well have been directed by Jennings. Credits in the traditional sense, especially for directing and camerawork, do not really apply to EMB-GPO-Crown films. Individuals were taken on for specific sequences—even occasionally to provide individual shots—for films to which several members of the team may have contributed. Also, it was not unusual for shots taken for one film to be preserved and used again in later films, as is characteristic of Jennings's own subsequent work.

One last acting role in Jennings's first GPO period was an appearance in Stuart Legg's *BBC, Voice of Britain* (1935) as a radio actor, circling the microphone and intoning as one of the three Weird Sisters in a broadcast of *Macbeth* which was actually produced in the GPO studio, not in the BBC's.

There is another interesting reminiscence of this period recorded by Noxon:

> . . . the brief and improbable association with a Methodist film production company headed by the heir to a flour-milling fortune, J. Arthur Rank. I have forgotten exactly how this came about, but Humphrey was asked to do a shooting script from a novel entitled, as I recall, *Three Fevers*, by Leo Walmsley. . . . I know that Humphrey worked on the script for we discussed it several times and in considerable detail. Whether the film was eventually produced I do not know.[6]

Produced it certainly was. It became, from another's script, *The Turn of the Tide*, the film that prompted Rank's full-scale entry into the British film industry in order to get it shown.[7] Its editor, curiously enough, was Ian Dalrymple, who was to become Jennings's great friend and producer; but Dalrymple reports that he did not meet Jennings until June 1940.[8]

Three GPO films attributed to Jennings at this time might well be regarded as his "editing trilogy." All three are basically instructional assemblages of pictures, models, and a few live shots. The first, *Post Haste*, consists for the most part of historical prints and drawings; Stuart Legg has suggested it may be one of the earliest examples of a film composed of still pictures.[9] In one instance at least, the camera pans across a picture to imply motion of its subject, and toward the end there is motion picture footage of mail sorting: vans, trains, ships, and planes, with appropriate sounds.

A history of the General Post Office would seem to be a natural and reasonable project for the young film unit, and Jennings's interest in English history and the development of communications shows clearly in this film, as does his fundamental lucidity in describing processes and their development. The soundtrack is a relatively complex one for the period. A variety of voices are introduced reading aloud; hoofbeats and train noises fill out the background. Fanfarelike calls of the post horn introduce and close the film. They also underline the two key changes described: from postboy to coach and from road to rail transport. There is an early use, too, of an editorial device which Jennings was to employ to great effect later (notably in *A Family Portrait*)—the direct engagement of the audience by a phrase such as "Here is . . ." or "Look!"

Several of Jennings's lasting interests and motifs are to be discerned in embryo in *Post Haste*. St. Paul's occupies one scene; the transformation brought about by the railroad is illustrated by an early traveling sorting office and a mailbag-snatching device ("an ingenious contrivance, the invention of Mr. Ramsey from the General Post Office"), accompanied by suitable steam engine noises; Jennings's reliance on existing, public imagery is evident throughout in the frequent use of contemporary descriptions and documents.

There is a little uncertainty about the authorship of the next film ascribed to Jennings, *The Story of the Wheel*, which contains little that could be identified as his essential style. There are only perfunctory references to Post Office matters, and one feels that the film was primarily intended for the elementary classroom. The commentary is single-voiced, female, precise and didactic, with frequent pauses to study the pictures. It is perhaps worth noting that, again, there is an occasional direct appeal to the viewer's involvement ("You can see how difficult it was . . . ," "Here you can see . . . ," "You see here . . ."). Museum models and displays are often shot with either the models or the camera in motion. Diagrams are occasionally animated very simply. Real-life shots sometimes break up the procession of historical prints and engravings which constitute the bulk of the film. Titles are interspersed to classify the seven sections of the history—a reminder of the fact that many classroom films were made in both sound and silent versions for a long while. (See the later discussion of *Penny Journey*.)

The third film, *Locomotives*, although not especially innovative in its style, is much more clearly a Jennings film. Again, a woman's voice delivers a didactic narrative commentary. Even though the viewer is not addressed directly, the predominant tense is the present one, even when referring to historical material ("It is in the collieries that the first locomotives are made"). This carries a more personal charge than would the past tense, evident especially in the description of Stephenson's Rocket. A mild excitement is engendered—"The success of the Rocket makes the future of the railways certain"—underlined by a long circuslike drumroll.

Jennings's near obsession with locomotives, which apparently he associated with the Chariot of the Tarot pack,[10] becomes very evident from this midpoint climax. Sir William Coldstream remembers seeing him enthusiastically laying out the model railway from which he obtained some subjective-camera shots.[11] The final portion of the film presents several romantic night shots of trains in the style that Jennings later made his own. There is also footage demonstrating the mailbag-grabbing device, which was later to form the climax of Watt's and Wright's *Night Mail*.

About 1935, Jennings became involved with color filmmaking outside of the GPO unit. Noxon tells us:

> Humphrey was interested in and employed in an advisory capacity by two color film development companies, Gasparcolour and Dufay-colour. As a producer I experimented with both these systems and I suffered with Humphrey from the bizarre and unpredictable results which both commonly yielded at that time.[12]

Both systems were pioneered by Major Adrian Klein, M.B.E., who later changed his name to Cornwell-Clyne and wrote three editions of an authoritative book on color cinematography.[13] In it he describes Gasparcolour, a subtractive process, as "the first 35mm integral layer tri-pack film . . . to be used commercially. . . . In 1934 Gasparcolour Ltd. was formed in Great Britain and . . . a number of very beautiful release prints were made."[14] About Dufaycolour, an additive system involving a mosaic of filter elements, one million to the square inch, Cornwell-Clyne shows obvious pride:

> As a technical achievement in manufacture nothing more remarkable has been done in the history of photography. Had the whole project been put before experienced photographic manufacturers in the first place, it would probably have been rejected as chimerical.[15]

Jennings seems first to have worked with Gasparcolour, in collaboration with his friend Len Lye, on a film for Shell Oil called *The Birth of the Robot* (1936). Lye and Jennings had met at the GPO unit, where Lye pioneered hand-painted color films. According to C. H. Dand, "When I was producing an experimental color film (*Birth of a [sic] Robot*) and needed someone with a painter's eye for color and design to direct, I chose Jennings."[16] Dand is credited only with the script of *The Birth of the Robot* in *World Film News*, which also notes "a formidable roster of experts" contributing to this film.[17] John Banting, a celebrated surrealist painter, was one of the designers, and Alex Strasser, the cameraman, was a refugee from Hitler's Germany, where he had worked on many of UFA's great films.[18]

The robot referred to was a figure originally designed for Shell by McKnight Kauffer, the important graphic designer. At the end of the original scenario, Dand tells us, after Venus has fashioned the robot from the dry bones of an incautious motorist, we find that Father Time and his antiquated machine for revolving the planets have been replaced by "the Robot and a fine modern piece of machinery. The Robot dances and over his dancing figure appear the words: 'Modern worlds need modern lubrication—Lubrication by Shell.'"[19] This ending was modified in the finished film, probably as a result of the conditions that Jennings described in an addendum to Dand's account:

> Although each member of the unit was working in a separate department, . . . the departments were allowed to overlap and influence each other's work, and the day-to-day discoveries of the unit were allowed to modify the original scenario and to alter the unit's conception of the film itself.[20]

Watching the film today with hindsight, one can see it reflecting several of Jennings's preoccupations, notably the dangers of technology and his love of rural England. This latter is epitomized by the use of Holst's "Jupiter" movement—from *The Planets*—the "English" movement, as it has been described.[21] There is also a delicate reference to Botticelli's *Venus Anadyomene*, where she rises from the waves standing on a shell. Unfortunately, another delicate joke—a mirage in which a car thinks it sees a garage—had to be underlined by the commentary. It is an interesting visual pun, since it depends on a verbal base for its humor.

Although, as Dand indicates in his later article, Jennings responded excitedly both to the 1936 surrealist exhibition and the 1937 coronation survey for Mass-Observation, low finances and the demands of his growing family dictated continuing involvement with the more lucrative film world. He contributed a piece to *World Film News*, criticizing the use of color in *The Trail of the Lonesome Pine*, the first outdoor Technicolor film,[22] and a press release of 5 October 1937 implied that he had directed, or was directing, three Dufaycolour films for Adrian Klein:

> Work is practically complete on three short colour films. One of these will be named *English Harvest*. . . . Another picture has been made of the last few top-sail schooners. . . . A third film is promised in which an attempt is being made to break entirely new ground in rhythm and colour. The films are being directed by Mr. Humphrey Jennings, whose work in recent colour films awakened considerable attention.[23]

These are mysterious references, since the only Jennings color film known up to that date is *The Birth of the Robot*. The film *English Harvest* has recently been discovered, but its release date must have been delayed considerably. It is a brief but very attractive depiction of an English pastoral scene, as warmly bucolic as the music from Beethoven's Sixth Symphony which accompanies it. Each shot's composition reflects the classical balance and harmony of the romantic, Constable-like view of the land that Jennings celebrated throughout his life. Once more apparent, too, is the lucidity with which he explores and explains a basic process: in this case, one simple portion of a ceaseless annual cycle. The commentary, detached, sparse, and simple, is by A. G. Street. Street was well known before and during the war as the BBC's "voice of the country" and the author of several books and articles on country matters.

There is evidence to suggest that *English Harvest* was incorporated into—or possibly extracted from—a slightly longer Dufay-colour film entitled *The Farm*. Part of a contemporary review of this film runs:

> The lovely colour photography—ranking with the best we have ever seen on any screen—secures charming scenes of animal life involving cows with their calves, mares with leggy colts, and sows. . . . *Finally, we have further beautiful vistas of harvest-time, complete with revealing detail of reaping and thatching—and the grateful break for "elevenses"*—the whole building up into a truly attractive slice of rustic life.[24]

Comparison of the lines we have emphasized with the summary of *English Harvest* in Appendix A indicates that these scenes are extremely likely to have been the same.

If the harvest of *English Harvest* was that of autumn 1937, then by the winter of 1937–38 Jennings was engaged in another Dufaycolour film—*Design for Spring*. This film depicted work done by and for the famous dress designer Norman Hartnell, another Cambridge contemporary of Jennings's and coproducer of the film with Adrian Klein. The film was previewed in February 1938. A trade paper "Onlooker" commented on the "fashionable audience," and went on:

> I must say that I found much of the colour work entirely pleasing, although some of the background detail left something to be desired. The softer shades in blue and red appear to dominate the scheme, and some of them are delightful in their unobtrusive realism, not least in their artistic contrasts and finely composed groupings.[25]

Only one reel of this film is extant in positive form, as described in Appendix A. It is this reel (the first) which, apparently, was finally registered and released under the title of *Making Fashions* in 1939. Brian Coe's article on color cinematography in *The International Encyclopedia of Film* wrongly describes *Design for Spring* as "Humphrey Jennings's first."[26]

Although nearly all of the film is shot in the interiors of Hartnell's workrooms, there are one or two exterior shots. One in particular is interesting in that it introduces another of Jennings's favorite images: smoking chimneys. "As the January winds tangle the smoke around the chimneys," says the commentary, which presages the first line of his 1949 poem: "As I look out of the window on the roofscape of smoke. . . ."[27] In Jennings's affinity for smoke and chimneys, and on the basis of the poem's phrasing, one might not be far afield to hear an echo of T. S. Eliot's "The Love Song of J. Alfred Prufrock."

Marius Goring recalls Jennings's enthusiasm for Dufaycolour. In fact he told Goring at the time that he wanted to make *all* his future films with the aid of this process, which he regarded as ideal. Goring suggests that Dufaycolour appealed to two of Jennings's deep interests: his joy in complex technology (recall Cornwell-Clyne's comments, quoted above), and his painter's understanding of delicate color combinations.[28]

The summer of 1938 seems to have brought Jennings back to the GPO Film Unit. An article in the Winter 1938–39 *Sight and Sound*, on the work of the unit, discusses his film *Penny Journey*:

> Another experimental undertaking is the making of the first educational silent film for schools which the Unit has so far essayed as a special production. It is called *Penny Journey*. . . . In former years a considerable number of educational silent films have been produced, but they have been made generally speaking out of cut-outs from sound films. *Penny Journey* has been scripted, shot and edited as a separate undertaking.[29]

At first sight, this is confusing, since the print of *Penny Journey* held in the National Film Archives and described in Appendix A is a sound film, with commentary and a few cello chords to introduce its first scene. Rachael Low comments: "I would imagine the 'experiment' would be that Jennings would plan the film in such a way that it was perfectly intelligible whether it had its voice-over sound track or not."[30] This seems a reasonable explanation; for many years, even after the war, there was a firmly held belief among teachers, especially of young children, that educational films should be silent. Indeed, sound film projectors were initially restricted to secondary schools in many educational authorities' areas.

It is clear from *Penny Journey* that Jennings now had full experience, both of directing people as they did their jobs and of organizing cameramen to shoot scenes of the beautiful English countryside. There are a number of GPO stock shots in *Penny Journey* (including the inevitable railway scenes), but it is the final sequence that sticks in the memory. In the rural community of Graffham, Sussex, the grocer-postmaster and his postman sort out the mail on the shop's floor. The cat stalks haughtily past them; then the postman completes the simple odyssey of a boy's postcard addressed to his aunt, first cycling, then walking, through idyllic sylvan scenery, to the isolated farmhouse. Here is the peaceful England which never quite returned after the war; and here, expressed in the simplest and most human terms, is part of the Griersonian documentary philosophy: It is our communications systems which bind us in community.

3   JENNINGS AND SURREALISM: 1936

It was, of course, inevitable that Humphrey Jennings should involve himself in the surrealist movement. There was, after all, no serious aesthetic enterprise that did not arouse his interest. By 1936, when Humphrey joined the forces behind London's first International Surrealist Exhibition, the movement had attracted a formidable array of painters and poets, many of them Jennings's personal friends, and had developed a fully articulated philosophy.

For their literary and painterly pedigree, the surrealists claimed a notable heritage—Rimbaud, Lautréamont, Apollinaire, Reverdy, Chirico. Like dadaism and futurism, surrealism reflected a need of its time to discard an image of reality based on everyday human experience and conscious memory. It was claimed that the logical order of things was false and superficial, that man was ready to be introduced into a new and broader domain of experience, where the boundary between the exterior world and his own internal one would be erased.

André Breton, who drafted the *First Surrealist Manifesto* in 1924, expressed his faith in "the future resolution of the seeming contradiction between the states of dream and waking in a kind of absolute or super-reality." The magazine *La Révolution Surréaliste* was also founded in 1924, and in 1925 the catalogue of the first surrealist exhibition was published. It included important names: Picasso, Man Ray, Arp, Ernst, Chirico, André Masson, Pierre Roy. In 1926, the

Galerie Surréaliste was founded; in 1927 Yves Tanguy was introduced to the surrealist movement, and in 1930 Salvador Dali joined.
In the *Second Surrealist Manifesto* of 1929 Breton attempted to state
the underlying motive of the movement more exactly:

> There is every reason to suppose that at a certain spiritual level life and
> death, the real and the imagined, the past and the future, the utterable
> and the unutterable, the above and the below cease to be perceived as
> contradictions. It would be pointless to look for a motive for surrealist
> activity outside of the desire to attain to that level.[1]

No simple statement of the aims of surrealism could possibly do
justice to the wide variety of ideas and artists that the movement en-
compassed. If we look at it as a style of life as well as an artistic
movement, it becomes easier to understand how it influenced Jennings and others who may have had serious objections to some of
its basic tenets. Breton himself suggests that some participants were
simply "hunting in the neighbourhood without becoming a member
of the surrealist house-party."[2] There are undoubtedly those who
are not likely to be identified by art historians as surrealists who
were nevertheless influenced by the movement. For example, it was
probably Alexander Calder's contact with surrealist thought that
contributed to his realization of the poetic possibilities of natural
rather than fully controlled movement. He borrowed biomorphic
shapes from Miró and began to think of mobiles as similes of organic structure.

The surrealist belief in pure psychic automation, free from the
exercise of reason, did not work in practice. The notion that a dream
can be transposed directly from the unconscious mind to the canvas, bypassing the conscious awareness of the artist, turned out to
be a typical exaggeration of the generally accepted importance of
spontaneity in the creative process. This did not mean that rigorous
discipline had no place in the work of those artists (including that of
Jennings) whom the surrealists claimed for their own. But the idea
of automatism did in fact stimulate some novel techniques for so-

liciting and exploiting chance effects, the element so beloved by Jennings.

The surrealists' love of shock effects took many forms. Some were outrageous and probably not intended to be taken seriously; others would later become quite respectable in the context of art criticism. Miró once compared the effect exercised by a good painting to that of a blow with the fist—"the spectator ought to feel the impact without having time to think about it."[3] The British painter Francis Bacon, commenting on the mysterious process by which art communicates, said: "It's a very, very close and difficult thing to know why some paint comes across directly onto the nervous system and other paint tells you the story in a long diatribe through the brain."[4] If Jennings did not subscribe to some of the basic surrealist tenets (he was certainly at odds, for instance, with their insistence on breaking with all tradition), he agreed with the importance of chance and coincidence, and of the irrational juxtaposition of images. We have no evidence that he agreed with the extreme position that mental layers most remote from consciousness are the most valuable for artistic creation. His view was probably closer to the position that "accident is a shrewd helper and the unconscious a powerful one."[5]

Especially in his filmmaking, Jennings deliberately renounced the surrealists' use of private imagery from the unconscious and adopted instead a repertoire of public images that were accessible to almost every English person. His use of such images and the concept that "any two shots can be cut together—the soundtrack will connect them"[6] are important keys to understanding the power of his wartime films.

Before filmmaking claimed most of his energies, Jennings's long-standing and abiding interest in painting and poetry was powerfully fanned by his involvement with London's first International Surrealist Exhibition. In spite of basic differences with some of the participants, he was undoubtedly attracted by the high spirits with which the event was launched. Had it not been for chance and coincidence, those elements so beloved by Jennings and the surrealists, their first major show might have taken even longer to reach and scandalize England. Had David Gascoyne not been in Paris to do research, and had Roland Penrose not gone there on business, the two would not have chanced to meet on a Paris street in 1935. They decided to organize a show upon returning to London. Although their meeting had been coincidental, their planning became very deliberate. For the better part of 1935, the two of them organized meetings, activities, and surrealist readings in preparation for the following year's exhibition, assisted by Jennings, Paul Nash, Hugh Sykes-Davies, Henry Moore, and others. Breton, Eluard, Georges Huguet, and Man Ray comprised the French committee. The show opened at the New Burlington Galleries on 12 June 1936.

More than sixty artists from fourteen countries exhibited their works. (One of them, of course, was Jennings.) Included in the show were children's drawings as well as African, American, and Oceanian primitive objects. Surrealist objects included Penrose's *Captain Cook's Last Voyage*, a wire sculpture with a woman's bust inside, and Meret Oppenheim's *Fur-Covered Cup, Saucer and Spoon*.

It was a remarkable show in every way. There were enough accidents and problems to satisfy even the most devout surrealist. To add to the unplanned incidents, the surrealists instigated enough pranks to amuse all who cared to exercise their sense of humor. Before it opened, for example, but after the show was hung and the catalog printed, Breton demanded that the exhibition be rehung. His tantrums generated even more confusion later among puzzled viewers, who concluded that the paintings, which had no relationship to their avowed titles, must be put-ons. Dali's *Aphrodisiac Dinner Jacket* was the victim of an unusually hot summer's day, and his glasses filled with crème de menthe attracted much attention. Before too many could quench their thirst, however, the liqueur had evaporated in the steaming gallery. The ingenious secretary, Ruthven Todd, solved the problem by drinking the remaining liqueur and substituting green ink. Serving boiled string in tea cups, Dylan Thomas asked visitors, "Weak or strong?" After lunch one day, composer William Walton returned with *his* addition to the exhibits—a kipper, which he attached to Miró's *Object 228*.

At the later 1936 International Surrealist Exhibition in New York's Museum of Modern Art, a Fantastic Art section highlighted the connections between surrealists, illustrators, humorists, and (significantly) Blake's engravings.[7] The unrealized plans for the last major surrealist exposition, to be held in Paris in 1947, included tributes to "Surrealists Despite Themselves" (Arcimbaldo, Bosch, Henri Rousseau, and Blake), as well as to those who "Ceased to Gravitate in the Movement's Orbit" (Dali, Dominguez, Masson, and Picasso).[8] Humphrey Jennings should perhaps have been included here, but in fact he had already been excommunicated from the London surrealist circle for accepting an O.B.E. for his wartime films.[9]

As we study Jennings's paintings, it is worth noting Julian Trevelyan's recollection that, in his own youth, "I drew . . . with a spindly single line, never taking the pencil off the paper, as I had remembered Humphrey doing."[10] Jennings's 1929 line drawing *An Essex Group* is an example of his devotion to the elegant, self-directing line at that stage in his artistic life. Automatism appears to be the means, if not the goal.

When it came to preparing to shoot a film, however, Jennings made detailed instructions and drew precise sketches for his cameramen.[11] Chance, in regard to film at least, was to be avoided. In only one sense did the approach of the filmmaker resemble that of the painter: details in both sketches and paintings had to be as exact as those in an architect's rendering.

In 1938, in one of his relatively rare articles, Jennings explained how painting and photography are and are not related:

Photography itself—"photogenic drawing"—began simply as the mechanization of realism, and it remains *the* system with which the people can be pictured by the people for the people: simple to oper-

ate, results capable of mass production and circulation, effects generally considered truthful. . . . Freud . . . says that the feeling of *Deja Vu*
"corresponds to the memory of an unconscious fantasy." The camera is
precisely an instrument for recording the object that prompted that
memory. Hence the rush to see "how they came out."[12]

In another 1938 article, Jennings made an interesting assessment of
Magritte:

> In Magritte's paintings beauty and terror meet. But their poetry is not
> necessarily derived from the known region of romance—a plate of
> ham will become as frightening as a lion—a brick wall as mysterious as
> night. . . . Precisely his passionate interest in the concrete world has
> made him remember that a painting itself is only an *image*.
>
> [The disparate elements in Magritte's paintings occur] in a passive
> sense in the painter's imagination. Hence their simultaneous irra-
> tionality—since nothing is chosen "on purpose"—and their evident
> truth—since their "bringing together" is in fact an "event" beyond
> choice. It is of the likenesses and discrepancies between the image and
> reality that these events are composed, and it is in the relentless logic
> of these likenesses and discrepancies that Magritte sees the central sit-
> uation: *La Condition Humaine*.[13]

In Magritte's works, the disparate elements may have been the
result of chance; in Jennings's paintings, however, a relentless logic
prevails, the logic which underscores the comments he and his collaborator Noxon made in 1931:

> Of Surrealist paintings two things can at once be said: their principle of
> construction is that of dreams and their unity depends, not upon de-
> monstrable composition, but upon mental reconstruction of elements
> which are in themselves pictorial unities; and not, as in cubist pictures,
> wedge-like fragments. The one follows from the other; a dream has
> two aspects: its obvious shapes and the impulses these shapes repre-
> sent. So that, for example, a picture by Dali has in it a group of recog-
> nizable objects, which by arrangement, lighting, and so on, form a
> piece of phallic symbolism. It is a kind of pictorial pun.[14]

In their paintings, both Magritte and Jennings give viewers
forms from a real, exterior world which they interpret surrealisti-
cally. For example, in *Apple, Prism and Mountains*, Jennings placed a

dark apple against a white prism. Both are enclosed by dark mountains in the foreground's left and right, and light gray, snow-topped mountains in the background's center. This painting suggests two worlds: the real one, from which objects have been extracted, and an imagined one in which they are "illogically" placed. By removing the objects from their natural surroundings and inserting them in unfamiliar or unexpected territory, Jennings gives them new life and encourages viewers to study the new relationships he has created.

Not all of Jennings's paintings made use of private objects connected by the "illogic" of personal associations. Most of his later paintings of the 1940s emphasized subjects which the public knew— from prints, postcards, and photographs. These "documents of mechanized reality," as he called them,[15] formed a readymade store from which he selected the images he so frequently used in his paintings and films.

Thameside and St. Paul's is based on one of these images: the cathedral's dome. Composed as a long shot, the canvas shows the blue and brown buildings and rooftops as well as the black and white clouds. The clouds and diagonally slanting roofs direct the viewer's eyes to the dome. Here, too, one finds, as Kathleen Raine has remarked, every brushstroke "made with meaning, deliberately placed according to a complex operation, involving both conscious thought and instinctive sensibility."[16] But then, these are the qualities that imbue all Jennings's creative works—on stage, on film, in words, as well as on canvas. Tarot cards, too, were part of Jennings's (perhaps less "public") store; he made both instinctive and conscious use of them.

Like William Blake, Jennings used St. Paul's dome to illustrate the belief that history is the culmination of what human beings have imagined. For Blake the dome suggested the forehead of Newton; for Jennings it also suggested Darwin. Unless an artist expanded his range of references, Jennings thought, his chosen images would function only on a literary level.[17]

Jennings shared another concern with Blake: the dehumanizing effect of industrialization. In *Workers' Houses (Bolton)*, for example, Jennings's view is as despairing as Blake's. With black, gray, and white, he shows the grass and weeds in the foreground and workers' flats in the center. In the distance chimneys belch so much smoke that one can barely see the factories and clouds. The linear treatment separates weeds, houses, chimneys, and factories; the bleak atmosphere unites them as reminders of the defilement of England's green and pleasant land.

The Blakean yet fluid lines of *The House in the Woods*, on which Jennings apparently worked for five years (1939–44), produce a picture decidedly cubist in style. Its verticals and diagonals form sparkling diamonds, a house and outside path that appear to be balanced on a cliff or rock. The painting, however, shows something not obvious in previously described works: the arbitrary yet careful placement of forms such as the circle and semicircle near the gate, and the leaf placed on it.

Jennings's very whimsical *Portrait of Purcell* further illustrates his bold emphasis of line and abstraction. In the canvas's center is the composer in semiprofile, his features made even more pronounced by heavy dark strokes. Black lines surround his head: the curls and lines project a double image—wig and fingers. Double images pervaded Jennings's paintings and films. Film editor R. Q. McNaughton has said that Jennings's main interest was in juxtaposition: "He tried to get two ideas on the screen at the same time."[18] His old associate Edgar Anstey notes: "Ambiguities excited him."[19]

When he applied them to his canvases, the very precise sketching methods Jennings used for his films produced generally disappointing results. The paintings are *so* well composed; the forms are *so* precise that one looks for a mistake—a misplaced line or a questionable patch of color, something that would lift the canvas beyond the domain of The Immaculate Academician.

At the same time, however much one wishes individual canvases showed more risks, an interesting contradiction between Jennings's several aesthetic commitments begins to emerge. On one hand he insisted on clarity and precision. On the other, the material he loved to treat—whether on canvas, celluloid, or the written page—was characterized by movement, historical transformation, and contemporary surprise. Charles Madge, referring to objects in Jennings's paintings, might also have been speaking of his poems:

> The thing is, that if you try to put Humphrey into an image, you are up against the nature of the image, because in Humphrey's mind, anyhow, the horse would rapidly dissolve into the steam engine and this would dissolve into something out of *Paradise Lost* and so on. Everything was always dissolving into something else.[20]

Dissolving is, of course, a film technique, and the use of dissolves was already evident in Jennings's poems by 1941.

Consider the third stanza of "I See London," written the same year Jennings filmed *Heart of Britain* and *Words for Battle*:

> I see a thousand strange sights in the streets of London
> I see the clock on Bow Church burning in daytime
> I see a one-legged man crossing the fire on crutches
> I see three negroes and a woman with white face-powder reading
>   music at half-past three in the morning
> I see an ambulance girl with her arms full of roses
> I see the burnt drums of the Philharmonic
> I see the green leaves of Lincolnshire carried through London on the
>   wrecked body of an aircraft.[21]

Besides dissolves, which allow one image to melt so that another may take its place, there are here the surrealist tactics of juxtaposing such disparate, contradictory elements as the one-legged man on crutches and the fresh green leaves on a mutilated airplane.

Like the third stanza, the preceding section of "I See London" relies on a photomontage:

> I see London at night
> I look up in the moon and see the visible moving vapour-trails of
>   invisible night-fliers
> I see a luminous glow beyond Covent Garden
> I see in mind's eye the statue of Charles the First rising in double
>   darkness of night and corrugated iron

On the corrugated iron I see wreaths and flowers
I see the black-helmeted night and the blue-helmeted morning.
I see the rise of the red-helmeted sun
And at last, at the end of Gerrard Street, I see the white-helmeted
    day, like a rescue man, searching out of the bottomless dust the
    secrets of another life.

Although Jennings's poems suggest dissolving images from line
to line, his films only relatively rarely employ the optical device of
dissolves between shots. (Jenny Stein, who, as Jenny Hutt, helped
to edit *A Diary for Timothy*, pointed out that there are quite a few
dissolves in the first reels of *that* film. She ascribes the lack of them
in other Jennings films to the influence of editor Stewart McAllister.[22] One must make allowance, too, for the effect of laboratory
costs on wartime budgets.) The poems—"camera poems"—do
more than record dissolving images: they telescope them, too. Jennings's views of a war-distorted London include observations of
contradictory situations: although the bombers have left, their
damage remains. Between the second and sixth lines Jennings has
telescoped the destruction of the night and the restoration of the
morning. Finally, he transforms the "vapour-trails" left by the bombers into still another hazy, impressionistic image: the "bottomless
dust," the debris that must be removed to restore the city to life.

"The Plough," written in 1948, provides another illustration of
how Jennings synthesized public and private images. Taking the simple machine that formed the historical foundation of British agriculture, Jennings transforms it into a kaleidoscope of personal, albeit
historical, references:

The gallows, the vine, the gang, the beet, the subsoil, the hoe
The Norfolk wheel
Whether in Tull's tune-book, Jefferson's design, on the Illinois prairie
    or pagoda ground,
All, all I see reflected in the giant shadow plough:
The gallows coloured green, the vine coloured red, the gang-plough
    lemon yellow, sombre purples and browns,
And the Norfolk wheel itself deep blue, standing alone in the snow.[23]

In "The Procession" (1939), one of his "Two American Poems," Jennings adopts the subjective view of a character in a film. After inviting the reader to share his imagination, he lists the flashing colors and sights the reader/passenger/viewer might see as he looks out of the window of a speeding train:

> Let us in imagination turn our faces westward
> The green cars of the Union line running out Ninth Street
> The red cars of the Second running out Third Street
> The yellow cars of the Eastern Penitentiary
> The white marble of the pure Methodist
> The rich brown of the First Baptist
> The splendid Episcopal Church of the Incarnation
> The pioneers of the piano business
> The pleasant spots in which repose the dead of this great city.[24]

"War and Childhood" (1943), which begins as a nostalgic piece about childhood with its memories of soldiers and horses, later shifts to images of shock ("Scaly hands running in fish-blood") and violence ("fish kicking the net"). Jennings follows these images in his prose poem with a litany of objects and sights the war destroyed: the girls, boats, nets, and fish market:

> I remember as a child by the ferry watching the soldiers testing horses for France. Farm-horses chasing them naked down to the river while the men on the banks hallooed and shot off guns in the air. I remember the Scots fisher-girls on Blackshore gutting the herring and singing in Gaelic. Scaly hands running in fish-blood, the last vessel dropping her sail at the pier's end, the last fish kicking the net. But to-day there is nothing—nothing of the girls on the boats or the nets or the songs or even the fish-market itself. Utterly gone—only the wind and broken glass and rough tiles made smooth by the sea. Only still visions of bloodshot eyes brimming over with fear. Nothing. War. Childhood.[25]

4 MASS-OBSERVATION, THE CORONATION SURVEY, AND *SPARE TIME*: 1937–1938

Through 1935 and 1936 a group of young people gathered at the house of Charles Madge and Kathleen Raine in Blackheath, South London. They included Jennings, the poet David Gascoyne, and Stuart Legg. Long discussions were held about surrealism, Blake, the Industrial Revolution, Freud, the relationship between art and science, "mass wish-situations," and the phenomenon of coincidence, which Jennings saw as a key to human behavior.[1]

The catastrophic year of 1936 ended for Britain with the national upheaval of the abdication crisis. Just before the news broke of the Edward/Mrs. Simpson scandal, a spectacular fire gutted London's famous Crystal Palace, the huge greenhouselike structure that had housed Victoria's and Albert's Great Exhibition of 1851. Many people, including the novelist Compton Mackenzie, saw this fire as what he called "a portentous coincidence. That it was significant," he said, "the superstitious agreed; it was when they tried to interpret the significance that opinions differed."[2]

In December 1936 *The New Statesman* published a letter from one Geoffrey Pyke. Pyke was a remarkable figure, who has been described by David Lampe as "the Unknown Genius" and whose career was documented by him in a book of that name.[3] In his letter Pyke commented on the tremendous amount of correspondence received by newspapers about the King and Mrs. Simpson "from obscure and eminent people alike." These letters, Pyke suggested, represented "material for that anthropological study of our own civilization of which we stand in such desperate need."[4]

In response to Pyke's call, Charles Madge reported that a group had already been formed, before the crisis, to study the anthropology of the British. British anthropology, he claimed, represented a special case, because its elements were "so repressed that only . . . a first-class upheaval brings them to the surface." Anthropological, psychoanalytical, and other sciences dealing with the behavior of man had been "applied by the group to the Crystal Palace/Abdication situation." But, Madge concluded, "only mass observations can create mass science."[5]

One of those who responded to Madge's call for the cooperation of voluntary observers was a young man who had just returned from an anthropological expedition to the tribes of Malekula, in the New Hebrides. As a result of his experiences there, he had concluded that the only way to combat one's own ethnocentricity was to live fully the Malekulan way of life. He was now applying a similar approach to the observation of workers in a Lancashire cotton town. This person was Tom Harrisson.[6] He journeyed down to Blackheath to meet Madge, Jennings, Raine, David Gascoyne, and several others. Gascoyne, who was the youngest present, recalls the meeting clearly:

> Humphrey Jennings had a habit of talking with his elbow on the mantelpiece—and he was at one end of the mantelpiece talking at the top of his voice, and Harrisson was at the other end doing exactly the same thing, talking at the top of *his* voice. That was very typical, I thought, of the situation.[7]

A month later, a fresh letter in *The New Statesman*, this time signed jointly by Harrisson, Jennings, and Madge, announced the formation of Mass Observation, an organization which later defined its object as "to make a scientific survey of the British Islanders, their

habits, customs and social life."[8] Madge has attributed the name
(which soon acquired a hyphen) to "one of our early observers,"
and calls it "a name which . . . could be interpreted as meaning observation either 'of the mass' or 'by a mass of observers.'"[9]

During the early months of 1937, as a result of this letter and
publicity in several other organs of the British press, Mass-Observation became an organization with more than a thousand voluntary
observers. (It still exists, but now as a market survey organization.) A
particularly ambitious project was undertaken for a series of "mass-
observation days" on the twelfth of each month. The description in
the group's first annual report begins:

> On February 12, 1937, thirty people made an experiment. They had
> never met each other, they lived in widely scattered parts of the coun-
> try and they differed greatly from each other in their surroundings,
> their work and in their views about life. What they had agreed to do
> was to set down plainly all that happened to them on that day. That's
> how Mass-Observation began.[10]

It was decided to extend the "twelfth-of-each-month" concept, so
that a particularly ambitious project was undertaken for May 12,
which was set as Coronation Day for the new king, George VI, who
had reluctantly succeeded his brother.

Published only eight months after the events it records, *May the
Twelfth*, the compilation by Jennings and Madge of reports from
over 200 observers all over the country and in parts of Europe, is a
monumental work.[11] In its preface there is a note about the relative
responsibilities of the three founders—"Humphrey Jennings is
responsible for the business of presenting results"[12]—and there
seems little doubt that the overall style of the book is Jennings's
work. (Harrisson, despite later claims, appears to have had little to
do with the survey.)

The book opens with a chapter detailing some of the preparations for the coronation:

> Eighty-five thousand seats were provided for viewers. . . . Paramount
> used the world's largest telephoto lens to film the event. . . . Manufac-

turers planned a Coronation Day colour scheme: linoleum, toiletware, goldfish, pianos, and mice were decorated red, white and blue.[13]

In what was later to become typical of Jennings's film style, these "news-snapshots" were juxtaposed with overheard comments such as: "There won't be no Coronation. The King will be dead by then. He's dying on his feet. They're keeping him alive artificially";[14] "the gypsies prophesized that he'd have a fit and choke . . . but they didn't ought to say such a thing after all the money that's been spent";[15] and (from an American): "Say, your gelatine of pork pressed into coronet shapes and cased in crimson jelly just gives me the creeps!"[16] The heading for this first chapter was a quotation from *The Book of Records*, edited by Confucius: "The Eight Means of Government are: Food, Goods, Sacrifice, Labour, Instruction, Protection against Crime, Entertainment of Guests, and the Army."[17] The chapter concluded, somewhat tendentiously perhaps, with the Communist *Daily Worker's* message for May 12:

> It is this Britain [working class] which will yet conquer. And on that day, the workers in all their majesty, dignity, and power will so organize the resources of this country that in a fraternal alliance with the freed people of present colonial countries, they will transform it into a paradise on which the sun of joy will never set.[18]

Other chapters ("London on May 12," "National Activities," and "Individual Reactions") juxtaposed quotations from *Henry V*, Baudelaire, and Freud's *Totem and Taboo* with accounts of conditions in the crowd watching the procession to the Abbey, reactions to the broadcast ceremony, and the return to Buckingham Palace. Several of these observers' reports seem strikingly similar to images found in Jennings's later films. For example:

> A middle-aged man walked slowly to the pillar-box, fetched a letter out of his pocket, stared hard at the collection plate, scratched his leg through his overcoat pocket, spat twice, then reluctantly posted the letter, bringing it half-way out again before finally dropping it in the box. After staring hard at the collection plate again and wiping his nose on his hand, he walked waveringly across the road.[19]

Compare characters in *Fires Were Started* (the penny-whistler) and *Listen to Britain*. And, almost certainly, the inspiration for the controversial scene in *Spare Time*:

> Walking towards the bus stop in Albert Street we saw the Deritend Jazz Band getting into marching order, in Union Passage. There were four men and about thirty girls all dressed in yellow blouses, black trousers and white canvas shoes. The men carried drums and the girls megaphones—through which they hum tunes. They marched away to the beating of a drum.[20]

The final section of the book, "The Normal Day-Survey," opens with a quotation from Pavlov's "Conditioned Reflexes—Lecture XXIII: Applications to Man." Jennings and Madge point out that May 12 had its own unifying element in the coronation. But: "We do not claim to have been able to hunt down unifying elements on February 12, March 12 and April 12 with any great success."[21] There follows an analysis by "social areas," and a number of March 12 surveys analyzed by this method.

The reviewer of the book in *The New English Weekly* commented that this was "probably the best book so far about the Coronation; these notes, or reports, appear to have been treated as though they were so many film 'shots,' to be put together by a process of cutting, editing and effective juxtaposition, in short, by a process of *montage*."[22] But the editors, in their closing remarks, stress that "Mass-Observation is more than journalism or film documentary, because it has as its aim in view not only of presenting, but of *classifying and analysing*, the immediate human world."[23] Nevertheless, this laudable goal was not achieved, if it ever was, until after Tom Harrisson had taken over the reins during the war. *May the Twelfth*, although wearing a respectable scientific white coat, reveals underneath very many of the more impish attributes of surrealism and poetic free association. It is probably significant that Jennings dropped his leading role in Mass-Observation after the coronation.

Madge remained with the dominant Harrisson until the latter made an arrangement linking the organization to the British Government's Ministry of Information. This struck Madge as bringing Mass-Observation too close, perhaps, to spying on its fellows. Nevertheless, according to Harrisson, Jennings, while at Crown making such films as *Heart of Britain*, would often call Mass-Observation for information and advice about the British people's wartime morale and its implications.[24]

In some ways *May the Twelfth* compares with James Agee's and Walker Evans's *Let Us Now Praise Famous Men*, published four years later.[25] In spite of its claim to objectivity, *May the Twelfth* presents a curious paradox: while the organizers encouraged observers to be unprejudiced in their reporting, the editors paraded their bias by inserting editorial comments. Agee, too, in the preface to his text, invokes a scrupulous objectivity:

> Ultimately, it is intended that this record and analysis be exhaustive, with no detail, however trivial it may seem, left untouched, no relevancy avoided, which lies within the power of remembrance to maintain, of the intelligence to perceive, and of the spirit to persist in.[26]

Nevertheless, as Jennings and Madge did in *May the Twelfth*, Agee inserted passages from other works—*King Lear*, *The Communist Manifesto*, a third grade geography text, and Ecclesiastes—all of which were selected to highlight and poeticize some aspect of human misery.

Beyond this, both the English and the American writers seem to imply that the man in the street and the downtrodden are the heralds of unique insights into the human condition. Mass-Observation believed that workers, merchants, professionals, and housewives (they excluded politicians) could be trusted to report reality. In their search for three typical Alabamian sharecropper families, Agee and Evans spoke of workers having "human divinity."

The differences between the two works, however, are just as significant as the similarities. Whereas *May the Twelfth* showed the individual linked to the British Empire, *Let Us Now Praise Famous Men* stressed that its three families suffered from the effects of social evils. Walker Evans's photographs documented the conditions and possessions of Agee's people: "The photographs are not illustrative. They, and the text, are coequal, mutually independent, and fully collaborative."[27] Mass-Observation's survey recorded volunteers' attitudes and feelings in print, but it is worth mentioning that a great deal of "candid camera" photography was also going on for Mass-Observation at the time, some by Humphrey Jennings and a great deal by another observer, Humphrey Spender.[28] If *May the Twelfth* was an attempt at a systematic record to be read silently, *Let Us Now Praise Famous Men*, not intended as a scientific study, "was written with reading aloud in mind. It was intended also that the text be read continuously, as music is listened to or a film watched."[29]

The most superficial difference is, perhaps, the most important. *May the Twelfth* is a book, and was always intended to be so. Agee, on the contrary, wanted a packaged collage:

> If I could do it, I'd do no writing at all here. It would be photographs: the rest would be fragments of cloth, bits of cotton, lumps of earth, records of speech, pieces of wood and iron, phials of colors, plates of food and of excrement.[30]

But both works reflect the strong documentary idea that was taking root in the thirties on both sides of the Atlantic, a movement which affected literature, painting, photography, and film.

For Jennings the poet, there was another aspect of Mass-Observation that must have peculiarly engaged him. Several of the prose poems he wrote about this time are, in effect, Mass-Observation reports, of horse races, a nobleman's funeral, and so on. Indeed, the published collection of his poems selected by him begins with "Three Reports" of this nature.

The documentary film *Spare Time*, made by Jennings for the GPO Film Unit, might just as well have been sponsored by Mass-Observation. Indeed, it says much for the freedom of choice and action available at the GPO, described by Harry Watt in his auto-biography.[31] Apart from one shot in a short sequence illustrating the weekly purchase of postal orders for football pool entries, the Post Office does not enter into the film at all. Indeed, several commentators have referred to it as Jennings's "Mass-Observation film."

According to the *Monthly Film Bulletin's* reviewer, *Spare Time* was "made primarily to be shown at the New York World's Fair to give Americans an idea of how the Englishman spends his spare time."[32] "Between work and sleep there comes a time we call our own. What do we do with it?" asks Laurie Lee at the film's beginning. The answer is shaped in terms of images, sounds, and music, rather than words, which are sparsely used. Three industries are identified—steel (Sheffield), cotton (Bolton and Manchester), and coal (Pontypridd)—and the people of the representative cities are shown in their leisure activities. It is against a background of music made by ordinary folk that we see these activities. They range from the most mundane—eating a meal at home—to the rehearsal of an amateur drama production and (most notorious) the kazoo performance of the Manchester Victorian Carnival Band.

This is the sequence which, according to Lindsay Anderson, "aroused the wrath of more orthodox documentarians."[33] Hillier claims they suspected satire at the expense of the pathetically drab performers of "If You Knew Susie" and "Rule Britannia" in a cold recreation field.[34] But Basil Wright, who in the 1950s used the term "cold disgust" to describe Jennings's attitude and confirmed the violent attacks on him, also affirmed that "as a piece of movie, it is both brilliant and unforgettable."[35]

Looked at today, *Spare Time* is slightly amusing in its incongruity, "the wind blowing chilly through the imitation silk uniforms, the Britannia tableau tottering along on its undernourished pallbearers, and the drum-majorette aping, like a grey ghost, the antics of a transatlantic and different civilization."[36] But, especially in the light of the previously quoted passage from *May the Twelfth*, there is no doubt the band was an example of the jazz bands (which had nothing to do with true jazz) that were common in northeast England and parts of South Wales in the twenties and thirties.

> It is a significant fact that the jazz bands flourish in periods of unemployment. They completely disappeared between 1938 and the early fifties. Between 1935 and 1938, the years of the arms boom, at least three hundred bands vanished, according to Elizabeth Bird. And when they resurfaced after the Second World War they were a different kettle of fish altogether.[37]

No other activity in the film is presented without evidence of respect—despite Wright's reference to the juxtaposition of "shots of a terrible tastelessness to shots of a traditional grace."[38] (Compare, for instance, Jennings's scenes of Belle Vue amusement park to those in Lindsay Anderson's *O Dreamland!*)

It is in *Spare Time* that Jennings, for the first time, explores what later became his most accomplished technique: the counterpointing of soundtrack allusions and images that may be only remotely related to each other. He invites viewers to make their own associations among them all. ("Only connect," as Anderson, writing about Jennings, quotes E. M. Forster.) It seems reasonable to assume that a great deal of credit for this technique must go to Stewart McAllister, Jennings's editor here for the first time. Paul Rotha, who describes McAllister's skills in editing and experimenting with sound, insists that "right from *Spare Time* onwards, McAllister contributed a very great deal. . . . [He] was a very, very remarkable collaborator."[39] At an early point in *Spare Time*, for example, Jennings establishes that one basic leisure activity in Pontypridd is choral singing: a woman arrives at a piano, plays some notes, and is gradually joined by men who begin to sing Handel's "Largo." Jennings then carries the sound of the rehearsing choir across several unrelated other leisure activities, periodically cutting back to the singers. This says not merely "While the choir was rehearsing, these other things were happening." It invites the viewer to reflect on their relevance

and common elements, while the meditative tone of the music accentuates the mood of gentle evening melancholy—even though the activity on the screen may be that of boys energetically playing handball in their club.

The final evening pithead and chimney shots underline with gentle irony the narrator's last detached words "a chance to be ourselves," as another shift enters the pithead cage to descend to the mine, and the work cycle reasserts itself.

5 WARTIME: 1938–1945

FORESHADOWINGS OF WAR

The making of *Spare Time*, with the opportunity to express Mass-Observation ideas and emphasize the value of popular music, obviously stirred Jennings's creative impulses and resulted in his first truly personal film. Yet it seems that in the prewar days he did not regard filmmaking as anything more than a useful means of obtaining money. The two GPO films which, with *Spare Time*, immediately preceded the outbreak of war confirm this. They bear the hallmark of official assignments reluctantly undertaken and have to be considered the least interesting of all Jennings's film work.

Speaking From America's subject matter—the improvement of transatlantic radio communication—is now interesting only to a historian of technology. The form of the film is restricted to a continuous, chattily instructive commentary ("a big bunch of sunspots is expected in 1940"), some animated diagrams, and an occasional shot of a workman that reflects the respect accorded by Jennings and other fellow documentarians to those who work with their hands. Nevertheless, Jennings once again clarifies and presents a complex process simply and efficiently. There is one sentence which reminds us of Jennings's lifelong awareness of the interacting worlds of technology and nature. It also contains an example of the repetitious style which frequently distinguished his commentaries: "The system does not intend to alter nature—the sun still has sunspots, the ionosphere still flickers, the waves are still out of rhythm." In the final scene of the film, the presence of President Roosevelt, literally speaking from the United States, suggests the gathering clouds of war in Europe under which this and Jennings's next film were made.

If coming events cast their shadows before them, it can be argued that the imminence of World War II caused the jingoistic tone of *S. S. Ionian*, commissioned by the British Council.[1] The film makes frequent reference to the Royal Navy ("the greatest navy in the world"), its armaments and fighting strength and its protective role. But the film is a rather dull account of a British merchant ship's routine round-trip voyage to the Near East. The film was quickly renamed *Her Last Trip* when the *Ionian* sank soon after the film was made.

Despite a somewhat convoluted attempt at the start to link the *Ionian*'s dull run with the epic odyssey of Ulysses, there is a distressing lack of incident and very little beauty in her slow and plodding journey. Occasional images, such as a misty shot of Gibraltar or of the ensign being lowered against the ship's sunny wake (two shots that Jennings used again in *Words for Battle*), indicate his potential. One or two casual references to crew members ("Here's Joe, one of the apprentices; that's Jim, the other apprentice") slightly humanize an otherwise detached commentary. But even the repetition of the *Ionian*'s cargo list ("steel, explosives, cement") does nothing to suggest the romance of the merchantman, which Poet Laureate John Masefield celebrated in his poem "Cargoes" on the same subject ("Dirty British coaster with a . . . cargo of Tyne coal, road-rails, pig-lead, firewood, iron-ware and cheap tin trays").

One might indeed suspect that Jennings, although credited with the direction, was not present during the voyage, and merely edited material shot and delivered by an anonymous cameraman. But this, apparently, was not so.[2] Nevertheless, one would want to know more about some of the crew. If there are occasional Jennings touches, they lie mostly in his use of music: an Eastern-style tune which "mickey-mouses" the gestures of the stevedores in Alexandria, and Elgar's "Pomp and Circumstance" for the return home. In an occasional trope ("Imperial Airways planes . . . like enormous flying fish," destroyers "fast as whippets") and in the absolutely typical closing shots of moonlight over the Thames, chimneys and cranes, sailing-barges and gasholders, there are other faint traces of the film poet. But Jennings abroad did not have the poetic power of Jennings at home.

THE FIRST PHASE

No one who was in Britain between 1939 and 1945 can look at Jennings's wartime films without an emotional throat-catch of recognition and memory. From the moment of the signing of the Nazi-Soviet pact in late August of 1939, all surviving hopes of continuing peace faded and died. War now was inevitable. Official preparations, which had been heralded by gas mask distribution some months earlier, were supplemented by further trench digging in London parks and installation there and on the Thames of anti-aircraft guns and balloon sites. These preparations were accompanied by the inevitable shortages and disappearance from the shops of flashlights, sticky paper (for protecting windows against shattering), and all kinds of dark material suitable for blacking-out windows and doors.

On Friday the first of September came the news of the invasion of Poland. The Saturday that followed was the last day of peace. People looked apprehensively around their own familiar environments for what, for all they knew, might be the last time, while futile debates raged in Parliament. The somber tones of Prime Minister Chamberlain at 11:15 on the sunny Sunday morning of September third sounded the death knell of peace. They were immediately followed in London by the wail of air raid sirens. For years there had been widespread expectation of the instant Armageddon-like destruction of the cities if war came (as in the H. G. Wells film *Things To Come*). "Old 'Itler didn't take very long, did 'e?" says a man in *The First Days* as he goes into a shelter.

The incident, although probably staged later, as were several others in the film, accurately reflects a Cockney attitude toward the enemy that, in general, persisted throughout the war. It reduced the monstrous impersonal threat of Hitler to the ridiculous "evil Chaplin" form of the Fuehrer, or the more amorphous "old Jerry." Up to the outbreak of war, the BBC had sedulously referred to *Herr* Hitler and carefully suppressed hostile or comic comment on him. It was a great and delightful shock, therefore, to hear the popular radio comedian Tommy Handley celebrate the return of live programs (after three days of organ music, gramophone records, and interminable official bulletins) with a song called "Who Is This Man Who Looks Like Charlie Chaplin?"[3]

Harry Watt has described the anticlimactic confusion and indecisiveness which seized the GPO Film Unit in common with much of the country during the ensuing autumn days, and how he, Jennings, and Pat Jackson were impelled to prepare a film record of events.[4] Credit for *The First Days* (originally called *A City Prepares*) properly goes to Watt, Jackson, and Jennings, and to Cavalcanti as producer. But it seems reasonable to suggest that a good deal of the material was Jennings's. The recurrent images of people listening to radios are unmistakably his, as are the evening silhouette shots of barrage balloons over the Thames. The "goodbye" sequence, where the word is repeated more and more desolately over the scene of departing troops ("going like the children but . . . the other way") was surprisingly ill received by the anonymous reviewer of *Documentary News Letter* at the time: "The most deliberately built-up sequences are the least successful, as for example the good-bye scene between boy and girl over a bunch of roses."[5] *Documentary News Letter*, founded by Arthur Elton, Edgar Anstey, and Basil Wright, was almost consistently hostile to Jennings's wartime films. Wright has pointed out that

> there were internal quarrels going on—different arguments as to how you should pursue film propaganda during a war. I'm not saying they were right, but the Film Centre group were not always in favour of the

Crown Film Unit attitude. . . . Grierson, from Canada, was in almost constant communication with us and was certainly on the side of the Film Centre group . . . so that you will find, in *Documentary News Letter*, a bias against Crown, or against Humphrey, if you like.[6]

The First Days and the later *London Can Take It!* certainly contain a great deal of Harry Watt, but the overall tone of the great Jennings/McAllister war films is present in them both. Watt was to take a bluffer and more belligerent path with *Target for Tonight* and later films. Jennings, in *his* wartime films, depicted a gentler, perhaps less aggressive but equally determined Britain, which nevertheless retained its sense of humor and humanity. "This is not twilight that has come to England," says the commentary, "it is dawn." For Jennings, too, it was the dawn. His great wartime work was about to begin.

His next film was in fact begun in the winter of 1939–40, but its release was delayed for several months, until after that of *Welfare of the Workers*.[7] Released originally as *An Unrecorded Victory*, it is better known by its alternative title, *Spring Offensive*. Gerald Noxon says that the film was made at a time when documentary production had come under the control of the Ministry of Information, "whose ponderous bureaucracy and continuous internal struggles for power had virtually eliminated [it]."[8]

The location is once again the East Anglia of Jennings's birth and love, the wheat shocks ranked as they were in *English Harvest*. (He was to return to exactly the same location for scenes in *Listen to Britain*.) There are several painterly images of the countryside and its machinery that haunt the visual memory—the flock of gulls following the plough; the dismal, misty, neglected farmland with old wheels, barrows, and tractors overgrown with weeds; the extreme long shot of a steam engine against the winter landscape, belching smoke like a factory isolated in the fields. Jennings's favorite juxtapositions of town/country, technology/agriculture, machines/nature, so splendidly realized by the time of *A Family Portrait*, are ingeniously invoked by Hugh Gray's script, involving a city boy evacuated to the farm, and given life by sequences such as that of the mechanical tiller (first embodied as the boy's Meccano toy model) churning and tearing through the weeds, with the dogs, horses, and pheasants fleeing from its rumbling, lumbering advance.

Once more, as Hillier has noted,[9] news from the radio plays a significant role. The evacuee arrives just as the BBC reports news of the War Agricultural Committees ("Don't miss the News!"). And it is of interest, perhaps, that the shot of the grumpy farmer shaving at his window is an almost exact copy of that of the village postman in *Penny Journey.*

Gray's script emphasizes two themes: the resurrection of land once neglected and the repetition of life's cycles. The *Spring Offensive* is a project for the restoration of a farm neglected for twenty years. Only technology can achieve this restoration. The film suffers from the self-conscious performances of the nonactors invited to play roles and the invented dialogues provided for them. Scenes of committee deliberations, which are less painfully heavy than in the later *The Cumberland Story,* are also relieved by the portraiture of splendid English faces. One of these, apparently, was the father of Hugh Gray:

> I . . . remember that [Jennings] found my late father (also Hugh Gray) a most suitable "type" for a farmer. In this he was probably correct, since my father was the son of West of Ireland farmers and may have inherited the look—altho' he himself was an engineer.[10]

There seems to have been some rather happy-go-lucky casting in the making of this film: poet Laurie Lee, who had narrated *Spare Time,* had a part as a young tractor driver,[11] and the evacuee's father was played by the film unit's electrician.[12]

The present-tense commentary, delivered again by A. G. Street, strikes an occasional self-conscious note (for example, the introduction of Land Girls—"Many colts have joined up, so the fillies come to the rescue"). Years later, Hugh Gray disclaimed this particular line:

As to my authorship of the script, I frankly have no clear recollection and wonder if there may not be some confusion between father and son! I certainly cannot imagine myself (at least in retrospect) writing such lines. . . . However, nothing is impossible—I only feel it is improbable! Maybe it was A. G. Street's. It might have been Humphrey's![13]

Released a month earlier, *Welfare of the Workers* was almost certainly shot after *Spring Offensive*. The reviewer in *Documentary News Letter* found it "scrappy and shapeless. . . . Its principal fault lies in the patronizing attitude which it takes towards the workers (simple childlike folk)."[14] Joe Mendoza, who had the job of recutting it, describes it as "the most boring film I've ever seen. I used to drop asleep in the cutting-room."[15] Most of its images are simple illustrations of the commentary's narration or provide neutral, generalized shots of factory workers, etc., as background for its generalities. Although the film brought together again the team of Watt (as producer), Jennings, and Jackson, they seemed to lack enthusiasm for the task of explaining and justifying regulations which were introduced to sustain the health and morale of workers in the armaments factories and elsewhere. These regulations, of course, were essential to what had become, after Dunkirk, Britain's solitary struggle against Nazism. (It should be added, perhaps, that Mass-Observation, with which Jennings undoubtedly maintained contact, was investigating similar health and morale problems for the government at this time.)[16]

Two BBC initiatives to aid workers' morale after Dunkirk included broadcasting "Music While You Work" twice a day (cf. *Listen to Britain*), and a regular lunchtime variety program ("Workers' Playtime") presented by teams of entertainers in factory canteens across the country. In *Welfare of the Workers*, the Scottish comedian Will Fyffe and the Minister of Labour, ex-trade-unionist Ernie Bevin, are seen on the canteen platform. But at least two shots of workers in the audience are identical to those in *Listen to Britain*'s "Workers' Playtime" sequence. This lifting of material from one film to another

(note the opening music, which is the brass band march from *Spare Time*) conforms to Jennings's long-standing concern with public rather than private imagery. (On the other hand, of course, one should make passing reference to the need for wartime frugality, which might well have conditioned *some* of Jennings's repetitions. The later *Words for Battle*, for instance, was created entirely from existing material.) The film's commentary, spoken by one who was to become increasingly well known as a popularizer of scientific matters—Ritchie Calder, later Lord Calder—depends on the same direct present-tense presentation that other Jennings films of this period do.

As Roy Armes notes, the early wartime films that most strongly anticipate Jennings's mature style are, "paradoxically, the two he codirected with the experienced Harry Watt."[17] Watt's own ebullient accounts of the making of *London Can Take It!* give due credit to Jennings's involvement from its inception.[18] He also describes Stewart McAllister's meticulous editing, "insisting on making each word drop exact on the right visual shot, even the right half of the shot."[19] There is little doubt that the quiet, modest Scot had considerable influence on Jennings's work; they were partners on almost every one of the "great" films, up to and including *A Family Portrait*. Elizabeth Sussex, however, claims she found no evidence that the two worked physically together on *London Can Take It!* Jennings was shooting much of the material in London, while McAllister was working continuously at Denham—so continuously, according to Watt, that he had no sleep for the final "forty-six or sixty hours" of the two weeks it took to make the film.[20]

After the fall of France in June 1940, there was every expectation that Germany would quickly follow up its successful continental blitzkrieg by invading its last enemy, Great Britain. Many—possibly most—of the children and others who had been evacuated from London at the outbreak of war had returned during the "phoney war" period and had once again to be moved—although not this time to the south and east "invasion areas," which now had their own evacuation problems. United States Ambassador Joseph Kennedy was reporting to Roosevelt that Britain could not win the war, and U.S. war correspondents thronged London to report on the devastation of the capital. According to Merralls, it was at this time that Jennings evacuated his wife and two young daughters to America and went to live in London with his producer, Ian Dalrymple, who had succeeded Cavalcanti at Crown. As Dalrymple recalled it to Merralls, Jennings came for a night's sleep during the blitz and his visit lasted two and a quarter years.[21]

The blitz came to London on 7 September 1940 and continued almost unabated in its first violent phase until mid-November, when heavy attacks were diverted to provincial cities and towns. Tom Harrisson, in his thoughtful retrospective study *Living Through the Blitz*, concludes that London's great *advantage* (in addition to its size) was the continuous length of the bombardment, which allowed Londoners to adapt to the new circumstances:

> By or before the middle of October 1940 millions of Londoners had "got over the worst" effects of being intensively bombed. Very few remained in town who had not developed a new normalcy of their own—not a carapace so much as an outer sponge for inner protection. The bomb-baptisms of September had been sufficiently widespread for everyone to feel personal identification with escape from death. . . . And if, by then, the whole thing was losing its excitement to become boring, that was a state of mind familiar in peace, powerfully accentuated by blackout and the other restrictions of war.[22]

The title of the Watt/Jennings film originally intended was "London Carries On," and its intention, of course, was to reassure American audiences that Britain was not indeed finished. *Documentary News Letter* called it "the first real message from the British people to the American people."[23] In view of contemporary American criticism that British propaganda films overemphasized Britain's non-aggressive attitude toward the war, it is mildly ironic that the film's more passive title was suggested by an American war correspondent, Quentin Reynolds—albeit with an exclamation mark that is rarely used in reference to the film but that appears in the title.

Reynolds, the correspondent for *Collier's Weekly*, broadcast regularly to America, as did Ed Murrow and others. He was to delight British listeners in August 1941 with a BBC "Postscript" addressed to Hitler in which he claimed that the Fuehrer's real name was Schicklgruber, and his deep-voiced, breathily ironic "Dear Mr. Schicklgruber" was a national catchword for some time.[24] Watt tells how Ken Cameron conceived the method of recording Reynolds's famous growl—"Let's sit him down in an armchair, stick the microphone nearly down his throat, and let him whisper"—and how, when the film was finished, Reynolds took it to the States in a bomber:

> Only Quint's name appeared on the titles, with no British credits at all, so all America imagined that this was an unbiased personal report made by one of their own people, a belief that Quint did not battle to belie.[25]

The film was initially disliked by the Ministry of Information, but the editor of the influential *The Daily Express* called it the best war film made so far. It became an enormous success in the United States and, in its shorter version (called *Britain Can Take It!*), in British cinemas. A book of the commentary, illustrated with stills from the film, sold sufficiently well to go into at least two editions.[26]

The visual material was shaped around Reynolds's words, which he wrote in the style of his radio dispatches after seeing an initial rough-cut of the film. This method of working very possibly suggested to Jennings the form of *Words for Battle*, where the images interact with words already written and existing in their own right. The association of words and images in *London Can Take It!* is more direct, less impressionistic, than in later films, and one "typical Jennings shot" of well-dressed civilians riding on a junkman's horse-drawn cart is, in fact, claimed by Harry Watt as his own.[27] Watt, however, confirms that the final shot, showing a jaunty young warden getting a light for his cigarette from a cab driver, "was one of Humphrey Jennings's touches of genius. He shot that."[28]

By 1941, the mood of Britain at war was changing: the long, grim struggle ahead was apparent to all. The nervous hesitancy of *The First Days*, the crushing defeats of 1940, which had been perversely turned into "the victory of Dunkirk," even the heady excitement of the summer and autumn Battle of Britain—"our finest hour"—had developed into the first winter of discontent: the wearying, droning nights of the blitz, culminating in the horror of the bombing of Coventry. This was the time when, as Jennings quotes Kipling in *Words for Battle*, "the English began to hate"—even though the old habit of referring to the enemy familiarly as "Jerry" still persisted, as the commentary to *Heart of Britain* indicates.

The changing mood is evident throughout this next film, with its quotations from *Spare Time*, its frequent evening shots of factory chimneys, spires, and moorlands, its masterful overlay of Beethoven's Fifth Symphony on shots of Coventry Cathedral wreckage, and its climactic defiant battle cry of Handel's "Hallelujah Chorus" against shots of war factories and bombers taking off. ("People who sing like that in times like these cannot be beaten.") *Heart of Britain*, often underrated, might well be considered the prototypical Jennings war film, blazing the trail for the masterpieces that were to follow.

The production team—Dalrymple, Jennings, Fowle, McAllister, and Cameron—was to remain virtually intact for the years up to *A Diary for Timothy*, and (with the exception of Fowle) to reassemble for the culminating summation of *A Family Portrait*. The commentary for *Heart of Britain*, spoken with conviction by Jack Holmes, is powerfully poetic ("the valleys of power and the rivers of industry"). A slightly longer version, *This Is England*, was exported to America with an Ed Murrow commentary. Despite the standard criticisms from *Documentary News Letter* ("Even Americans must be tired now of pictures of raid damage . . . and the usual defensive commentary. . . . Not even Americans, surely, need all this bullying and special pleading"[29]), the 1941 films were effective calls for help across the Atlantic. They were no longer reassurances that "Britain can take it" but assumptions of comradeship based on a common English-speaking democracy.

This is especially apparent in *Words for Battle*, which epitomizes perhaps the purest form of documentary, in that the words of documents themselves are used as material for documentary and the images are taken entirely from other documentary films such as *S.S. Ionian*, *London Can Take It!*, and *Britain at Bay*. Ken Cameron has said regarding Jennings's use of already existing material: "Humphrey used whatever he wanted. No matter who owned it, he'd have it."[30]

Deceptively simple, the film comprises seven short pieces of prose and poetry—from William Camden, Milton, Blake, Browning, Kipling, Churchill, and Abraham Lincoln—all read by Laurence Olivier. The accompanying images do not merely illustrate the words. They reverberate with them, providing fresh associations in the same manner as do words in poetry. Thus, we see RAF cadets assembling round a Spitfire plane as Milton's *Areopagitica* is describing "a mighty and puissant nation . . . as an eagle mewing her mighty youth." Then, as the Spitfire takes off and one cadet follows her flight, shading his eyes in closeup, Olivier reads the line "kindling her undazzled eyes at the full midday scene." This is followed by a moody, obscure shot of Hitler and Goering blurred by intervening trees, which accompanies the reference to "those that love the twilight." Then, at "amazed at what she means," comes a clip from a Nazi newsreel that pans past Goebbels and other German leaders gazing upward in a parodic illustration of the words.

Blake is introduced by a shot of the London County Council plaque affixed to his birthplace, while the soundtrack provides the voices and footsteps of evacuee schoolchildren and their teachers, who seem to be passing it on their way by train ("chariot of fire") to where we later see them, "in England's green and pleasant land." Jennings uses several shots of the fleet, Gibraltar, and others from *S.S. Ionian* to illustrate Browning's "Home-thoughts from the Sea" and a strikingly bitter, albeit little-known, Kipling poem, "The Beginning," which seems almost to have been prophetically written to accompany the misty, mournful shots of blitz damage and a victim's funeral.

Churchill, introduced in person rather than by memorial statues or book pages, stumps grimly past the camera as we hear his "We shall go on to the end." St. Paul's, freshly revealed through new blitz damage, stands indomitable to illustrate "We shall never surrender." Beethoven's trumpet call from *Leonora No. 3* underlines the increasing tempo and urgency of the images of empire troops as Churchill calls to "the New World" to "step forth to the rescue and liberation of the Old." Lincoln's words, seemingly in response ("It is for us, the living. . . . We here highly resolve"), are heard over remarkable shots of a cavalcade of tanks that rumble past his statue in Parliament Square, as Big Ben strikes. The roar of London's traffic combines with Handel's *Water Music* in a surging march movement. Telephoto shots show servicemen and women mingling with civilian pedestrians, all moving purposively across London streets, blurred by the passing vehicles but symbolizing the movement onward toward victory of the ordinary people of Britain. This sequence was originally intended for the conclusion of *London Can Take It!*, according to Joe Mendoza:

> Humphrey imagined a sequence of life going on—of people just walking and moving. . . . So Chick Fowle was sent into London to get shots of people. Being very literal, he put himself in the middle of Piccadilly Circus with a 600mm lens on, and did following shots. . . . We couldn't use it, it wasn't the right tempo."[31]

But the material was put in a can and saved, and Jennings used it to end *Words for Battle*.

This exquisite little masterpiece, combining the quintessence of Jennings's love of England with a clear call for assistance from the as yet uninvolved United States, was surprisingly ill received in Britain. (Its original title, *For Us The Living*, was abandoned as being "too lugubrious.") It remains relatively unknown today. The combination of Handel's music with wartime London, although ridiculed then, is a splendid illustration of Jennings's belief in the continuity of English culture. Unlike some of his surrealist friends who had suggested, however facetiously, that the art of previous generations should be destroyed to accommodate the new, Jennings believed that the art of the past breathes life into the art of the present and sustains us in times of danger.

Most, if not all, of Jennings's films can be seen to arise out of his preceding works. The origins of *Listen to Britain* lay in several different ventures with which the Crown Film Unit was concerned during the post-Dunkirk blitz period. The unit was moved from Blackheath to the safer and more commodious Denham studios, where it became known facetiously to commercial filmmakers as "the Half-Crown Unit." One of Jennings's early projects there was a short film drawing parallels between Britain's contemporary expectation of invasion and her similar mood previously during the Napoleonic wars. He worked on this with a feature-film writer from Korda's London Films, Wolfgang Wilhelm, but the idea was eventually abandoned.

As did many others in the unit, Jennings worked on *Britain at Bay* (director Harry Watt, commentator J. B. Priestley) and on a second Quentin Reynolds "report" entitled *Christmas Under Fire*, also directed by Watt. Another venture was "National Gallery 1941," reflecting Jennings's long and firmly held belief that *music* was an essential element in Britain's day-to-day life. (See *Heart of Britain* and *Dim Little Island* for two further examples.) It was intended as a five-minute film based on the lunchtime concerts instituted by Myra Hess in London's National Gallery, where, as Jennings's treatment concludes, "hundreds of men and women still find time in their lunch-hour to listen to Mozart and to invigorate themselves for the final battle."[32] Myra Hess was filmed playing the first and last movements of Mozart's Piano Concerto in G Major, K. 453, with an arranged audience.

Then Jennings was diverted to the direction of a film that was intended as a sequel to *London Can Take It!* and *Christmas Under Fire*. One of Quentin Reynolds's BBC "Postscripts" had been addressed to Goebbels ("Dear Doktor"), and it was felt that a film of this would make a suitable export to America. Before Jennings lost faith in the idea and it was abandoned, several sequences which appear in *Listen to Britain* were filmed: the opening scene of Spitfires flying over Suffolk cornfields (in exactly the same location as for *Spring Offensive*); scenes of bombs being loaded onto night bombers; of tanks being built; and of troop carriers rumbling through the Sussex village of Alfriston.

The raid of 10 May 1941 destroyed Queen's Hall (home of London's Promenade Concerts for many years) and burned all the instruments of the London Philharmonic Orchestra. (The last music played there was a special recording of Handel's *Water Music* and the *Leonora No. 3* trumpet calls, used by Jennings in *Words for Battle*.) Jennings and McAllister took a short break and came back with a new treatment, "The Music of War." The treatment begins: "Do you think that modern war has no music? What an error." McAllister later noted on a copy of the treatment that it was "written in 'cold' language for the civil servants who had to find the money."[33] This treatment contains the Blackpool Tower Ballroom sequence, the Canadians in the train, "The Ash Grove" sung to ambulance workers in the basement of the Old Bailey (a scene witnessed one night by Jennings and McAllister), Flanagan and Allen, and the already shot National Gallery concert. Jennings's search for the significant public image led to the jotting down on the treatment's cover the titles of possible "public tunes" he might incorporate into the film—"Old [*sic*] Lang Syne," "John Brown's Body," "I Love [*sic*] Sixpence," and "She'll Be Riding Down [*sic*] the Mountain." (This last song was not familiar to the Canadian soldiers, who eventually sang something more "transatlantic"—"Home on the Range.")

At about this time, H. M. the Queen (now the Queen Mother) decided to attend another National Gallery concert, at which Myra Hess—newly created a Dame—was to play. Dame Myra arranged with Jennings to include "his" Mozart Concerto in the program, and Her Majesty consented to be filmed, in a special postconcert session, as a member of the audience, with Sir Kenneth Clark (then director of the Gallery).

In addition to the problems caused by wartime conditions in Britain—the blackout, shortage of materials, and other difficulties—it must be remembered that recording optical sound on location was a much more difficult, less precise operation than it is with today's magnetic recorders, directional microphones, and other new devices. Joe Mendoza, the assistant director of *Listen to Britain*, recalls problems with the sound van, a heavy and clumsy but essential item of equipment in those days:

> We did some shots of workers going to work at five in the morning. . . . I remember getting the whole bloody unit up at four o'clock . . . we'd worked our whole location out; we had a hidden camera, and we'd tucked the sound-van round the corner. We were all ready when we discovered that the sound assistant had overslept and had got the key of the sound-truck in his pocket! [34]

The film eschews commentary and dialogue—with the exception of Leonard Brockington's introduction, obviously added by a nervous civil servant and best eliminated from any screening. (Ken Cameron, in some notes written in 1957, records that the film was rejected after completion because it had no commentary. This was "the only reason" for the unnecessary prologue. "The film is all the better for its removal," says Cameron.) The only other words are from BBC radio voices and an occasional remark emerging from general noise. But the masterful use both of music and a wide variety of sound effects is truly remarkable. Indeed, the film is still a model of the use of sound. McAllister himself modestly described it once to one of the present authors as "a sound-recording experiment" in which they sought to record every conceivable sound in terms of tone, amplitude, and pitch—*except* the sound of speech. The film also breaks new ground in being probably the first to use an "anticipatory soundtrack"; one frequently hears over one shot the sound belonging to the next, a device since overworked by others into a cinematic cliché.

The images and sounds in *Listen to Britain* complement and counterpoint each other so effectively that each viewing intensifies the experience of having actually *lived* at that time, in those places. Viewed silently, the film is a Family of Britain photograph album; heard without images, it is the random turning of a wartime radio dial. Three moments at least linger in the memory as examples of Jennings's and McAllister's genius: the complex of movement in the traveling shot down the road under the railway bridge, counterpointed by the fanfare and summons of "Calling All Workers!"; the cutting, to the swelling cadences of Mozart's concerto, of the shots of sunshine in Trafalgar Square, the silvery barrage balloon in the sky, the coat of arms on the gallery's pediment, Nelson on his column, and a sailor leaning over the balustrade; and the splendid effrontery of introducing the soaring soprano voices singing "Rule Britannia" behind the pounding of the steel mills.

FIRES WERE STARTED

By 1943, the storm center of the war had shifted from Britain to Russia. Ian Dalrymple, Jennings's producer, says:

> The Germans had taken all their aeroplanes to go and hit the Russians, and after May 1941 we were more or less at peace so that one could take many more risks in the blackout and that kind of thing, and it was suggested that a film should be made about the National Fire Service.[35]

In fact, as the preliminary subtitles indicate, "This is a picture of the earlier days," before the National Fire Service as such had been established. In an unusually warm and lengthy review, *Documentary News Letter* called it the "Film of the Month" and said:

> You're just as much interested and the film means just as much now as if it had been made and shown in the middle of the raids; and it will mean just as much in a few years' time when the war is over.[36]

The film was Jennings's only feature-length work. Daniel Millar, analyzing the film in 1969, claims that although *Fires Were Started* may be termed a "classic documentary," it is also "an exemplar for future filmmakers."[37] Today it would probably be dubbed a docu-drama, because it depicts real firemen and firewomen doing what they were accustomed to do during the blitz, even though the fires themselves were artificially started.

In filming, various blitzed warehouses were set ablaze again— one of them at least five or six times, according to Fred Griffiths. Blackout regulations were, of course, still in force, so permission was sought to light fires for the film. But no one in Britain's wartime bureaucracy wanted to take responsibility, so, as Nora Lee (Dawson), the assistant producer, relates:

> We had a sheaf of letters which proved it was nobody's concern. If a policeman came up, you merely showed him a letter from the police which said, it's not our concern. So we just carried on. . . . In fact, we had all those lights on in the dark areas, during the blitz, without anybody's permission at all![38]

William Sansom, the novelist, who was then serving as a fireman, found his assignment to a film unit as an actor a welcome change from what had become, in the absence of air raids, dull routine. He describes how Jennings operated without a script, making up dialogue on the spot, co-opting a street penny-whistler discovered in an East End square, and calling for impromptu piano music from Sansom. Sansom provided "Please Don't Talk About Me When I'm Gone" and the "rumba-type reach-me-down, and this went into the can within the day."[39] Sansom comments ruefully that "most of us had been through the blitz with hardly a scratch—but in this job we all got burned, and so did Humphrey and his assistants."[40] But he also insists: "The film was true to life in every respect. Not a false note—if you make the usual allowance for the absence of foul language which was in everybody's mouth all the time."[41] The same sentiment was expressed by Fred Griffiths when he introduced the film at London's National Film Theatre several years after its production:

> In the audience tonight I've brought along a couple of my mates who were in the Fire Service with me, and—well, I shall live, and they will live, those nights over again when they see this picture. And I tell you this: that as you see it depicted here—so it was, and sometimes far worse."[42]

It is sometimes argued that the characterization of most of the eight members of Sub-station 14Y's Heavy Unit One is rather cursory, that it is not easy to identify each man individually. As was his habit, Jennings refused the use of professional actors, but there are several impressionistic touches by which he gives us information about his characters, their environment, even their private lives. Several times during the preliminary sequences, for example, there are premonitory remarks made about the full moon, which Londoners had very quickly come to associate with the heaviest raids. Jacko's wife's "Don't do nothing silly," as he leaves his corner newsagent's shop, and his tale of the fire in his own home, followed by Vallance's ironic response, foreshadow his death, as do, Millar claims, two separate shots of him lighting a cigarette on the burning roof of the factory.[43] Hillier, in fact, postulates a mystical "ritual sacrifice" of Jacko and his replacement by "new boy" Barrett, based on some interesting if inconclusive speculations about Jennings's concern with the Tarot card La Maison-Dieu, the house struck by heavenly fire.[44]

The character which comes across strongest is that of Johnny

Daniels, the ex-taxi-driver. Fred Griffiths, who plays the role, had never acted before, but his hearty Cockney personality charmed Jennings, who devised a number of scenes deliberately to show it off. Griffiths went on to play essentially similar roles in some two hundred more films.

B. A. Brown, a small clownish figure, is associated in the film with kippers and braces (suspenders)—both standard English music hall joke objects. Joe Vallance is briefly seen bargaining for a secondhand statue; Walters, the deputy submaster, with a military moustache and grammar school accent, emerges from his front door reading a newspaper; and Rumbold, a gaunt, gloomy Scot, provides the two "classical readings" that, for Eric Rhode at least, represent crude touches of "little point."[45]

The shape of the film, Sansom points out, follows "the swelling-dying theme and repeat-theme notation of a kind of musical composition."[46] Beginning with the return from the repair shop of the Heavy Unit vehicle, the film's early scenes introduce each of the men who will ride it, a sequence accompanied by music that will give way later to the gentle penny-whistle tune as they enter the substation's gates. These introductions are not all absolutely clear, since other firemen appear in some scenes.

Johnny and Jacko are the only two who receive full-scale treatment at this stage, although Barrett is distinguished as he asks his way from a local Chinese resident. Alwyn's scherzo-style music accompanies two finely edited montages of checking equipment and carrying out a fire drill, climaxing in a trumpet lunch call, as two extending ladders, with firemen, rise against the sky. In the afternoon, Johnny and Barrett visit the substation's "ground," a sequence again accompanied by music that emphasizes the romance and beauty of the docks and the Thames sailing-barges. Then the late afternoon "recreation" sequence includes the putting-up of the blackouts, Barrett's piano playing, kitting-up, and the eventual departure of the team for the fire on Trinidad Street.

The blaze itself and the methods of dealing with it are handled in excellent narrative style, with periodic cutbacks to fire watchers, Control, and the substation. (One recalls the simple clarity and direct exposition of Jennings's early "educational" films.) With the exception of music to celebrate the arrival of relief water and a brief musical climax when Jacko falls, the soundtrack is restricted to natural blitz noises and shouted commands. Once the fire is mastered, a briefly triumphant march ends with the "all-clear" and the grey dawn of "making-up," and a sad dirge underlines the filth and wretchedness of the weary men.

There is a moving sequence depicting the relationship of the firemen to the neighborhood as Heavy Unit 1 clanks slowly over the hose protectors, and the returning residents and day workers wave to the crew through the smoke and dust. Griffiths has described how the film unit itself was slowly accepted by the local people, many of whom found themselves bit parts in this sequence:

> At the finish they were snatching little bits of film, like pushing the old pram with the baby in, or "Did you see me with my little boy Ernie yesterday?" and "I got in a bit last night, I was that woman standing on a corner with the second fireman standing by the first appliance," and all that. They just wanted to enjoy it, y'know, get into it, because of the background. . . . It was a sort of family concern after we'd been here a little while. Because we took root and became part of the neighbourhood."[47]

The next sequence, back at the substation, is introduced by a shot of a single almond tree in full blossom against the dreary brickwork. Apparently Jennings intended a shot (again, made up on the spur of the moment) of the submaster returning from the fire and passing by a single flower in the hedge outside—the first flower of spring. Unhappily, the clapper-boy, in marking the shot, guillotined this solitary blossom. As Nora Lee (Dawson) comments, "It wasn't funny. Not only did he ruin that day's shooting . . . he ruined the complete film, because never again were you going to get that exact moment."[48]

The final sequence intercuts the formal funeral of Jacko with shots of the munitions ship, saved from the fire, sailing triumphantly downstream. Sansom tells us of the resistance from the firemen-actors:

> The only revolt occurred over the funeral episode. Some of the men had already attended the real funerals of burned-up friends. They refused to carry this false coffin. Beneath this, I suspected deeper superstitions: they did not like acting in the old weed-grown churchyard, on holy ground, and among the symbols of death. They were, in fact, shocked.[49]

There is almost total agreement among critics that *Fires Were Started* is Jennings's masterpiece. Gavin Lambert, for example, asserts:

> There has been no other British film about the war like *Fires Were Started*, and when seen again to-day its poetic statement, its wide human sympathies encompassing both particular figures and particular happenings, and yet evoking the whole atmosphere of London under fire, appear as something unique.[50]

The lasting worth of the film is reflected in more recent comments:

> *Listen to Britain* and *Fires Were Started* are among the few war films that can be seen decades later without embarrassment. In these, nothing of humanity has been sacrificed for assumed strategic needs. They are films of affirmation.[51]

And one last tribute, from Millar: "*Fires Were Started* . . . seems to me the highest achievement of British cinema; and Jennings is not only the greatest documentarist but also . . . the greatest film-maker that this country has produced."[52]

THE LATER DAYS

The Silent Village was based on an idea by Viktor Fischl of the Czechoslovak Ministry of Foreign Affairs.[53] The Nazis' destruction of the Czechoslovak mining village of Lidice as a reprisal for the assassination of Heydrich, the "Protector" of that occupied country, had deeply shocked the Allies when the news reached them. (Fritz

Lang's *Hangmen Also Die*, dealing with the same theme, was made at roughly the same time and indeed was in competition with *The Silent Village* for release time in London cinemas.) Fischl submitted a note to the Crown Film Unit pointing out the similarities between Lidice and the South Wales mining villages he had seen. Jennings visited the area and chose the village of Cwmgiedd as the locale for the film. The Lidice story was re-created there with the enthusiastic collaboration of the entire village, which adopted the unit and the film as their own.[54]

In the first part Jennings opens at a leisurely pace, with shots of people in chapel, the mines, school, gardens, a grocery. He follows these with miners showering, then walking home singing "Men of Harlech." People in the local cinema watch Donald Duck, others drink in the pub, a girl tries on a wedding gown. (She was wed in actuality during the film's shooting.) This last shot, its placement and length, and the overall relaxed editing of the sequence arouse the viewer's suspicion. Surely such an idyll will be violently interrupted.

It is, in the second part. After rushing waters, we see a black car with a Nazi emblem and a loudspeaker mounted on its roof. The announcements from the car's loudspeaker (we never see its occupants) warn that property will be confiscated and uncooperative villagers executed. Later, even the radio, that constant Jennings symbol of community involvement, begins to broadcast Nazi warnings, and is switched off. (The announcements made were translations of actual German radio proclamations at Lidice.)

The villagers rebel. The miners strike, resort to sabotage. In retaliation, the Nazis shoot the men and send the women and children to concentration camps. The epilogue, in which we return to the peaceful Cwmgiedd of the opening, shows the Welsh villagers reading about Lidice and resolving to keep its memory alive. This has a spurious ring, a clumsy lack of conviction that makes one want to end the film before this sequence. Again, as with *Listen to Britain*'s prologue, one senses the intervention of a Ministry of Information bureaucrat, lacking confidence in, and understanding of, the deliberate ambiguities of art.

Hillier describes the film as "very impersonal . . . the tribute of an outside sympathizer rather than of one involved."[55] A sense of involvement with occupied Europe was, however, almost impossible to create during the war itself. Witness the well-meant but disastrous cycle of Hollywood "resistance films." (Relatively few British filmmakers ventured into the trap, perhaps because they were closer to the scene.) In any case, Jennings's translation of Czechoslovakia into Wales has a further distancing effect.

It is interesting to note that only here and in *The True Story of Lilli Marlene* does Jennings attempt to depict the enemy in person, rather than as the impersonal menace faced throughout the war by Britain. In neither film is he especially convincing. In *The Silent Village*, the occupying Nazis are ingeniously kept off the screen for most of the film, being represented by the loudspeaker voice, marching steps, and gunfire on the soundtrack. The German sentry who is killed in the mine is a mere lay figure, although the only other German soldier seen is movingly posed on guard beside the village's First World War memorial, reminding us perhaps of Jennings's repeated use of children astride World War I cannons outside London's Imperial War Museum. (This shot, in its turn, may have further resonances: recall Kipling's *Kim* and his friends on the gun Zam-Zammah in Lahore.) Here, however, no children play in safety; the mood of *The Silent Village* is the grimmest of all Jennings's films.

By this time, Jennings's interests were increasingly turning toward feature films. Nora Lee and Pat Jackson speak of a project he developed to make a feature entitled *Two Cities* (London and New York). This would have been made for Filippo Del Guidice's company, which bore that name, and would apparently have had a plot involving "an international operator."[56] As Pat Jackson comments, "It would have been his first step into the 'commercial drama' world."[57] But it came to nothing.

On a June night in 1944, Hitler's long-heralded secret weapon arrived in London. Pilotless bomber, unmanned aircraft, flying bomb, buzz-bomb, doodlebug—many were the names which came to be applied to the V-1 rocket. By this time the Allies had acquired a firm foothold on the European continent, and the end began dimly to be discerned. The new bombardment seemed to herald a return of the classic blitz situation, but there were variations. The morning after the first attack, and for some days afterward, there was excited speculation about German planes that seemed to have been hit and exploded as they came down. Not until some time later did the government deem it wise to inform the populace of the new menace, which made nonsense of air raid warnings and all clears, yet provided its own alert in the form of an unmistakable snarling, throbbing, engine roar that would suddenly cough and stop. In the succeeding moments of silence as it fell, one took shelter—and prayed, as did Bill and his wife in *A Diary for Timothy*.

In a sense, it could be said that the air attacks on Britain became progressively more easy to endure as the war progressed. In the beginning, a few bombers roaming the night skies could set off an alert that did not end until dawn, ensuring a sleepless and anxious night for millions. Later concentration of antiaircraft guns and rockets made for noisier but shorter alerts. The V-1, however, could safely be ignored until its hiccuping cutout; its successor, the V-2, traveled faster than sound, so that its swishing arrival and explosion were heard *after* it had struck. If you heard it, you were safe.

It was very clear that the V-1 had to be the subject of a film, and Nora Lee, with cameraman Cyril Arapoff and assistant director Jack Kranz, was sent to shoot material on the coast depicting the antiaircraft and, later, Spitfire attacks on the mechanical marauders. Further material was shot by Teddy Catford and his camera crew, and some sensational action shots of bombs being exploded in mid-flight were supplied by the R.A.F.[58] The film, then known under its working title of *V-1*, was rejected by the Ministry of Information officials as being too "artistic" and insufficiently informational.[59] It was relegated to a back shelf, and a new version was hurriedly prepared and released for overseas use, with the title *V-1* officially confirmed. Script, direction, and commentary were credited to Fletcher Markle. Markle was a Canadian airman with previous broadcasting experience, who later had a brief Hollywood career. (Compare the role of Quentin Reynolds in earlier Crown films.) Jennings, as senior Crown director at that time, may be honorarily credited as producer of *V-1* but had little or nothing to do with its shaping.

Much later, Jennings's original film was resuscitated under the title *The Eighty Days*. It has a commentary by Ed Murrow, yet another transatlantic reporter, and takes a gentler and more retrospective look at the V-1 campaign.

According to Adrian de Potier, who had just joined the Crown Film Unit on coming down from Cambridge, a great deal of the credit for *The Eighty Days* must go, as so often, to Stewart McAllister:

> I was put in charge of listing cans of films as they came in. . . . Stewart McAllister came up and said, "Hey, Adrian, will you go and clear up that cutting-room in the corridor?" . . . It was three feet deep in film. "We've got to work there tonight, we're making a film." . . . I did just that, but in between, I held it up to the light. The first thing I saw was a shot of Queen Victoria. Then there was a shot of a dustbin with a cat walking round it, then a shot of a woman looking up at the sky: a totally disenchanting conglomeration of shots. . . . I said to someone, "Do you know what's going on in this cutting-room?" He said, "Yes, they're making a film about the flying bomb." I said, "That's fine, but . . . I haven't come across a V.1. yet. I've seen cats, I've seen dustbins." . . . He said, "Well, you're in for a rough time; there's a chap called Jennings making a film with some of these things." . . . Anyway, I cleared up that stuff into some kind of order, and old Mac said, "I want you to help me tonight—we've got a panic on." I watched him put together these shots, holding them up to the light. About ten o'clock, we went to the theatre with Ken Cameron. Ken looked at it and said, "Oh my God! Am I supposed to do anything with this?" Mac said, "Take it easy. . . . Jenny, go and get me some sandwiches." By five o'clock that morning, there was a rough-cut. . . . I couldn't even distinguish the relationships between the stuff.[60]

Comparisons of *V-1* and *The Eighty Days* are revealing. There are two or three examples in *V-1* of Jennings-style "organized reality"—the girls donning their tin hats as they leap into the water for safety, the boys smoking in tall grass, a bowls game which ignores the passing buzz-bomb. These were directed by Nora Lee, who pays tribute to what she had learned from Jennings during their long association on *Fires Were Started*. But Markle's commentary hectors the audience throughout, seeking its sympathy through identification. ("You can sit back in your seat in this theater and see and hear V-1 . . . but you cannot imagine how London suffered.") Most of the images are used as direct illustrations of the commentary ("You're an attendant in a first aid station . . . you're a G.I., an MP . . . you're the man on the street.")

In contrast, Murrow's commentary for *The Eighty Days* is restricted to the opening and closing sequences, and this underlines the formal tripartite division of the film. Music accompanies the opening and the close—heavily threatening at first, mournful later (a theme from *Fires Were Started*), but triumphant toward the end with "La Marseillaise." The central sequence—the longest—relies on a soundtrack of natural noise only—and silence, so that we strain to hear the faint grumbles of the bombs on their way across southern England to the capital, or hold our breath during the silence that precedes an explosion.

The opening sequence to *The Eighty Days* shows a V-1 exhibition that was organized in London, with the bomb squatting on a platform looking remarkably like a piece of iron surrealism such as might have appeared in the 1936 exhibition. The closing sequence attempts an upbeat tone by showing General de Gaulle visiting a stricken coastal town (probably Rye in Sussex). This is less effective than the very telling shot which closes *V-1*: office books and ledgers piled on a chair in the ruins, surmounted by a disconnected telephone, while a man shovels rubble in the background—a scene which might well have been contrived by the most ardent surrealist.

Such surrealistic scenes were commonplace in wartime, and

Jennings was usually alert to them. (Notice, for example, the buses in the craters in this film and *London Can Take It!*, and the school easel burning in *The Silent Village*.) Occasionally, of course, the significance of such images is ambiguous: the Union Jack in the rubble at the end of *The Eighty Days* is comparable to shots taken by German cameramen of Nazi flags in Berlin ruins after Allied raids. When these latter appear in *A Defeated People*, the impact is very different from that originally intended.

Taking into account his fascination with those popular songs that become part of a nation's culture, one might have expected Jennings to have made a compelling documentary about the song "Lilli Marlene." But he did not. Although the credits promise a reconstruction of its history, *The True Story of Lilli Marlene*—"the most fabricated of all Jennings' films"[61]—seems ultimately not to be about the song, and certainly is not "the true story."

Marius Goring, the actor and Jennings's old school friend, narrates most of the film, which begins in 1944, returns to the inflation-ridden Germany of the twenties, moves from the occupation of Belgrade to the battle of El Alamein, comes up to date again with Lucie Mannheim (Goring's wife) singing new lyrics in a BBC studio ("Hang Hitler from the lantern of Lilli Marlene!"), then swoops into a speculative future with a scene of a postwar London East-End market.

As the film lurches from one incident to another, each sequence betraying its artificiality through Edward Carrick's sets and art direction, not to mention the surprising appearance of Jennings himself as the Hamburg lyricist of the song, one can only exclaim with Alice, "Curiouser and curiouser!" With the passage of time, the ambience in which the film was made and shown has faded. Even the song is now a half-forgotten antique, so that it becomes more and more a museum piece, incomprehensible almost, yet full of quaint interest and, for Jennings students, offering stimuli to considerable speculation.

There is the failure once again to treat the Germans as anything other than conventional (albeit unintentional) caricatures. This was a failing not peculiar to Jennings, of course; similar "villainous Nazis" were commonplace in other wartime (and later) films. But there are brief newsreel shots in *Lilli Marlene* of real Germans, of General von Paulus after the surrender at Stalingrad. These painfully point up the contrast between manufactured and real. Usually Jennings took real-life material and shaped it into significance by adding some rehearsed scenes. But here he attempts the reverse, and the real shows up the fictional as shoddy.

All in all, in its extreme theatricality of style, *The True Story of Lilli Marlene* raises important questions about Jennings's potential as a director of fiction films—as it happened, a potential never to be truly tested. Nevertheless, the film does possess certain strengths and many points of interest. For example, it is one of the few films made in wartime which recognizes the *humanity* of Germans, however ill depicted they may be. (Jennings was able to realize this more fully in the postwar *A Defeated People*.) The scenes of the Afrika Korps and the British Eighth Army both listening to German "messages from home" are touching, even though Denis Johnston's commentary sarcastically punctures the sentiment. ("We will see whose home thoughts serve them best.")

The final sequence, too, which carries us to an imaginary postwar scene at "the London docks on a Saturday night," is a fascinating evocation of the peacetime 1930s during which Jennings developed his typical L-R camera sweep. (Recall the lighted shopfronts in *Spare Time.*) In its final images of the corner tobacconist's, *The True Story of Lilli Marlene* also resurrects the memory of Jacko who died in *Fires Were Started*.

In the autumn of 1944, as the Allied forces pushed toward Germany on all fronts and hopes were raised that the war might end that year, Jennings embarked on what proved to be the last and most complex of his wartime films—*A Diary for Timothy*. Originally conceived as a film about the lives of six people during what was hoped would be the last six months of the war, it was later cast into the form of a "diary" for a baby born on 3 September 1944, the fifth anniversary of the war's outbreak. Diana Pine, Jennings's assistant, describes the consequent search:

> We had to find a baby that had to be the baby of a soldier and I rang one hospital and the doctor in charge said, "yes, I think we can manage that date . . . we're expecting several. Ring me up on Monday and see what's happened."[62]

Betty Jenkins, Timothy's mother, continues the story:

> Two days after Timothy was born about eight people came to the nursing home. They didn't explain what it was all about at all. Then a very serious-looking man who afterwards I was told was Humphrey Jennings walked round my bed, looked me up and down—and Timothy— and eventually after several minutes said, "I'm quite satisfied, are you?" to Diana Pine, and she said, "Yes, oh perfectly!" It wasn't until after he decided he wanted to do it or not that they told me what it was all about.[63]

Basil Wright, who took over the Crown Film Unit in January 1945, found a great deal of material for *A Diary for Timothy* already shot:

> There was no script—there couldn't be a script—and as you didn't know how the rushes were going to fit with anything else, it was an awful job for the poor old producer. And Humphrey was never available, because he was always out shooting again! Eventually the pattern emerged in the cutting-room.[64]

The scriptless creation of the film led to some difficulties with Ministry of Information sponsors, but their fears (and Wright's) were allayed by screening a rough-cut sequence in which Jennings brilliantly and typically fused two totally disparate wartime events.

The first of these was the introduction by the Germans of their second secret weapon, the V-2, a faster-than-sound missile launched against London that autumn. For some time, Londoners were periodically startled by sudden, if infrequent, loud explosions unaccompanied by any siren, aircraft, or other noise. Because it was basic government policy not to provide news that might assist the enemy, no one knew the cause of the mysterious explosions, and rumors were rife. (The first and most common one was that a gas main had exploded somewhere, but this quickly became untenable as the days passed and the explosions multiplied.) Finally, information about the V-2 was released, and Londoners had reason for gloom and apprehension, since no defense appeared to be possible, save to discover and attack the launching sites on the Continent.

The second event was the very popular production of *Hamlet* that was then playing at the Haymarket Theatre, with John Gielgud. Jennings organized a canteen discussion scene between two Civil Defence workers about the V-2 and intercut it with shots recording Gielgud's performance in the gravedigger scene. This, as Basil Wright comments, "is what in earlier times was called a Conceit." But, as he continues, it is a stroke of cinematic genius and "gave a focus to what otherwise tended to look like a rather tattered sketchbook."[65]

Jack Beddington, the able man who was Crown's chief supporter at the Ministry of Information, suggested a narration to be written by either Max Beerbohm or E. M. Forster. Wright "felt that Beerbohm would satirize it too much," and chose E. M. Forster.[66] It should perhaps be added that Basil Wright has since taken responsibility for what has been called "an extravagant phrase" in the commentary: the line "and death came by telegram to many of us on Christmas Day." Wright says it was, "with its surrounding paragraph, written by myself to fill a last-minute gap left by the not-always-too-industrious Forster."[67]

Other events dealt with in the film include the Allied failure to secure a bridgehead at Arnhem; significantly, Jennings uses the news of this and other battles to illustrate the immense communicative power of the wartime BBC. There is also a subtle reference to the forthcoming end of the war, as Mrs. Jenkins and her mother check the "demobilization group number" of her husband, based on age and length of service.

Now relegated, so to speak, to support Tim's "starring role,"

Jennings's original six characters were reduced to four. Three of them are predictable in the light of his long-standing interests. These are: Alan, a farmer; Goronwy, a miner; and Bill, a locomotive engineer. The fourth, Peter Roper, is an R.A.F. pilot grounded because of wounds, whose gradual recovery in a hospital provides an upward movement for the final phase of the film. On 7 September 1960, Granada Television rescreened the film in a program called "Timothy's Second Diary" and added interviews with its participants, sixteen years after the fact. Alan had abandoned his farm for a horticultural nursery; Goronwy was still a miner, but suffering from pneumoconiosis; Bill had retired and was surviving on a tiny pension; and Peter Roper, who in the film had said he intended to be a beachcomber after the war, had become instead a psychiatrist in Canada. Timothy was then a schoolboy, quiet and rather daunted by his unsolicited fame.

Mention should also be made of Myra Hess, who provides for the film a kind of repeat performance of her *Listen to Britain* National Gallery concert. A recorded film of her playing the first movement of Beethoven's "Appassionata" Sonata, obviously made from the material shot for *A Diary for Timothy*, was released by Crown at about the same time and is included in Jennings's filmography (see Appendix A).

The difficulty of writing critically about this complex and moving work has been referred to by several Jennings commentators. Lindsay Anderson quotes critic Dilys Powell as saying: "It is the general impression which remains; only with an effort do you separate the part from the whole. . . . The communication is always through a multitude of tiny impressions, none in isolation particularly memorable." But Anderson disagrees with Powell's last remark. He feels the impressions *are* memorable especially for "the intimate and loving observation of people." Jennings's people, he concludes, "are ends in themselves."[68] Gavin Lambert says the film "shows Jennings' impressionism stretched to its utmost, and the result, like the period it reflects, is almost too transitional."[69] Eric Rhode is concerned about moments of bathos in E. M. Forster's commentary, but also points out that the main concern of the film is with future peace, not with the war. "From a historian's viewpoint," he concludes, "*A Diary for Timothy* is a wonderful illustration of why Britain went Labour in 1945."[70]

The most detailed analysis of the film is one not easily obtained—that made by Evan Cameron while he was a student at Boston University.[71] In addition to his careful study of Jennings's "overlap sound" technique—employed here even more effectively than in *Listen to Britain*—Cameron demonstrates the symmetry of the work, showing how its six sections, while following a monthly, chronological order, also have a dramatic pattern in which the central section represents a nadir of disappointed hope. In this central section, Jennings abandons his major characters to concentrate on the world surrounding them—a world still full of danger and uncertainty. When we rejoin them, the news is still bad—the Germans are counterattacking in the Ardennes—but, with the throat-catching beauty of the white Christmas frost and the Cambridge King's College Chapel choir singing "Adeste Fideles," hope begins slowly to return. Scenes of recovery and rebuilding are counterpointed by BBC announcers' mounting excitement as they report new victories.

At the film's close, Richard Addinsell's opening theme, with its hesitant solo violin, returns to underline the uncertainty of the ending. The fact that a slightly different version of this ending exists, which incorporates shots of victory celebrations, does not invalidate the uncertainty. Indeed, it rather enhances it. In both cases, the final dissolve is from flames to Tim in his cot, but in the later version the flames are those of a victory bonfire. The end of the war brought with it new dangers and decisions to be made. Peace has its dangers no less than war. Although some of Jennings's fears have proved to be unfounded, we have lived to see some of them realized.

Walberswick

Walberswick, the picturesque fishing village on the eastern edge of England, a coast washed and eroded by the North Sea. Here, Humphrey Jennings was born August 19, 1907.

The Perse School, c. 1920. *Second row, sixth from the left* is "F. H. Jennings."

Jennings's set design for Purcell's *King Arthur*, performed at the New Theatre, Cambridge, February 14–18, 1928.

The Birth of the Robot (directed with Len Lye, 1936). Unable to find a garage while driving through a sandstorm, the motorist chokes on sand and dies. His skeletal remains are scattered in the desert.

The Birth of the Robot (directed with Len Lye, 1936). Originally designed by McKnight Kauffer, the film's robot was created from drops of Shell Oil that touched the motorist's bones.

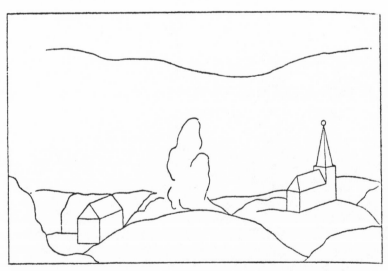

In *An Essex Group* (1929), Jennings's drawing shows his early devotion to the elegant line.

Jennings's *The House in the Woods* (1939–44).

Spare Time (1939). One spare, or leisure, time activity: playing "Rule Britannia" on a kazoo in the Manchester Victorian Carnival Band. Even today, viewers may think this sequence slightly bizarre.

Spare Time (1939). As the camera shows the factory chimneys against the sky in early morning, the narrator explains, "This is a film about the way people spend their [spare] time. Between work and sleep there comes a time we call our own. What do we do with it?"

The First Days (1939). The shot of an empty London street after warning sirens suggests Chirico's paintings and Atget's photographs of deserted streets and alleys.

The First Days (1939). From their barracks windows soldiers watch recruits train and drill (next illustration).

The First Days (1939). Recruits: "These were London's children. . . .
The defense of London is in young firm hands."

The First Days (1939). The empty picture frames at the National Gallery after the paintings were removed for safekeeping.

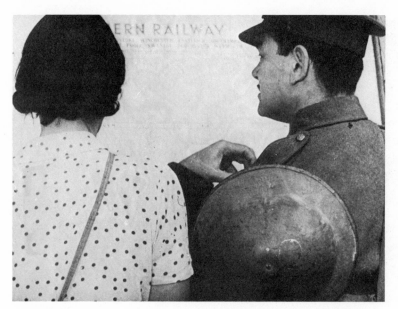

The First Days (1939). At Waterloo railway station, young lovers realized, "It was a time to say 'Goodbye' . . . 'Goodbye' . . . 'Goodbye' . . . 'Goodbye.' . . ."

London Can Take It (1940). During wartime, unusual behavior—like leaving a clothing store through the window—becomes ordinary and acceptable.

London Can Take It (1940). As commentator Quentin Reynolds explains, "Everyone is anxious to get home before darkness falls—before our nightly visitors arrive."

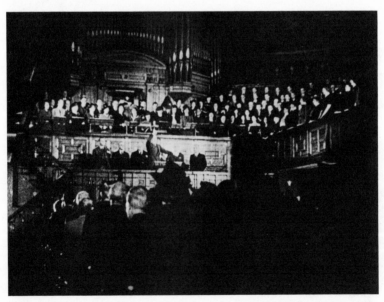

Heart of Britain (1941). A choral society sings Handel's "Hallelujah Chorus," a defiant battle cry against the Nazis.

Words for Battle (1941). As the camera records the bombed streets and funeral procession of a victim of the blitz, Laurence Olivier recites Kipling's "It was not part of their blood, it came to them very late . . . when the English began to hate . . ."

Words for Battle (1941). As the cadets look into the sky, Olivier recites Milton's "Methinks I see her [a mighty nation] as an eagle, mewing her mighty youth."

Listen to Britain (1942). In the Tower Ballroom in Blackpool, servicemen and their dates dance "The Beer Barrel Polka."

Listen to Britain (1942). The sounds of workers pounding steel become the melody of "Rule Britannia."

The Silent Village (1943). In the Welsh coal-mining town of Cwmgiedd, the loudspeaker on the roof of a Nazi car warns, "Attention, attention! Put trust in the Fuehrer."

The Silent Village (1943). Refusing to cooperate with the Nazis, the Welshmen sing "Land of My Fathers" before they are lined up and shot.

The Eighty Days (1944). Against the London ruins created by Nazi bombs, the Union Jack hangs on a line.

The Eighty Days (1944). A man waits in silence for Hitler's secret weapon against London, the V-1 bomb, to fall.

A Diary for Timothy (1944–45). Humphrey Jennings confers with Dame Myra Hess, who performed the first movement of Beethoven's "Appassionata Sonata" in the film's National Gallery sequence.

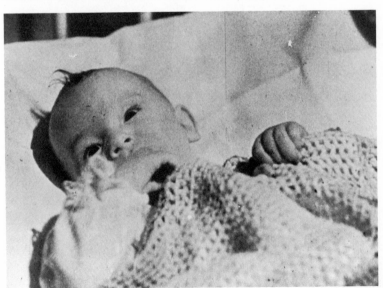

A Diary for Timothy (1944–45). At the end of the film, Tim looks up from his crib as the off-screen narrator asks him, "Are you going to have greed for money or power? . . . Or are you going to make the world a different place—you and all the other babies?"

The Cumberland Story (1947). In 1934, coal miners marched and protested against working conditions and worse—unemployment.

The Cumberland Story (1947). This machine restores the Lady Pit to a productive and safer mine.

Dim Little Island (1949). The tune played on an Elizabethan lute reminds composer-narrator Ralph Vaughan Williams of "a time when people, of necessity, made their own music. . . . They made what they liked, and liked what they made."

A Family Portrait (1950). Humphrey Jennings and the crew of his last film.

A Family Portrait (1950). A shot of the lighthouse at the seacoast Beachy Head begins the live action section of this family tribute made for the Festival of Britain.

A Family Portrait (1950). Jennings follows the narration, "We can only thank Heaven we produced a Blake, a Shaftesbury, a Dickens to proclaim love, and health, and life," with a shot of cricket beneath towering gas holders at South London's famous Oval ground.

A Family Portrait (1950). In his last film, Jennings juxtaposed his beloved St. Paul's dome with shots of docks, clouds, and chimney smoke.

6 POSTWAR—*A DEFEATED PEOPLE* TO *A FAMILY PORTRAIT*: 1945–1950

Immediately after V-E Day in the spring of 1945, Basil Wright went to Germany to examine what sort of a film should be made about that country's occupation. He then sent out Rex Warner, the poet and novelist, to prepare a scheme for a film to which Jennings was assigned immediately after the completion of *A Diary for Timothy*.[1] Although Jennings and two members of the unit spent two months shooting in Germany, according to the official handout, there is some justification for Hillier's remark that "it is hard to see in *A Defeated People* very much of the author of the great British war films."[2]

In *A Diary for Timothy* the commentary had been directed away from us, the audience, and toward the baby who represented the future. But in this film the commentary bluntly addresses the viewers ("*Our* military government—that is, *your* husbands and sons"). The chosen commentator was William Hartnell, who had recently played the tough British sergeant in *The Way Ahead*, Carol Reed's film tribute to the army. After a brief opening discussion among various British voices that sets out the argument of the film—vengeance or pity?—Hartnell, backed up by Guy Warwick's strongly emotive music, seeks to involve the audience in the first of the postwar problems that were to confront the victorious Allies.

There are several points of interest in this little-known but historically valuable study, made at a time when the Allies' sharply focused war effort was blurring and fragmenting into a peacetime kaleidoscope of conflicting national interests. For one thing, the Germans finally appear *as people* in a Jennings film, as distinct from the impersonal, bodiless menace that haunted the skies of Britain and the handful of stereotyped lay figures best epitomized, perhaps, by the grotesque dummy soldier in the background of *The Eighty Days.*

Because Jennings was a humane and responsive person, he could not exult in the devastation and misery his cameras portray. But—perhaps from diffidence—he mostly refrained from the kinds of closeups that study the humanity of the defeated Germans although such closeups frequently appear in his treatment of the British.

At this stage, the Germans were regarded as untouchable lepers, all likely to have been infected with nazism, regarded almost as a communicable disease. Fraternization with the Germans was for a time forbidden to Allied soldiers, and the general attitude of deep suspicion darkened English hearts for many years after the war. Jennings's film argues for the distinction between Germans and Nazis, but the suspicion is still there—note the treatment of the Krupp family and the interrogation scenes. In the latter, musical leitmotifs are used—a melancholy violin suggests the German's pleas, and a bold, vigorous trombone represents the determined British refusal to fall prey to pathos.

The intercutting and overlapped sound of the final sequence, which has a typical Jennings quality, makes an effective ending to a film that was almost certainly answerable to too many official sponsors. But the images of flaxen-haired German damsels dancing in a circle are perhaps too close to Leni Riefenstahl for comfort. Set against the harsh reality of devastated postwar Germany, Jennings's attachment to the symbolism of children, street barrel organs, and ordinary folk seems here, for the first time, overly romanticized.

In King George VI's Birthday Honours List of 18 June 1946, Frank Humphrey Sinkler Jennings Esq., Director, Crown Film Unit, Ministry of Information—as he is described in *The London Gazette*—was admitted to the Order of the British Empire. In the same year, the newly elected Labour government was embarking on Britain's "silent revolution," introducing the National Health Service, nationalizing the railways and vital industries. One of its most significant moves was to end the long, bitter resentment of the private ownership of coal mines. The passing of the act to nationalize them was greeted in the House of Commons by the singing of "The Red Flag," a gesture of victory that scandalized many but that is very revealing of the mood of the immediate postwar years.

Harry Watt to the contrary,[3] *The Cumberland Story*, Jennings's last film for Crown, was not *about* a mining disaster. It might have been better if it had been. Until this time (*Coalface* being an honorable exception), almost all films about coal mining had featured disasters (*Kameradschaft*, *The Stars Look Down*, etc.). But Jennings, working under the sponsorship of the new Ministry of Fuel and Power, could hardly make disaster the climax of his film—contemporary disaster, at any rate. Circumventing the problem, he showed a past cave-in caused by the reckless greed of the earlier owner's manager. He then depicted the resurrection of an old, imaginative plan to mine beneath the sea and its successful application through modern daring and vision. To meet the new situation of nationalization, he added an anticlimactic sequence at the end that serves no apparent purpose except to lengthen the film and perhaps to indicate (as did *A Diary for Timothy*) that fresh troubles might yet loom ahead despite everyone's sense of accomplishment.

General opinion tends to dismiss *The Cumberland Story* as a dismal failure, although Basil Wright prefers the term noble failure and sees the film as a logical outcome of Jennings's deep interest in mining, as well as an expansion of the coal miner episode in *A Diary for Timothy*.[4] Lindsay Anderson, a fervid admirer of Jennings, says that he was "overwhelmingly disappointed" when he saw it.[5]

In sum, one is forced to agree with Anderson and with Eric Rhode, who conclude that Jennings's enthusiasm for

> melancholic collieries, the dawn shift, the discovery of a coal seam beneath the sea . . . somehow doesn't transmit to the screen. *The Cumberland Story* . . . may tell us a great deal about coal mining, but like its subject is seldom more than a bore.[6]

The years 1947–49 mark a fallow period in Jennings's film work, although he was by no means idle or bereft of ideas and enthusiasms. He painted and continued to work assiduously, as he had done for years, on his "Pandaemonium" papers. Edgar Anstey tells us of long discussions with him about a filmed history of railways, to be made for British Transport Films. This, of course, would have been an ideal subject, and the project was still being enthusiastically discussed shortly before Jennings's death in 1950.[7] Nothing came of a 1946 plan to make a film version for the Rank Organization of Thomas Hardy's *Far from the Madding Crowd*, with Laurence Olivier and Vivien Leigh. Ian Dalrymple, the producer of Jennings's best wartime films, and who was to re-employ him later, had always hoped to film Hardy's novels—so much so that he named his company Wessex Films. But, as he says, "It was never a real proposition as far as Humphrey was concerned."[8]

In late 1946 a major project developed for the filming of H. E. Bates's novel *The Purple Plain*, about the struggle back to civilization of an airman shot down in the Burmese jungle. Diana Pine recalls that the project was overly ambitious and was eventually shelved for lack of funds.[9] It was finally filmed by Two Cities in 1954, with Gregory Peck in the lead, and directed by an American, Robert Parrish. The *Sunday Chronicle* critic spoke of "talk of filming this . . . novel of wartime Burma for years."[10]

In December 1948, Jennings made copious notes for another intended film, about the London Symphony Orchestra. But the postwar world seemed to have no space or time for Jennings. Denis Forman, who had served with the Ministry of Information and knew

Humphrey well, says: "After the war, there was no launching platform for Jennings's films, because they didn't meet the needs of any
one department."[11]

By the end of the turbulent forties, the mood of Britain was
changing profoundly. The élan that had accompanied the Labour
government's immediate postwar reforms had evaporated, and the
first realizations of what life in Britain would be like without the British Empire were beginning to seep into national consciousness. Ian
Dalrymple tells of how he was approached by J. Arthur Rank to
make a film about what Britain had contributed to the war effort:

> I said, "I don't see any point in doing that now. Why don't you do a film
> about the decline of the British Empire?" Of course, that shook him.
> . . . But the scrapings out of that really became what we made for the
> Festival of Britain [*A Family Portrait*].[12]

Julian Trevelyan says that as early as 1946 Jennings was talking about
a new film he wanted to do:

> It sounded rather ghastly, but, as Humphrey did, he talked us into it,
> and then it seemed marvellous. It was a project about "Sons of Brit-
> ain," all sorts of people—Ralph Vaughan Williams and so on—who
> were thoroughly English. He was working for some propaganda thing,
> and it seemed rather corny, but he made it seem rather marvellous at
> the time.[13]

These two sets of ideas seem to have come to fruition in the two
meditations upon England and Englishness which Jennings, having
finally left Crown, made for Dalrymple's Wessex Films. As it turned
out, they were to be his last films.

Dim Little Island, less complex than *A Family Portrait*, is also less
cohesive in its arguments. There are echoes both of *Heart of Britain*,
with its emphasis on the saving glory of English music, and of the
(now rather hollow) calls to "work harder" that concluded several of
his wartime films, as well as *The Cumberland Story*.

The film's titles, set in Blake-like typography and with an eighteenth-century use of capitals, include the phrase "A Short Film

Composed of Some Thoughts on our Past, Present and Future from Four Men." The multicommentary format is relatively unusual for Jennings, and the four commentators have distinct views to offer that he is not completely able to orchestrate. Dalrymple, indeed, has suggested dryly that the four sections arose from notes jotted on the backs of four separate envelopes in Humphrey's pocket.[14]

Osbert Lancaster, whose witty drawings have poked fun at English foibles for forty years or so, opens the proceedings with a less flippant judgment than his drawings might indicate. Calling the cartoonist a "guardian of reality," he reminds the viewer of Ford Madox Brown's painting *The Last of England*, which shows emigrants leaving the country in the 1850s. Despite the optimism of that period, "to them England was the land of the 12-hour day." Later, he cynically reminds us (over a shot of a ship called *British Genius*) that "we remain deaf to appeals to reason . . . the experts are invariably wrong."

Next James Fisher, the naturalist, extols the beauty and mystery of the English countryside, and Vaughan Williams develops this into a panegyric of English music. Not until John Ormston's somewhat naive discussion of Britain's engineering and exporting fall from grace do the sour notes return. Ormston's remarks merely restate what Jennings seems always to have had in mind—that it took a national cataclysm to wake up British genius. Vaughan Williams also says in the film that in times of upheaval people take their music more seriously. The quotation shot from *Fires Were Started* underlines what Richard Winnington said Jennings once told him "firmly and passionately, that good films could only be made in times of disaster."[15]

It was the war that quickened Jennings's (and many of his contemporaries') spirit. Peacetime left him (and them) seeking a comparable challenge. For Jennings, the search was to end abruptly in death at the foot of a Greek cliff. For others, it was to continue into a morass of failed hopes and diverted intentions. Perhaps *Dim Little Island* failed because, at a time when the public did not feel it needed it, there was more morale-boosting in Jennings's last films than in any of his war works.[16] Nevertheless, it was a film he had to complete before he could make his last, most personal statement, in *A Family Portrait*.

Some have called *A Family Portrait* a confusingly detailed, impersonal film, devoid of the passion of the wartime films. Yet it points to Jennings's continuing fascination with two of his previous concerns. If *Spare Time* was his Mass-Observation film, *A Family Portrait* owes a great deal to "Pandaemonium." Suggesting, though not duplicating, the purpose of that collection, *A Family Portrait* anthologizes fragments of Britain's scientific, literary, and intellectual history. Secondly, Jennings's use of images evokes the concept of "spontaneous gesture" associated with surrealist automatism.

Probably as a result of its long gestatory period, *A Family Portrait* was, according to Dalrymple, the only Jennings film that was fully scripted, both for words and images.[17] Conceived first as an ambitious full-scale film, it was reduced in length and scope when finally it was commissioned for the Festival of Britain.

The festival, originally proposed several years earlier by the editor of the now defunct *News-Chronicle* newspaper, was designed to celebrate both the arrival of the century's second half and the centenary of Prince Albert's Great Exhibition of 1851. It was intended as a tonic to the spirits of a people sorely tried by a decade of war and its attendant material shortages. As the film says, its intention was "to pat ourselves on the back." It celebrated the British heritage of art, music, and humor in a manner very similar to that used in *Heart of Britain* and, even more, to *Dim Little Island*. The relationship between the latter film and *A Family Portrait* is stressed by the use of the same shot of Beachy Head lighthouse in both films. In *Dim Little Island* it is the film's last shot, as Osbert Lancaster speaks of a beginning; in *A Family Portrait* it is the first live shot, and the commentator says, "Where to begin? Here."

In London, the dreary, abandoned, brewery and warehouse area south of the Thames, adjacent to the splendid new Waterloo

Bridge, which was the pride of the immediate prewar days, became the site of an excellent and exciting exhibition of British arts and skills. Its two legacies are the Royal Festival Hall and the National Film Theatre. The former may be seen almost as a direct outcome of the musical arguments proffered by Vaughan Williams and Jennings in *Dim Little Island*. It stands as a monument to the artistic hopes of the early fifties just as the Crystal Palace embodied the industrial optimism of a century earlier.

A Family Portrait certainly lacks the declamatory conclusions of the wartime films, several of which now seem to ring with a fervor that might even be regarded as outmoded jingoism. But it demonstrates beautifully the poetic, allusive skill that Jennings deploys both in his soundtrack and his images—and in the combination of the two. They play off, and with, each other with delicacy and assurance, like—and one has to use an English analogy here—a seasoned pair of batsmen stealing runs in a cricket match. "Prose" and "poetry," to use Jennings's own dichotomy, each feeds the other, so that a brass band march matches a foundry master's arm movements, the commentary refers to "the march of the machines," and we cut to Trevithick's locomotive "Catch Me Who Can," which took the place of horses. Then Stephenson, a modern train, horses racing, train again, and a horse race crowd at Newmarket, accompanied by the march from Handel's *Rinaldo*—"Let Us Now Take the Road." Or, in another instance, after shots of slums and children playing cricket in the street, the narrator mentions Blake, Dickens, and Shaftesbury—"Thank heaven we produced them to proclaim love and health and life"—and we see a modern school, followed by professional cricket under the gas holders at the Oval ground. In another segment, a closeup of Darwin, who studied the "struggle for existence," dissolves into a pan of fruit trees in blossom, which then become the daily mass of pedestrian workers crossing London Bridge. "The Lambeth Walk," Douglas Furber's popular prewar dance and Cockney song, is played delicately as a minuet to emphasize the reference to poetry and prose, then extended to underline Newton's discovery of the magnetism of the earth, as a ship's compass swings in gentle rhythm to the music.

With the denial to us of "Pandaemonium," we must take *A Family Portrait* both as Jennings's last testament and his legacy. In either case, to use British understatement, it is not an unworthy one.

7 UNCOMPLETED PROJECTS

THE LONDON SYMPHONY ORCHESTRA

Between *The Cumberland Story* (1947) and *Dim Little Island* (1949), Jennings wrote notes and sketches for a planned film about the London Symphony Orchestra,[1] a plan that was never to be realized. The published sketches, however, indicate that the film might well have been one of his best. During his six months' preparation for it, Jennings attended rehearsals, performances, recording sessions, spoke with the players, and watched them in their off moments before rehearsals, at tea breaks, and on tour.

The text of the "Working Sketches" shows Jennings's love for classical Beethoven, Handel, and Mozart, as well as for the more modern Benjamin Britten and Vaughan Williams. With his zest for observing and recording the unusual and the bizarre, Jennings, Mass-Observer still, reported on the individuals who make up an orchestra and on those who become its audience.

As individuals, the talented players of the London Symphony Orchestra might well have gone in for careers as soloists. How did these performers react as an ensemble, a team? What about their listeners? What happened to the teachers, factory workers, merchants, and others who, when the house lights dimmed, became the audience? We shall never *see* Jennings's answers. But to read the "Working Sketches" is to realize that the power of art aroused him as deeply as did the challenge of war.

Throughout, Jennings compiles the details of a rehearsal atmosphere: cleaning ladies carrying their buckets downstage while the
orchestra rehearses Fauré's *Masques and Bergamasques;* Josef Krips
leaning over "as though to pull the notes out of her mouth" while
Kathleen Ferrier sings Mahler's "Kindertotenlieder"; the photogra-
pher flashing his camera between the scherzo and finale of a Beethoven symphony; and the violinist who confessed that he didn't
like Beethoven but preferred the "good tunes" in Handel's *Water
Music.* After the first trumpet played a solo, his colleagues ap-
plauded—and then booed him. As a lighted cigarette's smoke floats
through the first horn's mute, the other horn players laugh. One
tells of a flute player past seventy so vain that he covers his bald spot
with shoe polish.

Of the orchestra's conductors, Jennings admired Sir Malcolm
Sargent, Clemens Kraus, and Krips. At one session, Krips admonished the first violinist for turning pages at a tense moment during a
Beethoven symphony. A cellist understood why Krips was upset: "It
is distracting to turn over, it does take your mind off your work."
Because of his attention to details, Krips becomes the master, the
musician who "wants you to play—he just moulds you—and you
want to play." Krips the perfectionist, it would appear, is like Blake
the painter, who believed that "without Minute Neatness of Execu-
tion the Sublime Cannot Exist! Grandeur of Ideas is founded on Precision of Ideas."[2]

The reference to Blake is indirect; the visual references to previous films are obvious. A puddle of night rain near the Albert Hall
reminds us of *A Diary for Timothy.* An image from *Listen to Britain*:

> The train to Mitcham Junction sweeps out of Victoria, over the river
> right under the chimneys of Battersea power station and out into the
> gray landscape of industrial streets, railway yards, and back gardens
> with washing and struggling trees. Then the train gets into more open
> country—lines of prefabs, nissen huts, allotments [Victory gardens],
> Tooting football ground; rows of seagulls on flooded furrows.

In *Listen to Britain* sandbags are piled against empty picture frames;

in "Working Sketches," at the Queen's Westminsters HQ Drill Hall, the orchestra's "cello cases are ranged next to ammo boxes and beer crates. The double basses huddle in their overcoats in front of 'Grenades, Anti-Personnel, Hand, No. 70, Mark 3, an enlarged coloured section.'"

Jennings wonders what the future members of the evening's audience do while the orchestra rehearses. "Quite an important question. Why is each of them coming? Their faces now, and the same faces in the evening—their wishes, and the Orchestra's wishes." In another sketch, he implies that the orchestra is there for the music. Music so completely unites the instrumentalists that, even though they might be thinking of something else while waiting, they can each enter on cue.

"Working Sketches" indicates that Jennings might well have divided his film into three parts, three special "moments" he witnessed when emotions overflowed. During one, after Navarra played the Dvořák Cello Concerto, many players exclaimed, "'What an artist!' If the Orchestra often seems to be hard in its judgments, it is because it reserves its enthusiasm for a concert and a player like this. The emotional and cathartic effect on the Orchestra . . . is great—it influences its players for weeks." During another "moment," the filmmaker spotted a girl with tears in her eyes as Ida Haendel played the last notes of Beethoven's Violin Concerto and the audience waited for the final beat before it released stifled coughs. The third "moment" occurred while Ralph Vaughan Williams, then nearly eighty, conducted one of his symphonies. "I remember our worry as the conductor's hand occasionally stole back to the rail to steady himself, that his fingers fumbled in turning the pages, that once the Orchestra carried on as if he was lost, that there were tears in his eyes."

This third "moment" would have an appropriate ending for Jennings's film because it happened while Vaughan Williams conducted his Second Symphony, The London: "not just as a piece of great music in the abstract—it is of us, written about us: this makes a performance in London a social event in the real sense. . . . All this one felt." One can't help concluding that Jennings would have made a film audience feel it too.

"PANDAEMONIUM"

To the layman, pandemonium is chaos. To Milton, Pandaemonium was the capital of Hell. Jennings's plan, cherished throughout his adult life but never finally realized, was to use Milton's concept as the title of a collage-anthology of quotations from contemporary Englishmen of the seventeenth, eighteenth, and nineteenth centuries. In his work, intended to be published as a four-volume paperback, indexed, cross-referenced, and profusely illustrated, Jennings planned to display and juxtapose ideas from those centuries, notably those commenting on the machine and its effects upon society.

The work would have been more than a mere panorama: it would have provided a unique kaleidoscope of political, social, artistic, and scientific currents of thought in the stream of English history. Original sources illustrate the changes that technology brought to Britain over the centuries. Because it includes passages that note the blights as well as the benefits science has brought, "Pandaemonium" inevitably reflects many of the ideas of Jennings's favorite poet and painter, William Blake: "Without Contraries is no progression. Attraction and Repulsion, Reason and Energy, Love and Hate, are necessary to Human Existence. Evil is the active springing from Energy. Good is Heaven. Evil is Hell."[3]

It is of more than passing interest that, at roughly the same time, another student of life and art, excited by surrealism, Marxism, and the other intellectual movements of the time, was bent upon a somewhat similar project. This was Walter Benjamin, a Berlin intellectual, author of the seminal essay "The Work of Art in the Age of Mechanical Reproduction." Hannah Arendt, editor of Benjamin's *Illuminations*, tells us:

> Quotations are at the center of every work of Benjamin's. . . . When he was working on his study of German tragedy, he boasted of a collection of "over 600 quotations very systematically and clearly arranged"; . . .

> like the later notebooks, this collection was not an accumulation of ex-
> cerpts intended to facilitate the writing of the study but constituted the
> main work, [which] consisted in tearing fragments out of their context
> and arranging them afresh in such a way that they illustrated one an-
> other and were able to prove their *raison d'être* in a free-floating state,
> as it were. It definitely was a sort of surrealistic montage.[4]

Although their life spans were roughly contemporaneous—Benjamin was fifteen years older and died fifteen years earlier—there is
no evidence that Jennings and Benjamin had any kind of contact, although it is just as impossible to prove that Jennings, with his wide-
ranging, magpielike acquisition of ideas, did *not* know something of
the German's work, especially in the early years before nazism.

"Pandaemonium," like Benjamin's "greatest ambition,"[5] was
neither published nor completed during its composer's lifetime. Jennings's papers still lie, untouched for years, in the vaults of a London
bank. After Humphrey's tragic death, Jacob Bronowski tried to have
the existing papers published, but found it difficult in those days
to duplicate the handwritten passages. Even when Charles Madge
and others had typescripts prepared for publishers, problems continued. "Pandaemonium" was a baffling work for publishers, who
must have wondered, How can we sell this commercially risky anthology? As Science? History? Art? Sociology? Perhaps a truly skeptical publisher might have rejected the work because, arguably, what
Jennings considered his life's work would have contributed relatively little to the world of scholarship. Yet it is interesting to note
that a smaller anthology with very similar aims was prepared and
published in 1970 for the students of Britain's Open University.[6]

Jennings's concern about the special power of science and the
machine to affect the quality of human life may well be traced to his
early days at the Perse School. About 1920, when Jennings was nearly
thirteen, Headmaster W. H. D. Rouse wrote "Machines or Mind?,"[7]
an essay imbued with the contradictions and paradoxes that mark
the poems of Blake as well as the films, paintings, and poems of Jennings. "Poetry cannot make a machine," Rouse said, "but it is the

food of the imagination."[8] Throughout their respective lives, Rouse used pedagogy and Jennings his arts to ask—and answer—the question, How can science enrich the quality of life?

> What is the use of machines? The world is full of machines. . . . Why are they made? To save time, trouble, money. They are a nuisance to everybody around, they spoil one's eyes and ears, offend the senses, make life dangerous; worst of all, the better the machine, the less we use our intelligence. It is quite possible to argue that they do more harm than good; but suppose they are all good, suppose time, space, money, labour is saved, what then?[9]

For Rouse, the answer was clear:

> He who can show the world how to use its leisure time will be a greater benefactor than . . . any maker of machines. The most highly civilized nation of history was Athens in the years 500 to 400 B.C., and they hardly knew what a machine was.[10]

Rouse taught his students that reading Latin and Greek literature, rather than relying on machines, would fill their lives with beauty and wisdom. Jennings, of course, knew and loved the classics. In his poems and paintings, and especially in his films, he amended, extended, and advanced his headmaster's definition of the epic poet:

> The epic poet depicts a real world in action. There it is, as clear as if we saw it with our own eyes; clearer, indeed, for the art of the poet lies in that he can, by selection, bring his world within focus for our eyes, which we could not do for ourselves.[11]

EPILOGUE IN GREECE

In 1950, Dalrymple's Wessex Films took on the task of making for the U.S. Economic Cooperation Administration a series of what he calls "six lantern-lecture films about 'The Changing Face of Europe.'"[12] The only one of these which seemed to offer any possibilities for Jennings's poetic style was one on health, to be called *The Good Life*, and he went to Greece for location work on this. His only companion on the location-seeking expedition that caused his death was his continuity girl, the wife of assistant director Harley Usill. She too is now dead, so that the most authentic and detailed account of what occurred on the island of Poros would appear to be that given by Ian Dalrymple to James Merralls:

> He went out from Athens one Sunday to one of the islands to obtain a representative shot for the titles. He did not go to the island he intended, having en route met a Greek acquaintance who misinformed him about the little steamers. He climbed a low cliff to get a comprehensive view; but the edge was very dry, his foot slipped, and he fell some thirty feet onto the shore, where his head hit a rock. A blood transfusion was not available, and he was dead within a few hours. He is buried in the British cemetary in Athens. A copy of Trelawny's "The Last Days of Shelley and Byron" was found on him when he died.[13]

Dalrymple, the man who probably understood him best, wrote a splendid tribute to him, the last words of which bear repetition here:

> His death came as a sharp shock to all of any sort who had met him, and to many who had not. . . . The two words which at once sprang to the minds of all the cognisant about him were—*unique* and *irreplaceable*.[14]

8 JENNINGS IN RETROSPECT

Three decades after his untimely death, some attempt may be made to assess Humphrey Jennings as a man—and mirror—of his culture and era.

First and undoubtedly foremost, he was an *English* man. Although his work celebrated Britain as a whole, it was always from an English point of view. Moreover, he was a product of a certain region of England—East Anglia. Because of this, he became a Cambridge man, as opposed to an Oxford scholar. In prewar England, the two major universities created a strict dichotomy of cultures, accents, and outlooks, a dichotomy that percolated down even to those who had no special connection with either. For example, some weeks before the annual boat race, children were expected to declare their allegiance either to the light blue of Cambridge or the dark blue of Oxford. Once selected, one's choice was made for life. (In the U.S.A., Yale and Harvard offer a comparable, but much less sharply defined, division.)

Jennings clearly loved the English landscape. Images of waving East Anglian wheat open *Listen to Britain*. Mindsmere Bird Sanctuary appears in *Dim Little Island*. Fenland countryside is the setting for *English Harvest* and *Spring Offensive*. Scenes of wheatfields and shocked corn are among the evidence that Jennings was involved in the making of *Britain At Bay*, which also contains several other of his trademark shots: waves breaking on the beach and smoking factory chimneys at twilight.

Specially significant to Jennings was the land itself, the need for its cultivation and preservation, and its protection from the depredations of industry and technology. Even in *The Birth of the Robot* it seems not too fanciful to ascribe to Jennings the final, futuristic scene of roads straddling the globe, traffic lights, machinery dominating all, and the robot triumphant over the ancient gods. One thinks of the influence on him of Perse's Rouse, who "had an almost Erewhonian horror of machinery . . . and was convinced that they would eventually enslave mankind."[1] At the end of *Spring Offensive* the viewer is directly admonished not to forget the land, an appeal repeated urgently in *A Diary for Timothy* and *A Family Portrait*.

Yet there is a paradox here, very characteristic not only of Jennings and his upbringing but of Britain itself since the Industrial Revolution. For *Spring Offensive*'s "unrecorded victory" was the rehabilitation of a neglected farm through the operation of technology, a victory of the pastoral made possible by the enemy of the pastoral, the machine. (Cf. Jennings's lifelong obsession with locomotives, ploughs, and other farm machinery.)

Agriculture and science were the opposing twins of Jennings's emotional life, the poetry and the prose of the England that he celebrated in his final film. "How to reconcile the farm with the factory?" asks the narrator of *A Family Portrait*. Over an image of farmer and scientist standing under the ancient Long Man of Wilmington comes the reply: "We should pray for these two to agree—our bread and butter depend on it."

Jennings, deeply concerned as he was with the Industrial Revolution and its consequences, frequently evinced a Blakean pessimism and despair at the blackening of England's "green and Pleasant land." Walking one evening with Kathleen Raine across London's Battersea Bridge, Jennings commented on the heavily industrialized Thamescape: "This has all grown up in less than 200 years. Has anyone ever suggested that this was the way in which human beings ought to live? It will all have to go, it has been a terrible mistake."[2] Yet his prediction that the river's polluted water would one day be converted into fish ponds has now almost come true, ironically through the technological development of a huge barrier downstream. Ironically, too, the land which was so painstakingly drained by the farmer in *A Diary for Timothy* was later flooded by its new owner to provide a sanctuary for water fowl.[3] Perhaps the crowning irony, however, comes with the suggestion in a recent BBC program, "The Vanishing Countryside," that agriculture is itself to blame for the disappearance of the beautiful British countryside over the past thirty years—not the more obvious blight of motorways and urban sprawl.[4]

Another variation on Jennings's nature/technology dichotomy is his concern with horses and with locomotives—iron horses, chariots of fire. His paternal grandfather and one of his uncles had been famous racehorse trainers at Newmarket from the 1860s onward. The French horse Gladiateur, trained by Jennings's grandfather, won the English triple crown of the Derby, the St. Leger, and the Two Thousand Guineas in 1865.[5] Many years later, Humphrey was to be himself described as having "survived the Theatre and English Literature at Cambridge, [and] is connected with colour film direction and racehorses."[6] Certainly, horses of all kinds obsessed him throughout his life and work. Stuart Legg, in fact, says

> he looked rather like a horse sometimes, this long face, great big nose, almost a sort of forelock on top. . . . He was a strange figure to look at . . . tall, lean, with a big nose, with a lock of hair down one side, and a very prominent adam's apple.[7]

It was like a horse, too, that he ran. He made his name at the Perse by leaping the barbed wire barrier erected to mark the end of the cross-country race.[8] He begins his nostalgic prose poem "War and Childhood" with references to horses being tested for shipment to World War I in France. Joe Mendoza ascribes the incident in *Fires*

Were Started, where a frightened white horse is led to safety, to Jennings's attendance at a wartime exhibition of drawings by Felix Topolski:

> There was one drawing . . . that fascinated Humphrey, and that was the fireman leading a horse up between two burning warehouses on the night of the City blitz. And he put that shot into *Fires Were Started*. He'd never forget anything.[9]

Jennings's feelings for what Kathleen Raine called "the organic whole of English culture"[10]—and, one would add, for the *people* of England—found expression in all his work, culminating in *A Family Portrait*, which has been called "a work of almost incoherent patriotism, a paeon of pure joy at the very existence of the English people."[11] His attitude toward the wartime British was one of profound respect and love. Lindsay Anderson has said of *Listen to Britain*: "This is what it was like. This is what we were like—the best of us."[12]

The best of us—the best in each of us—was brought out in Britain by the war: this is the thesis that informs all of Jennings's films of the period, a thesis that must stand as a truth against the skeptical, cynical probes of later generations. Consider, in *Listen to Britain*, the two female Civil Defence workers eating their sandwiches on the steps of the National Gallery entrance; the jolly working girls in a razor blade factory singing to the radio's "Music While You Work"; the faintly ridiculous little man who conscientiously persists in carrying his respirator and steel helmet to work, past bomb rubble and broken glass, while the BBC's "Up In the Morning Early" exercise instructor murmurs "Lift your chest . . . look to the front." People like these could be found on every street corner, and Jennings elevated them into immortality. They "carried on" not merely because they had no alternative but because they took for granted the necessity of the situation.

Rarely, however, were their feelings (or Jennings's) expressed overtly. Lindsay Anderson, a Scot born in India but educated in England, comments: "The English don't like strong statements . . .

they hide behind words like 'one.' 'One feels,' not 'I feel.' . . . War caused Jennings, the English, to declare themselves."[13] To some extent, his final remark is confirmed by such films as *Heart of Britain* and *Words for Battle*. But the earlier comment finds splendid illustration in the moment in *Fires Were Started* when the bomb falls on the local control headquarters. The girl on the telephone gets up from beneath the table, mopping her bleeding forehead, and merely says, "I'm sorry for the interruption—we have a message for you." Sangfroid can go no further.

The very English traits of modesty and joking understatement are especially evident in the cool, offhand commentary to *A Family Portrait*. The style conceals conviction behind the casual joke ("Our ancestors nearly all came as invaders . . . they had to be enterprising chaps and good sailors to do it"). This is an Englishman speaking to the English. Yet the overall tone of the film may be taken to be, as Anderson later suggested, that of an upper-middle-class Englishman presuming to speak for the nation as a whole, representing (he claims) a certain insensitivity.[14]

Although it is absurd to suggest, as some have done, that Jennings was an aristocrat, he was born and educated into a considerable degree of privilege. Pre-1914 England was a powerful country of settled, hierarchic order, where everyone knew his place in the scheme of things and there seemed little likelihood of, nor necessity for, change. Private schools like the Perse and, in particular, Oxford and Cambridge, twin bastions of classical English culture, gave their students a strong sense, not only of their own privileged status, but (of equal importance) the responsibility toward lesser mortals that privilege entailed: noblesse oblige.

World War I shook this settled state, but its overtones reverberated into the twenties and thirties. Jennings grew up in a world where you were defined by what you wore, how you spoke, and how you bore yourself. The possession and spending of money were not major factors in all this. It mattered little what you had; it was a question of who you were. Thus, when Jennings began to feel the financial strains of marriage and paternity, he followed the traditional old boy line and turned to his Cambridge friends to help him find employment. Gerald Noxon and/or Stuart Legg performed this function and brought him to film but, as Julian Trevelyan says: "He took up films only because he needed money. He was perennially short of money."[15] Noxon confirms this, writing about the Jennings of 1940:

> While he was glad to have film work at that time for many practical and other reasons and would be glad to continue making films during the war if he could help in that way, his real interest still lay in painting. . . . I still have the feeling that if Humphrey had inherited anything like an adequate income, he would have left film work and gone back to painting as the main occupation of his life.[16]

This belief in his essential destiny as a painter stayed with him until his death. David Gascoyne reports:

> The last time I saw Humphrey, he was on his way to that tragic expedition in Greece. I was in Paris and he was in Paris on his way there. We met on the terrace of the Deux Magots. I had a long talk with him. He said, "At last I've discovered what I really want to do, I think I'm ready for that—and that's painting." He said, "I've really found myself in painting at last." I remember quite clearly his saying that. I was a bit surprised.[17]

In the mid-thirties Jennings and young people of his class felt increasingly aware of their need to make some kind of gesture toward those less privileged than themselves. (A similar tendency was apparent in American students during the civil rights movement of the early sixties.) The result, among other things, was the Mass-Observation movement in 1935. Drawing on their widespread interests and backgrounds, Jennings and his friends brought a variety of sociological, poetic, surrealist, and other approaches to the general program of documenting everyday life in Britain—"the anthropology of the British Islanders."

Tom Harrisson, who coined this phrase, and some others of the group actually went to live in the neighborhood they were study-ing. Others, like Humphrey Spender, found physical contact with it somewhat embarrassing, as he has described in the book of photo-graphs he took for Mass-Observation at the time.[18]

The effect of World War II on the English class system (more ac-curately its caste structure) was considerably—even if only tempo-rarily—to diminish its strength. Richard Sennett describes the basic situation that occurred:

> The simplest way in which a communal identity is formed is when a group is threatened in its very survival, such as a war or other catastro-phe. While taking collective action to meet this threat, people feel close to one another and search for images that bind them together.[19]

Lindsay Anderson says something similar:

> During the war, it was valid to stress ideas of service, cooperation, love, help. The smallest detail of behaviour becomes of increased sig-nificance. . . . Humphrey Jennings was upper-middle-class . . . he was aware of class, but did his best work when class, *hierarchy*, was ac-cepted in order to win the war.[20]

The acceptance of hierarchy, of the natural authority of certain classes of people, was (and to a lesser degree still is) a basic British habit, developed over centuries of a monarchic and aristocratic tra-dition. It is difficult for Americans, whose culture is founded on re-volt and the constant *questioning* of authority, to appreciate this. As a contemporary Australian television critic, Clive James, puts it: "Britain might as well be Japan as far as class is concerned. I can see how Americans might not pick up the signals."[21] The signals are an integral part of all Jennings's films, and the acceptance of hierarchi-cal discipline is beautifully illustrated in *Fires Were Started*. The modification (deterioration?) of the English cultural system can be traced in a chronological study of his work and life. As Marius Gor-ing commented: "He'd have been saddened by the mess we've got into."[22] In the same interview, Goring suggested that had Jennings survived, BBC television "would have been the thing for him." The reference to the BBC reminds us that this very typically British institution operated on a parallel course to Jennings's work and life. Its founding father, John Reith, was a strict and stern Scot whose influence on the lives of young Britons in the twenties and thirties was comparable to that John Grierson. He shaped the BBC, especially in its radio period, into an instrument that defined British national culture in a fashion very similar to that of Grierson's documentary movement. Jennings's frequent references to the BBC as a cohesive community link, especially during the war, illustrate the point. If, as McLuhan pointed out, Vietnam was a television war, Britain's was a radio one. At the first screening of *A Family Portrait* at the Festival of Britain in 1951, one criticism was that it was more "television" than film, an unconscious tribute to Jennings's prescience, perhaps.

There has been speculation among Jennings's friends about the likelihood of his eventually entering the feature film field. There are, to be sure, fictional elements in many of his films—"creative interpretations of actuality," as sanctioned by Grierson's dictum. Many of these, of course, were dictated by the shooting conditions of the time, but Jennings went to infinite pains to present the appearance of actuality and spontaneity.

Fires Were Started, in fact, was a feature-length "docu-drama" much like many British features of the period (for example, *In Which We Serve*, *The Way Ahead*, and *Millions Like Us*) that incorporated realistic depictions of wartime actuality into essentially fictional narratives. But these films relied heavily upon professional stars and actors, whereas Jennings subscribed to the documentary tradition, derived from Flaherty and Grierson, wherein "real people" were used to play themselves. (There were a few exceptions—Laurie Lee in *Spring Offensive*, Marius Goring, and Jennings himself, in *The True Story of Lilli Marlene*.) A title at the start of *The Cumberland Story* proudly proclaims that the film features "the actual people involved."

Yet this film contains some of the worst examples of this prac-

tice. Most of the participants in the story exhibit the nonprofession-
al's faint air of uncertainty when delivering manufactured dialogue,
an uncertainty that mars many of the performances in Jennings's
films. Often, it would seem, this rather delighted him, making the
films in his eyes more "honest." There are indeed several instances
where awkwardness is genuinely attractive. (One thinks of Ken's
mother in *Spring Offensive*, William Sansom in *Fires Were Started*,
and Mrs. Jenkins in *A Diary for Timothy*.) But the poorly staged (and
dully photographed) committee discussions in *Spring Offensive*,
The Silent Village, and, most lamentable, in *The Cumberland Story*,
although possibly authentic, support Lindsay Anderson's criticism
that "the staged sequences in these films do not suggest that he
would have been at ease in the direction of features."[23]

Generally, Jennings was able to observe humans "intimately
and wisely," to borrow a phrase used by Richard Barsam about
Flaherty,[24] and generally he coaxed convincing performances from
them. Fred Griffiths, speaking of *Fires Were Started*, recalls:

> They said, "You can have actors and turn them into firemen, or you can
> have firemen and turn them into actors. . . . He wanted to have his way
> so much . . . he'd rather take an ordinary fireman like me, and the rest
> of the fellows, and try to turn us into something which he wanted to
> mould.[25]

But Nora Lee, discussing the weaknesses of *The True Story of
Lilli Marlene*, speaks of Jennings's being caught up, for the first time,
"in the trammels of the film studio." She says that the complex demands of commercial studio filming were "anathema to him. . . .
One has to ask oneself, 'Would he have been able to handle all
this?'"[26] Bill Megarry, the editor of *Dim Little Island*, tells of an argument with the studio's art department over a piece of furniture for
The Cumberland Story: "The art director and the rest of them were
saying 'Oh, go away and chase yourself!'"[27] Even with *Fires Were
Started*, on which she worked, Nora Lee hesitates to endorse the
scene in which Rumbold reads Macbeth's "Ay, in the catalogue ye go

for men," and sees it as one of Jennings's faults: "He loved certain things (e.g. literary quotations), and he just wanted to pack them in. And you just can't do this in film . . . at least, when you're doing a straight story."[28]

Nevertheless, it would seem that Jennings himself had few qualms about feature film work. At the time of *The Purple Plain* project, he was his customary enthusiastic self about the prospect. Bronowski recalls:

> I . . . saw Humphrey Jennings in Paris at the end of 1947. . . . We had a delightful afternoon, but now he talked only of pictures and films. He was in Paris in order to find a Burmese girl (I think) who would fit into some minor part in a film that he was making. I never learned why there should be better, or more, Burmese girls in Paris than in London.[29]

But, as Diana Pine, Jennings's assistant on *The Silent Village* and *A Diary for Timothy*, indicates, there was now a new and unusual note of cooperativeness with studio practices that he had always loathed:

> It was a time when . . . numbers on units were being increased, and you were being forced to carry more people than you needed. Humphrey was reacting to pressures in a typical Humphrey way. Instead of fighting them, he said, "OK, if I'm going to be forced to do all this, I will work in a BIG way." . . . He had tremendous plans.[30]

And Pat Jackson claims that, on Jennings's return from a location visit to Burma:

> He was a changed man. . . . I remember him saying, "Most extraordinary! I got a completely different sense of time there. I used to rush around much too much, get too impatient with everything. Then for two days I sat on an ox-cart going through the jungle, talking to the driver . . . one of the most wonderful things that ever happened to me."[31]

Certainly, the Humphrey Jennings of prewar and wartime was an impatient, overweening man of great loquacity and nervous intensity. He had little regard for his own personal safety, so that his fatal fall from a Greek cliff was regarded by several of his friends as something very much in character. During the making of *Fires Were Started* he had nearly walked backward off a warehouse roof while concentrating on his directing, and there was a myth, promulgated by Bronowski and repeated by Tom Harrisson many years afterward, that a similar accident had occurred in Greece, with fatal results. Bronowski retracted his story after Jennings's widow provided the true account of his death.[32]

There are many tales told of Jennings's violent moods. Nora Lee speaks, for example, of the intense hostility he displayed when he saw her takes for the V-1 film: "He decided that 'this thing was bigger than both of us,' and that he must take over and develop the theme."[33] He had total confidence in his own ability and talent, as is evidenced by the epigraph to Chapter 1 ("I know I am born to be famous").

Bill Pollard, who worked as cameraman with Jennings in the early GPO days and then again on *A Family Portrait*, tells of Jennings's self-assurance and skill:

> When you have a chap who takes the camera out of your hands, and starts pushing you around, and says "Now you're going to go there, it's going to point *that* way, you're going to do this," as a cameraman I usually resent it, because he usually doesn't know what he's about. . . . But in Humphrey's case, he knew *exactly* what he was doing. . . . He's the only person I can say this about: I didn't argue, because *I* learned from him! He had a wonderful sense of composition, filling the frame with exactly the right information and not wasting any of it, like a poet selecting exactly the right word.[34]

Timothy's mother, Betty Jenkins, has a revealing tale of Jennings's concern for authenticity in his characters and actions:

> I went to lots of trouble and expense to have a very elaborate hair-do. So soon as I saw his face I knew that I'd done the wrong thing. . . . I did so want to look glamorous and he said, "The average mother of Britain does not look glamorous. You were not meant to be a film star, you are meant to represent the mother of Britain." . . . [Timothy] was chris-

tened eight times altogether—two practices and five takes. . . . And the Christmas party, I'll never forget that! Normally, I only drink one glass of sherry, then I go off to sleep. Just to say, "Absent friends!" and raising our glasses—it took so long that we all drank four glasses of sherry.[35]

And Fred Griffiths's account of the shooting in *Fires Were Started* of the song "One Man Went to Mow" is a classic example of Jennings's persistence and single-mindedness:

I started on it at ten o'clock in the morning. We broke for lunch from one to two, and I was still singing it at half-past five at night! . . . I heard him turn round and say to the cameraman (this is a very great understatement, believe me): he said, "Penny, I think Fred's voice is going!"[36]

Jennings's almost mystical search for coincidences seems often to have been rewarded. His producer, Ian Dalrymple, relates that the camera's discovery of the ship named *British Genius* in *Dim Little Island* was "pure accident," but Jennings insisted that it was "the truth that won't be denied."[37] Diana Pine's anecdote of another occasion provides a gloss on this remark:

I remember . . . when I said, "What a good thing you shot it at that moment; did you see the cat walk across the road?" He said, "What do you mean, did I see it? That was the reason we shot it at that moment." It wasn't so much coincidence as it was all one thing, which it should be if you are following really the world as it is happening. It's all part of the inspiration.[38]

The partnership of this strong-willed and violent Englishman with his modest, unassuming (but equally strong-willed) Scottish editor, Stewart McAllister, provides a startling juxtaposition comparable to any contained in their films together. Adrian de Potier has described McAllister's quiet patience with Jennings's "completely incoherent, inarticulate" instructions, and the manner in which McAllister would secretly salvage sequences ripped out of a rough-cut by Jennings, store them away, then restore them later, much to Jennings's delight.[39] Tales of the incongruous, friendly-hostile relationship between these two permeate all their coworkers' reminiscences. Perhaps the best summary comes from Edgar Anstey: "Mac and Humphrey could only create by quarrelling."[40]

In an article written in 1935, Jennings deplored the growing obliteration of popular iconography, citing "beer ads, steam railways, Woolworths," and adding, "When the life has been finally veneered out of these it will be the end."[41] Perhaps the most significant aspect of his style, evident in his work in all media, is his continual use of quotation from existing popular material. Kathleen Raine insists that, for Jennings, "The image must be particularized, concrete and historical . . . above all, the image must never be invented. . . . The poet . . . must actually see such an image, for physical manifestation is the final test of imaginative truth."[42] Hillier adds:

> Just as in his poetry he preferred phrases from existing sources, so in painting he always worked from postcards or prints, never from nature. This is equally evident in his films, where he makes extensive use of popular song, familiar buildings, well-known literature, radio broadcasts and so on. . . . Certain images or subjects return again and again in Jennings' work.[43]

On the other hand, this refusal to create freshly, to rework instead what already exists, may perhaps be seen as an attempt at self-concealment on Jennings's part. Eric Rhode, one of the few to write adversely about *Fires Were Started*, complains: "I wish Jennings had been more influenced by Blake, who tended to create symbols out of himself, rather than to seek them in popular culture."[44] Perhaps Jennings's aggressively self-confident manner was an armor against his fear of self-revelation.

This, of course, is pure speculation. Perhaps we should turn instead to the assessment of his friend, Charles Madge. He believed that Jennings was deeply influenced by Thomas Gray's "very subtle technique of allusion to other poets" and that his "idea of poetry by quotation or allusion is at the back of his poems."[45]

Allusion and quotation from others may be seen as characteristic of British modesty and self-deprecation. Particularly noteworthy in this context is Jennings's allusive use of popular music of all kinds, ranging from the Christmas carols from King's College, Cambridge (a BBC tradition dating from 1928 and still extant), to *Listen to Britain*'s "Roll Out the Barrel" and "Rule Britannia," and Mozart, Handel, and Beethoven. It reflects particularly his long and deeply felt belief that the saving grace of the British, perhaps, lay in their making and enjoying music of all kinds. Musicologist Howard Ferguson (who makes an appearance in *Listen to Britain* as Myra Hess's page turner) claims that Jennings had no professional knowledge of music,[46] and Marius Goring has described how he "would hold forth at great length about music . . . which he knew nothing about at all."[47] But his "Working Sketches" for a film planned about the London Symphony Orchestra reveal that Jennings realized the enormous emotional *power* of music, even if he knew little about its techniques. His younger daughter Charlotte, in a television interview, recalls her father's stern injunction "not to use music like wallpaper."[48]

George Steiner defines poetry as being "knit of words compacted with every conceivable mode of operative force." He continues: "The poet attempts to anchor the particular word in the dynamic mould of its own history, enriching the core of its present definition with the echo and alloy of previous use."[49] If we enlarge Steiner's "word" to include images and music, we see how Jennings's brilliant juxtapositions of materials that resonate already from their own previous use can provide new and striking associations in the finest traditions of poetry.

APPENDIXES

APPENDIX A

FILMOGRAPHY, CREDITS, AND SUMMARIES

OF FILMS

Humphrey Jennings: Filmography

1934 (?) Advertising film for Socony-Vacuum Company about "Slum" (?)

1934 *Pett and Pott* (Cavalcanti)
        Art direction, and played a small role as a grocer

  The Glorious Sixth of June (Cavalcanti)
  Played Albert Goodbody, a Post Office telegraph boy

  Post Haste
  Sole credit as editor

  The Story of the Wheel
  No credits: assumed to be editor

1935 *BBC, Voice of Britain* (Stuart Legg)
        As a radio actor played one of the witches in *Macbeth*

  Locomotives
  Directed

1936 *The Birth of the Robot* (Len Lye)—Gasparcolour
        Color direction and production

1937 (?) Two Dufaycolour films for Adrian Klein (?)

1938 *English Harvest* (Dufaycolour)
        Directed

  Design for Spring (Dufaycolour)
  Directed

Penny Journey
Directed

1939 *Spare Time*
Directed and scripted

Speaking from America
Directed

S.S. Ionian (Her Last Trip)
Directed

The First Days
Co-directed with Harry Watt and Pat Jackson

1940 *Spring Offensive (An Unrecorded Victory)*
Directed

Welfare of the Workers
Co-directed with Pat Jackson

London Can Take It!
Co-directed with Harry Watt

1941 *Heart of Britain (This Is England)*
Directed

Words for Battle
Directed and scripted

1942 *Listen to Britain*
Co-directed, co-scripted and co-edited with Stewart McAllister

1943 *Fires Were Started (I Was a Fireman)*
Directed and scripted

1943 *The Silent Village*
Produced, directed and scripted

1944 *V.1.* (Fletcher Markle)
Honorary credit as producer

The Eighty Days
Produced and directed

The True Story of Lilli Marlene
Directed, and played the small role of the song's lyricist

1944–45 *A Diary for Timothy*
Directed and scripted

1945 *Myra Hess Playing the First Movement of Beethoven's Sonata in F Minor, OP.57 (Appassionata)*
Assumed to be Producer

1946   *A Defeated People*
       Directed and scripted

1947   *The Cumberland Story*
       Directed and scripted

1949   *Dim Little Island*
       Produced and directed

1950   *A Family Portrait*
       Directed and scripted

Credits and Summaries of Films

POST HASTE (1934)

GPO Film Unit

26 minutes

Editor: Humphrey Jennings

Post horn sounds behind credits. Credit: Based on documents from British Museum, Postal Museum and contemporary quotations.

"In the seventeenth century . . . General Post Office instituted." Document: An Act for Erecting and Establishing a Post Office, Charles II. Contemporary drawings. "The house of Sir Robert Bede, in Lombard Street. At these windows, letters were received. They were sorted into bags . . . each bag taken by a postboy. The postboys were instructed: *The post shall blow his horn so often as he meeteth company or passeth through any town, or at least twice in every mile.*

"General Post Office, January 6, 1782." Another voice: *The first boy carrying the Chester mail was attacked a little before Highgate, between the 5 and 6 milestones about half-past four o'clock, by two men, who broke open the cart and took away a number of bags.* Drawings, and "Caution to Post Boys—George III."

"Important letters were sent by the Express Extraordinary. Here's the Express receiving military despatches." Drawings. Camera pans across them. "The tollgate being shut, he has to waken the gatekeeper with his horn. At the next stage, he has to change horses . . ." Drawings. "The bridge is broken, he leaps the brook. Leaving his horse in the snow, he jumps a stile and delivers the despatches."

Horn blows. "In 1784, John Palmer persuaded the Post Office to try a new plan for carrying mail, namely, by coach." (Quoting voices from contemporary sources describe the new system. Drawings include one of St. Paul's.)

A hundred years ago, London postmen not only delivered letters but also collected them. They were taken to be sorted to the new General Post Office, a building considered to be (pompous voice) *more worthy of British commerce and in regard to architecture more honorable to British taste and British hearts.* "The postmen brought in the letters in these mail carts, and from here the mail coaches set out for the country." (Quoting voice: *The letters are conveyed by strong and well-guarded* coaches . . .) "The mails are being dropped and taken in at full speed. The postwoman hoists her letter bag up on a hayfork." Drawings.

"But during the great snowstorm of December 1836, the Christmas mails were delayed all over the country." Drawings. (Quote: *The last mail stopped by the snow . . .*)

Horn blows. "One of the most important events in Post Office history is the change-over from the road to the railway." (Quote: *. . . Letters received each evening are delivered in Manchester and Liverpool the following day.*)

"This is Rowland Hill (picture) who brought in uniform penny postage." (Quote: *The public may now procure a stamp for literally one penny* [CU, penny black stamp] *being a small engraving of the Queen's bust, on the reverse side of which is spread an adhesive substance which, being moistened, causes it to stick to the letter.*) Drawing of large sorting hall in GPO. Long quotation . . . *extremely animated scene . . .* Drawing of early sorting office on train. Long quotation . . . *a carriage sixteen feet long . . . Letter bags for other stations along the line are taken up by an ingenious contrivance, the invention of Mr. Ramsay from the General Post Office.* Early Victorian drawing of mailbag snatch. (Soundtrack of steam train accompanies drawing.)

"The parcels post originated in an independent company . . . in the eighties it was taken over . . . service extended all over the country. Finally, in 1902, motors took the place of horses . . ." Contemporary real-life shots of sorting, mailvans, trains, ships, planes, with appropriate soundtracks.

(Horn blows under THE END title.)

THE STORY OF THE WHEEL (1934)

GPO Film Unit

12 minutes

Editor: Humphrey Jennings

Credit: Photographed from models and drawings from the British Museum, London Museum, and Science Museum.

Title: Primitive Man

Models. "In the earliest times man lived in caves . . . hunted animals for food. He had to carry his prey on his back, for he had not yet discovered that animals could be used for other purposes besides food. Later, he tamed the wild horses, camels, and oxen . . . the heaviest loads had to be dragged along the ground . . ." CU model tree trunk dragging. "You can see how difficult and laborious this was on rough ground." Models. "People of the Old Stone Age used a rough kind of sledge . . . made of branches tied together and bent upwards in front, like the prow of a ship." Trunk dragging across rounded pebbles. ". . . this suggested rounded logs of wood placed under a load as rollers . . ." Models of rollers, with hand picking up rollers from behind and moving them in front of load. (Commentary describes the process.) Picture of Egyptians moving statue. "Egyptian slaves used this method . . ."

"The next step was to build a sledge with four short legs to hold a log in position . . ." Model of this dissolves into whittled-down "axle log." ". . . First type of axle and the beginning of the modern wheel . . . After this great discovery, many different kinds of wheel were made." Wheels preserved in museums, Egyptian frescoes. Model chariots, Assyrian and Egyptian. (Commentary describes these.) "Heavy loads were carried on wagons fitted with small stout wheels." Model. Real-life shot of a rough track. "Tracks like this were of course useless for these chariots and wagons—longer and better roads were required."

Title: The Romans

". . . Among first people to make roads scientifically." Maps. "Roman Empire . . . could only be held together by good roads . . ." Diagram of road structure in section. "Here you can see how deeply . . . they laid the foundations." Real-life shots of roads. Models. "When the Roman Empire was broken up by the barbarians it was a great disaster—not only for the Romans, but for the roads, which gradually went back to nature." Shots of Roman roads in Britain today.

Title: The Middle Ages

Models. "When . . . the Norman soldiers conquered England, the men preferred to go on horseback. But their ladies drove around in . . . very fine wagons . . ." Illuminated manuscript. "Some of them were like the covered wagons which the pioneers used in America centuries later . . ." Model Norman castle. But the roads were not as good as the wagons . . . Norman builders were too busy making castles to worry about roads." Pictures. "In the twelfth to fifteenth centuries, transport gradually fell back to primitive ways of pack horse and barge."

Title: Sixteenth Century

Picture of Elizabeth I and Elizabethan pictures. "In Queen Elizabeth's reign, there was a great growth of commerce, and great efforts were made to get merchandise from one place to another. But they went about it the wrong way—instead of building stronger roads, they built stronger, heavier wagons to roll over the rough ground." Picture of wagon. "You see here how stout they were."

Title: Seventeenth Century

"But the mistake of building stronger wagons was soon realized, and in the seventeenth century great progress was made." Real-life shot of country road with rider. Drawings. "Better and better roads were built and with better roads came the first, fine English carriages . . . fast and fashionable." Map. "The journey from York to London is 200 miles. By 1673, carriaages could do it in eight days."

Title: Eighteenth Century

Drawings. "Sedan chairs were introduced . . . to relieve the traffic, so popular had the carriages become . . ." Map, this time showing three days. "In 1750, the journey to York took only three days. Soon coaches were taking the King's mail at high speed from town to town." Shots of real-life coach and CU of speeding horses' hoofs. Map shows twenty hours. "With relays of fresh horses, the journey to York could be done in a day. This was a great advance on the old system of postboys . . ." CU hoofs. Models. "But however light the carriages, and however swift the stagecoach service, mail and passengers could go no faster than horses could carry them."

Title: Steam

Shots of locomotives. "A new power, quicker than horsepower, had to be found before faster journeys could be made . . . the power of steam revolutionized transport altogether, and made a new chapter in the history of the wheel."

LOCOMOTIVES (1935)

GPO Film Unit

21 minutes

Director: Humphrey Jennings

Music: arranged by John Foulds; incorporates part of Schubert's "Rosamunde"

Credit: From models in the Science Museum.

Music of "Rosamunde" under titles and first shot (CU of kettle boiling). "When water is heated . . . steam presses on the sides of the kettle and rushes out of the spout . . . But steam, once controlled, is power." Model pumphouse working. (Soundtrack of metallic chinks and clicks.) "In the eighteenth century, steam power was used to run pumps in mills and collieries. In this pumphouse, the fire is placed below, the water is in a boiler above it, and the steam escapes into an upright cylinder. Here the steam pressure forces the piston into movement." Model coaltrucks. "In the collieries, the coaltrucks are run from the pits on rails. For years the trucks were pulled by horses . . . But with the coming of

steam they are pulled with a rope which runs by a fixed steam engine." (Soundtrack carries trucks and steam engine sounds.) "And it is in the collieries that the first locomotives are made." Model of the first locomotive. "The steam engine has been placed on a truck. The cylinders are still upright, but the action of the pumping engine now drives the wheels. The wheels are coupled together with a chain." Model of locomotive crossing a bridge. "The colliery trucks are given seats and doors, and used to carry passengers." (Musicbox music.) Picture of *The Rocket*. "In 1829, Stephenson builds the Rocket. It will go 35 mph. The success of The Rocket makes the future of the railways certain." (Long drum roll as in circus.)

(Music begins.) "In 1830, the Royal Mail is transferred from the roads to the railways." Mailtrain picture. "Here is the inside of an early traveling post office. Letters were picked up, sorted, and dropped at stations on the journey." Picture of traveling sorting office. (Music ends.) "The railways began to grow." Map of Britain shows linkages animated. "From London the lines spread all over England" (names of towns given). "1862—The Lady of the Lakes." Picture. (Engine sounds on track.) "Subjective" shots along model rails, with model station, etc.

"Paddington today." Real-life contemporary shots of station. "The Cornish Riviera Express." (Train sounds.) Rails. Steam against embankment scenery. Romantic night shots of trains. "And this is how the Royal Mail is picked up . . ." Night shots of mailgrab. (Train music mixes with rhythmic train sounds until mailgrab crash climax.)

THE BIRTH OF THE ROBOT (1936)

Shell Oil Company

7 minutes

Producer and Director: Len Lye

Script: C. H. Dand

Photography: Alex Strasser

Color Direction and Production: Humphrey Jennings

Color Process: Gasparcolour

Design and Model Construction: John Banting and Alan Farmer

Sound Recording: Jack Ellitt

Music: Holst, "The Planets" suite

Holst's "Jupiter" from "The Planets." Father Time turning a kind of carousel from which are strung Mercury, Venus, Mars, etc., in human guise. "Once upon a time, high up in the sky, Father Time made the planets go round with an old-fashioned machine which he turned like a mangle . . . and Venus, from her shell, drew forth sweet harmonies as Mercury and Saturn and Mars and Jupiter went round and round and round . . ."

Car drives across desert, blithely running up the side of a pyramid. "In the trackless desert on the Earth below comes the happy motorist, so confident, proud in his up-to-date car . . . nothing daunts him."

(Music crescendo.) A sandstorm envelops the motorist and his car. "But wait—a storm!" The car's headlight "eyes" look upward. A service station fades in and out. "Choked with sand and grit, the car looks up to heaven for lubrication. Garage? Mirage!"

Skeleton in the desert. "In the trackless desert lie the bones of the heroic motorist, bleached and thirsty . . ." The notes emanating from Venus (crotchets, quavers, etc.) are changed into drops of oil. "In pity, Venus's notes are changed to oil." The oil drops onto the bones, which are transformed into a robot, which rises and stands erect. "And with the magic touch of oil, the Robot is born!"

(Music crescendo.) Robot creates traffic lights, roads begin to straddle the globe, machinery domintes the Earth. The Robot stands triumphant. "And so the Robot changes in [*sic*] a sign of Lubrication. Lubrication by Shell!"

ENGLISH HARVEST (1938)

Dufay-Chromex Ltd.

7 minutes

Producer: Adrian Klein

Director: Humphrey Jennings

Asst. Director: Cecil Blacker

Photography: J. D. Davidson

Commentary: A. G. Street

Music: Beethoven's Sixth Symphony

General landscape of wheatfields. "Farming England, the playground of the town, the workshop of the country. Farming is a slow business, but it never stops."

Harvester with scythe advancing on camera. Ears of wheat in foreground disappear as he cuts. "In August, the holiday month, the countryman is busy gathering his harvest. Today, one can still hear the sound of the scythe, and watch the beautiful rhythm of its swing." Horsedrawn binder in operation. CU the driver through the blades of the machine. "Opening the road to the modern machine—the binder, cutting the crop and tying it into neater sheaves than any made by hand." Stooking. "Following the binder come the stookers, setting up the sheaves to keep the heads off the ground." _

Landscape of stooks drying. "Now the stooks stand . . . drying." Loading carts. "Now pitchers fork the sheaves to the loader. At last they reach the dusty hot shade of the Dutch barn." Men sitting around eating. One brings can of ale which is passed around. "Midday. Here comes the harvest ale." CU can as it is picked up, and men return to work.

Woman opens a cottage window, emerges into garden. Women bring tea, sit in field with men. "The wives bring tea to their men in the harvest field . . . a picnic scene which hasn't changed since time out of mind."

Thatching the stack. "The overflow from the Dutch barn has made a chunky stack, which must have a hat on before the autumn rains . . . Last year's straw covers this year's grain."

Ploughing. "Now for next year's harvest—ploughing, the king of jobs, the most charming disguise that work can wear. Preparation for next year. Farming never stops."

DESIGN FOR SPRING (1938)

Dufay-Chromex Ltd.

20 (?) minutes

Producer: Adrian Klein, in collaboration with Norman Hartnell

Director: Humphrey Jennings

Photography: Jonah Jones

Asst. Director: Cecil Blacker

Color Director: Joan Bridge

Music Director: Harold Sandler

Cast: Norman Hartnell, Lady Bridget Poulett, Miss Peggy Hamilton, Miss Biddy Weir, *Members of the Hartnell Staff*

Summary of Extant First Reel

(Fanfare music behind ornate titles modifies into sugary waltz tune.) Exterior of British Museum. "The cold of a London's winter." Statue of Persephone, with CU's of it. "In the British Museum, this statue of Persephone, the ancient Greek goddess of spring, still retains the ageless beauty of the time, 3000 years ago, when, under endlessly blue skies, the fashions of the gods were created."

Wedgewood decoration above mirror. Camera tilts down to show Hartnell in front of it. "Today, in London, blue and white memories of Greece decorate the studio of a famous creator of society's fashions, Norman Hartnell." Intercut shots of Hartnell's watercolor paints, his design, and Wedgewood bas-relief. "He makes as many as 1500 individual designs for dresses in one winter. Blue and white Wedgewood has in fact suggested one of the most beautiful of this year's spring models—a tea gown in light blue crepe, with dark sapphire bows." (Music modifies to a more formal, gavotte-like tune.)

Hartnell's assistant (Lady Bridget Poulett?) stands behind him, talking on the telephone. She calls stockroom to bring up a model gown. Shot of Hartnell in CU. His sketch. He takes the dress, studies it, checks it against the sketch. *It's lovely!* says his assistant. (Music comes to a concluding note.)

"Now, the materials go upstairs to the workrooms, and the new model is added to the fitters' list." General shot of workrooms. ("Busy" music begins.) A dummy is draped. CU of the fitter. "First of all, they drape the material on a dummy, to get an idea of the hang of the dress without making a pattern." "Often, instead of using the actual material, the dummy is draped with white marque. When the material is cut out to the marque, it goes to the work-girls, to put together." Seamstresses at work. CU of one's hands, which tilts up to picture on the wall of Bing Crosby. "From the workroom walls, the stars look down."

(Music played by harp.) "When the dress is almost finished, it comes down from the workroom to the studio, worn by a mannequin, to be passed by the designer." The mannequin enters the studio. Adjustments are made to the dress. CU of the mannequin, tilt down to her dress being adjusted. Another CU of her. "It looks so easy, but it wants just that touch of art by the fitter to bring the designer's sketch to life."

(Violin music.) A Wedgewood vase, then an exterior shot of roofs and smoking domestic chimneys. "As the January winds tangle the smoke around the chimneys, thousands of starry sequins are then threaded . . ." Exterior shot shows work-girls entering back door, past commissionaire. Then, in the workroom, a long sequence of sequins being threaded and sewn on dresses. CU pan shot along the glittering sequins. CU work-girl. CU sequins. Repeat shot of chimneys.

(Foxtrot music.) Further shots of sequin sewing. Hartnell's drawing. Greek statue (Winged Victory of Samothrace?). Blue dress being fitted. "The embroi-

dered gown looks a very simple business, but the embroidery is a very special skill—just because it has to look simple, and not a stunt." CU of fitting and sewing the gown. Pictures on the wall of Robert Taylor and Spencer Tracy.

(Viennese waltz, "Voices of Spring.") Small ancient statue. "Statue of a picture hat, twenty-three centuries ago." Edwardian postcard. "A picture of a girl with a picture hat, 1911." Girls at work on hats. "Making picture hats, 1938." Shot of bare branches against sky. "While the bare branches wait for spring, artificial flowers for spring dresses are being made with scissors and paste . . ." Girl with artificial daisies, applies them to dress. Other artificial flowers. ". . . They are tied into bunches with garden bass." Real flowers being brought in. "In the grayness of January, bright flowers from hothouses in the warm South come to decorate the showroom." Mannequins at dressing tables, getting dressed. ". . . and the mannequins, prepared for long days of showing, get changed." (Waltz ends.)

PENNY JOURNEY (1938)
GPO Film Unit

6 minutes

Director: Humphrey Jennings

Photography: Henry Fowle, W. B. Pollard

Manchester—general view. "This is Manchester . . . a boy is writing a postcard." Map of Britain showing Manchester. CU postcard—a view of the city. "It's to an aunt of his who lives in a village in Sussex called Graffham." Map showing Graffham. CU reverse side of postcard. "Dear Aunt, thank you very much for your letter. It must be nice to be in the country."

Boy posts card, CU of clock. "The boy gets to the postbox just in time for the quarter-to-three collection." Postman at box. "The postman clears the box . . ." Commentary goes on to describe details of process, turning cards and letters right way up for stamps to be cancelled.

"Next comes the sorting . . ." Boy's postcard shown going into pigeonhole marked "South East Road," later into Redhill bundle. Many illustrative CU's. Commentary describes the details. "It's now 6 o'clock in the evening. Here is the mailtrain taking the postcard from Manchester." Evening shot from train's tender—probably stock shot from *Night Mail.* "The train gets to London; the mailbags are sorted into motor vans. The Redhill bag arrives at Redhill at half-past ten at night." Map, night shots of vans, and loading. "At Redhill, the postcard is put into the bag for Petworth. It arrives at Petworth; about five in the morning it is finally put into a bag for Graffham."

Scenic shots of Graffham village, which ". . . lies under the edge of the Downs. Graffham Post Office is also the grocer's shop. Mr. Prescott, the grocer, is also the postmaster. It's now seven o'clock—the bag from Petworth is coming down the Lavington road . . . In a cottage near the Post Office lives Mr. Money." From below through window shot of Mr. Money shaving. "He is the cyclist postman for all round Graffham. At twenty-five past seven he sets out for his duty." More scenic shots of Graffham exteriors. "At half-past, the van arrives from Petworth . . ." Exterior

of Post Office, van unloaded. "Mr. Prescott empties the bag on the floor at the back of the shop, and he and Mr. Money sort it." Interior high-angle shot of two men sorting mail on floor. Cat stalks by in background. "Letters for the village itself—letters for houses in the woods (this is Graffham Court) . . ." Interspersed shots of places mentioned. "Letters for farms—this is Haylands . . ."

Mr. Money on bicycle rides through splendid avenue of trees, other shots of sylvan scenery. "Every day, Mr. Money does nine miles of cycling." We now follow Money as he reads the address on the card, and sets out on his last act of delivery. "Teglees Farm. Teglees is up at the top of the Downs, and to get to it Mr. Money has to walk about three-quarters of a mile up through the beeches, with a stiff short cut through the saplings. At the top, you get clear of the trees and you can see right back to Graffham, Petworth, almost to Redhill. At half-past nine he delivers the postcard which was posted in Manchester yesterday afternoon." Aunt looks at card. Repeat "Dear Aunt . . ." CU postcard.

SPARE TIME (1939)

GPO Film Unit

18 minutes

Producer: Cavalcanti

Director/Script: Humphrey Jennings

Commentary: Laurie Lee

Photography: Henry Fowle

Editor: Stewart McAllister (?)

Music played by the Steel, Peach and

Tozer Phoenix Works Band, and the Handel Male Voice Choir, and the Manchester Victorian Carnival Band

Sound recording: Yorke Scarlett and Ken Cameron

(Brass band music.) Factory chimneys against sky. "This is a film about the way people spend their time. Between work and sleep there comes a time we call our own. What do we do with it?"

Workers leaving the steel furnace, moving to brass band music. (Same shot as in *Listen to Britain* and *Heart of Britain*.) "Steel . . . there are three shifts, so spare time can be morning or afternoon . . ."

Brass band rehearsal. The music stays on track through intercut shots of factories, steel mills, houses, interior of home. Woman serves a pie to family. (Band rehearsal.) Man goes out with his whippets. Another tends his pigeons. Boys with bicycles clean them. Cycle club outing in the country; they stop at pub, bring their drink and food outside.

Soccer game. (Natural soccer sounds.) Advertisements for football pools. At the Post Office, men buying postal orders. Crowd. Game. "Cotton." Mills. Carnival kazoo band plays. The music ("If You Knew Susie") continues over: Windows of houses dissolve to mother with baby. Kids draw on the sidewalk. Man wraps a parcel. Woman waters plants in greenhouse.

Back to kazoo band, which now "presents" in a pageant-style "Rule Britannia." Music of "Rule Britannia" continues over: Belle Vue (Manchester amusement park). Tiger, lion in cages. People watching. Wrestling.

Rehearsal of Restoration comedy (natural sounds of dialogue and producer with actors). Ballroom (band plays "The Bells of St. Mary's"). One woman pauses to adjust her shoe. A couple in evening dress pirouette in "exhibition dance" style. The motion of the dancers is very similar to the ballroom shot in *Listen to Britain*.

"Coal." The pits, against the dark landscape. (Sirens sound.) Rows of tiny houses. "Danters" (circus) lights in the surrounding night. Circus sideshow rides. Pits at evening.

Choir practice. Woman arrives at piano, ripples a few notes. Men begin to assemble around her. One helps her take off her coat. They begin to sing Handel's "Largo." Singing continues through: Exterior of window. Interior of pub. CU's men playing cards, dominoes. Puppet show apparently on a large stage: Welsh flax spinner and harpist models. The audience. (Return to choir rehearsal.) Shop window, then interior of shop. Outside shop, a man offers a girl sweets from a paper bag. They talk. (Back to choir, pan to pianist.) Taken from a car, long tracking shot along lighted shop windows. (See end of *The True Story of Lilli Marlene*.) Boys' club, handball game. Dissolve to home interior: mom serves food; dad reads paper, then comes to table when called. Exterior, men leave pub. Pithead.

(Music fades into siren.) Miners' shift comes on duty to clanking sound (same shot in *Listen to Britain*). "As things are, spare time is time when we have a chance to do what we like. A chance to be most ourselves." Cage descends. Rows of chimneys against evening sky. (Repeat brass band march over END title.)

SPEAKING FROM AMERICA (1939)

GPO Film Unit

10 minutes

Director: Humphrey Jennings

Commentary: R. Duff

Photography: W. B. Pollard, F. Gamage (?)

Diagrams: J. Chambers

Sound: Ken Cameron

("Busy" music.) CU phone ringing, man answering. "A business man in London gets a call from America . . ." (Behind the commentary, the telephone conversation continues.) Commentary describes the passage of the British voice through the international switchboard to Rugby radio station. CU radio valve (as used in *Listen to Britain*). ". . . at Rugby the voice is amplified 120 million times . . . it is carried from the shortwave transmitter to the 'array,' or system of aerials . . . from the array the voice is projected into the upper atmosphere in the direction of New York . . ." Model globe. New York shot. Models. Faraday House shot. ". . . The voice replying from New York is transmitted into the atmosphere from New Jersey . . . at Faraday House, the two voices are put together in a conversation . . ."

Long held ocean shot. "Now, on their way over the Atlantic, telephone voices meet various blocks . . . electrical waves are reflected up and down between the earth's surface and the ionosphere . . ." Models and animation. "Here trouble begins . . . the ionosphere is continually shifting about, also it flickers . . ." Model globe and animation. Cloud background to further animation. "Then there's another problem . . . one wave will arrive after the other . . . two waves cancel out, voice fades away . . ." Live photo of Rugby radio station as background to animated diagrams. "So a new station is wanted—a big bunch of sunspots is expected in 1940 . . ."

Map—live shot panning L-R down the Thames—map again. ". . . Opposite Canvey Island, there's a village called Cooling which overlooks a big stretch of marshland . . ." Landscape of Cooling marshes. Maps and diagrams. ". . . Engineers are planning a new receiving station . . . two miles of aerials—sixteen of them . . ." Landscapes. ". . . Away from factories and main roads . . . has to be dead flat . . . has to be wet to be a good conductor . . ."

Shots of raising poles, digging trenches, wiping tubes, detailed CU's with natural sound background. ". . . The tubes are taken out to the trench in thirty-foot lengths . . ." High-angle shot: men in a long line laying the cable in tube. "When about two hundred feet are ready, they're lifted up and put down in the trenches . . ."

Interior shots and CU's of receiving station. ". . . Inside the station the cables are fitted to receiving apparatus . . . The system does not intend to alter nature . . ."

Diagrams. ". . . Let's take two waves, call them A and B . . ." Commentary and diagrams follow process of delaying and synchronizing waves.

Twilight shots of station aerials and clouds. ". . . Cooling radio station is going to be important also for receiving radio broadcasta from America." Radio voice says: *We are now taking you over the the United States.* Newsreel shot of

Roosevelt addressing college com-
mencement. Roosevelt: . . . *the vast
amount of our resources, the vigor of
our commerce and the strength of our
men have made us vital factors in world
peace, whether we choose it or not.*

Music to END. Globe revolves, mast,
cables, station, radio listener superimposed.

S. S. IONIAN (1939)
(also known as HER LAST TRIP)

GPO Film Unit

*20 minutes (A shorter version, CAR-
GOES, was also released.)*

Director: Humphrey Jennings

Sound: Ken Cameron

Olive tree outlined against water. Broken Greek pillars. Print of an ancient
Greek ship. "Once upon a time . . . a
Greek sailor got lost on his way home
and sailed out of the Aegean Sea westward, past Malta and Gibraltar . . . the
Greek was Ulysses, and his voyage the
Odyssey." Porpoises in the water, sea.
"Today we've turned the tables . . . now
it's the Northerners who are running
their vessels South by East . . ."

Gibraltar. "In the Bay of Gibraltar lies
the *Ionian,* unloading stores for the
naval base . . ." Shots of *Ionian* unloading. "She has a Greek name . . . 4000
tons, Captain William Smith, new, clean,
fast . . . with a cargo of steel, explosives, cement, beer, telegraph
poles, corrugated iron, and airplane
spares . . ."

(Music and engine noise, the latter
continuing throughout sequence.) Captain with sextant. "The sun strikes full
on the sea . . ." Second Engineer going
below. Engines. Coal stoking. Funnel
smoke. ". . . The temperature of the sea
goes up and up to 70 to 90 degrees . . ."
Crew rig up awning, go about various
tasks, relax in sun. ". . . And here's Joe,
one of the apprentices, dobey-ing—the
sailors' word for washing." Shot of sea.
(Engine noises on track continuously.)

"From Gibraltar to Malta is two and a
half days . . ." Radio operator. Sea. Island comes into view. Cablegram: *Ionian will come into the Grand Harbor of
Valetta six o'clock Sunday evening.* Harbor slides past camera L to R. ". . . In
the floating dock, a battleship . . ."
Floating shots L-R. Unloading, battleship
in background. (Commentary details the
unloading.) "Now the tugs come and
pull the lighters away." (Engine noises
continue throbbing throughout.) CU orders. Funnel steam. Harbor slides past
R-L.

"All over the world there are big and
little ships . . . but tramp and liner belong to the same family, the family of
merchant ships. When a British merchant steamer passes one of His Majesty's vessels, they dip their ensigns to
recognize the relationship between the
two services." Ensign dips. Sea. Sailor
with canary. VLS naval vessel.

Crew at work. "Nobody waits on a
seaman . . ." Crew collect food. Oiling
cables. Wake. (Engine continues throbbing.) "From Malta to Alex is three and a
half days . . ." Radio operator. Cablegram. "Sparks radios to agents 'Expect
to berth eight-thirty Friday.'"

Dissolve to CU Egyptian mask. Flags
in rigging. Alexandria harbor. "Early Friday morning Alexandria lighthouse suddenly shows up out of the sea." Seaplane in harbor. "Imperial Airways

planes come down like enormous flying fish." Battleship. Ensign dipped. (Commentary gives description of battleship *Malaya*: *oil burning, armed to the teeth, 1150 men . . .*)

"That dark flag is red. It means 'explosives on board.'" Unloading explosives. "Dangerous cargo first . . ." (Eastern-style music matches gestures of unloaders.) "Carefully stowed inside these crates are airplane parts for the RAF depot at Aboukir Bay, where Nelson smashed Napoleon's navy over a hundred years ago . . . Now . . . unloading chains and anchor . . . cement for Egypt's new motor roads . . ." Dhow goes off. Cablegram: *Ionian sailed this morning . . .*

"From Alex to Haifa is a day's run. (Engine sounds.) "The *Ionian* ties up in Haifa harbor . . . that's Jim, the other apprentice . . ." He plays gramophone record of the Barcarolle from "Tales of Hoffman." View through porthole. Landscape in background, destroyers slide past R-L. Commentary gives details of names, tonnage, weaponry, etc. ". . . Fast as whippets . . . They can hear the Barcarolle across the water." (Barcarolle plays faintly, fades out.)

Landscape slides past L-R. "In the foreground, the oil dumps of the famous pipelines from Iran, in the background, Mount Carmel . . . The *Ionian* leaves the same day for Cyprus . . . Behind the harbor lies a sort of English gothic cathedral . . ." *Ionian* ties up alongside cruiser. "At Larissa, the *Ionian* unloads the last of her cargo . . ." (Cypriot music.) Seaplane. "Unloaded, she sails high in the water . . ." *Ionian* sails R-L. (Engine sounds.) Cyrene landscapes from the sea. Loading. Commentary repeats her outgoing cargo . . .

"Now she begins loading locust beans, oil and wine . . ." (Greek song.) "This is Limasol." Boats. "The last port is Stavros, where once upon a time stood the groves and temple of Venus . . ." VLS views of landscape from sea.

Egyptian flag. "Back in Alexandria again, the *Ionian* waits just long enough to pick up oilcake and cotton for London. The loading goes on into the night . . ." (Elgar's "Pomp and Circumstance" begins.) Leaving Alexandria for home. Shot of ensign at stern (as in *Words for Battle.*) "Past the cruiser *Antaeus* . . . Past the *Malaya* . . ." Battleships. Stoking, smoking funnel. "Past the *Warspite*." Crew member watches with binoculars. Navy on horizon. Ensign. Bows. Stern, with name *Ionian*. Navy. "Westward!" Gibraltar. Shots of fleet. "Throughout this voyage, the *Ionian* has met with ships of the Mediterranean fleet . . . North is where the Home Fleet guards the way . . ." Cliffs of Dover. (Music continues.) Notice: Butlers Wharf. Tower Bridge. "By the Tower of London she unloads her cargo brought safely from Cyprus and Alexandria under the protection of the British Navy, the greatest navy in the world."

Night on the Thames. Moon over gasholders, cranes, chimneys. "In only a week or two, the *Ionian* will turn round, steam along the Thames again . . . with a new cargo . . . Gibraltar . . . Malta . . . Alexandria . . . Cyprus and Palestine." (Music continues.) Navy shots intercut with Thames sailing barge shot to END.

THE FIRST DAYS (1939)

GPO Film Unit

23 minutes

Producer: Cavalcanti

Directors: Humphrey Jennings, Harry Watt, Pat Jackson

Commentary: Robert Sinclair

Editor: R. Q. McNaughton

Sound: Ken Cameron

Music (Sibelius's Second Symphony) behind titles—"A Picture of the London Front."

Outside the Imperial War Museum, boys play on a World War I cannon. (A shot to be used later in *The True Story of Lilli Marlene*). "Twenty years." "Tipperary" plays in background as camera roams the War Museum interior. Shells, etc., on display.

"September 3, 1939. London was at peace on this Sunday morning." Silence now through shots of: empty street, church spires, towers. A man, then more people, enter church. People pack their car for an outing. Vicar. Bikes. Church. Towpath. Big Ben, 11:15. 10 Downing Street. Chamberlain's voice: *I am speaking to you from the Cabinet Room at 10 Downing Street . . .* Clouds, aerials, man listening to radio. More radios, people listen everywhere. *. . . This morning the British ambassador in Berlin handed the German government a final note . . . unless we hear from them by eleven o'clock . . . I have to tell you now that no such undertaking has been received, and that consequently this country is at war with Germany.* Paper boy. People listening to radio. *It is evil things we shall be fighting against . . . Against them, I am certain the right will prevail.*

Clouds. "London is calling. London calling to the world. This is London. Here is London, calling to a world at war."

Sirens sound. ". . . An unknown plane approaches the coast." Rooftops. People go into shelters. Balloons rise. One shot contains balloon rising, people moving R to L. Warden stops a man in a car, sends him to a shelter. "The warden . . . his principal equipment is friendliness . . . Friendliness: it has become the wartime equipment of all Londoners." People inside the shelters. Sirens sound. Man in shelter comments: *Old 'Itler didn't take very long, did 'e? . . . What's that, rum rations?* "People joked, but in their hearts was devastation . . ." People chat in shelter.

"The devastation of war claimed even the blades of grass that brightened the gray winter . . ." Trenches being dug. ARP (air-raid precautions) on tractor. Sandbags. "The long-covered earth of London has seen the light after barren years. It is put to barren use . . . sandbags, sandbags, millions of sandbags." Sequence of sandbag filling, stacking. ". . . Those earthworks are rising like a tide in our streets. We want these to be the last earthworks . . . Men and women . . . ran to and fro like ants, each with his tiny burden. But the bags and the boarding and the trenches are but the external signs of a great upheaval in London's inner life . . . the hardening of London's face, the growing ruggedness of the streets, meant a warming of the heart and a quickening of the sympathies . . . The thousands of classes of London, some from their damp basements and some from their luxury flats, came to work for the public good . . . they did indispensable work which no leader could have ordered and no money could have bought . . ." Sequence of recruits training and drilling. ". . . A remarkable thing: a generation of young men, born in the last war, and brought up in contempt of militarism and the fruitless romance of the battlefield, went into uniform willingly and with clear understanding . . . These were London's children . . . now they carry on, but they are still our children." (Dramatic music.) Planes. "The defense of London is in young firm hands." (Music ends.)

"But some Londoners must keep their feet on the ground . . ." Workers in the streets. Policeman in tin hat. White paint on roadway. A car crosses it, painter looks up with resigned expression. "London's white warpaint was to be a guide on the darkest night—sometimes." Static water tanks. Hospitals being evacuated. "Children too were leaving London . . ." Tying labels on children. Mothers watch. "For this was a city of children . . . The real London was its children, its future . . . London is the cradle of tomorrow, and not just the slate and stone and the bricks and mortar of an ancient and toiling city . . ." Children in train. "The mothers stayed . . ." Women sweep up. Dialogue between them: *It gets that quiet, doesn't it? Funny, it takes a war to give us a bit of peace and quiet.*

Ambulance girls. ". . . Three thousand taxi drivers became godfather to a fire pump . . ." Taxi pumps. Balloons. The Mall, pan across roadway to other side. ". . . One side of a street might be sunny and civilized, the other like a road in France, with army convoys hiding under the trees . . ." Drills and training. "In quiet backwaters . . . its young men trained."

"It was a time to say goodbye . . ." Young lovers buy flowers. Troops at Waterloo. "Goodbye." Band plays as troops entrain. Steam. Train leaves. "Goodbye." (very quietly). Troopship. "They've gone off like the children—but they have gone the other way." Siren of ship. "Goodbye" (finality in voice). The girl we saw earlier is offered flowers by vendor. She passes him.

National Gallery. Empty frames. British Museum being emptied. Statue being lifted by neck. "Here is a hanging, another gentleman who is going to the country, when they can get him off his pedestal . . ." Gibraltar Walk, "Rock of Gibraltar," built from sandbags. Poster says "Let 'Em All Come." ". . . A living Cockney monument, built by Cockney hands . . ." In the East End, notices, ARP, in English and Hebrew. In shop window, "20,000 Sandbags for Sale." The docks: camouflage being painted. News placard: "*Athenia* sunk." A West End street scene. War map in shop window "with flags of hope pinned on Poland."

In a church, registration of foreigners who are reading newspapers in different languages. "A hundred thousand people of many lands. They are part of London . . ." Cat looks up. Barrage balloon flutters. Cat looks. "Many pets were killed to avoid suffering, others evacuated . . ." Nurse's uniform on a store dummy. Other uniforms. ATS (Auxiliary Territorial Service) girls admire dress in shop window. "In their new trappings was the old spirit . . ." Convoy of troops in lorries travels down Whitehall. (On soundtrack songs "Wish Me Luck . . ."

and "We're Gonna Hang Out the Washing on the Siegfried Line.") Barrage balloon. Women knitting.

Silhouette evening shots. "Night must fall . . . the gleaming river may yet betray London . . . from the ground, men watch." Evening on Thames, balloons in clouds. Observers. Plane. Traffic lights masked. Empty theaters, closed. "Locked for the first time since the Puritans closed them nearly 300 years ago . . . But no one has ever stopped the Cockney voice of London . . ." In blackout barrel organ plays "Keep the Home Fires Burning."

Docks. War factory, pan L-R. Plane takes off. "Night or day, it is always the birthday of an aircraft . . . and in the blackout, the hospital is awake, ready." Sign: HOSPITAL in silhouette. Nurses. "The hospital—and the arsenal." Blackout shots. Searchlight beam.

"London turns to a new day . . ." Morning shot. Cinema. Balloon rises. "This is not twilight that has come to England, it is dawn . . ." Factory, balloon, allotments (victory gardens). Clouds and balloons dotted in sky. Military drill outside Buckingham Palace. "In the clear daylight stands the London front . . ." Sandbags. Sentry at palace in battledress. "London calling . . . and when you hear it, you'll know that this front is still intact . . . that men still whistle at their work in England . . ." Balloon. King and Queen look up. Balloon rises. (Military-style music to END)

SPRING OFFENSIVE (1940)

GPO Film Unit, for the Ministry of Information

20 minutes

Producer: Cavalcanti

Director: Humphrey Jennings

Script: Hugh Gray

Commentary: A. G. Street

Photography: Henry Fowle, Jonah Jones, Eric Cross

Editor: Geoff Foot

Artistic Director: Edward Carrick

Sound: Ken Cameron

Music: Liszt, arranged by Brian Easdale and conducted by Muir Matheson

(Music.) Wheat stooks. "September 1939. The English countryside . . ." Several CU's of countrymen. "Its most important crop: the English countryman . . . in the midst of harvest comes news of war . . . what will war mean to the countryman?" (Music throughout.) Farm. "Here's Fred Martin's farm at Shottisham in East Anglia . . . on Monday evening, Mr. Martin is at Woodbridge, meeting a train." (Radio time signal.) Mrs. Martin moves to window. *Here comes the car . . .* Ken, the schoolboy evacuee, wearing his label, enters diffidently. *Don't miss the news . . .!* General greetings, with BBC news in background. CU of Fred from Ken's POV.

". . . Fred pulls his weight in all sorts of ways . . ." (takes in an evacuee). Radio: *The Minister of Agriculture and Fisheries has appointed a War Agricultural Executive Committee for each county in England and Wales . . . as free a hand as possible in their own areas . . .* [gives further details of scheme] *. . . appeals for men who know their jobs . . ."*

Shots of local committee. Many CU's of English faces as they discuss problems. ". . . First job, to get a million or more acres of grassland ploughed up . . . a big job . . ." Martin talks to various local farmers, gets their cooperation. One farmer shaving at window argues against him. Martin: *You'll get the Government grant of £64.* Response: *I'll give you sixty-four quid to mind your own business and clear off!*

CU oiling machinery. (Music begins a march rhythm.) LS machine steaming against countryside background. Tractor driving, flock of gulls across ploughed field. ". . . Extra tractors need extra drivers—a hard job for youth. If you don't find colts, you'll never get hosses. But many colts have joined up, so the fillies come to the rescue. Town girl—country girl." Land girls being trained on tractors (*It's not like a two-seater, is it?*). Long tractor sequence, pastoral scenes, CU's of furrows. "How they barked and stuttered through September and November!" (Music climaxes.)

War Agricultural Committee. Martin knocks out pipe in grate, reports on progress. *That is Grove Farm* . . . Thumb on map, dissolve to reflection of farm in millpond. *Derelict* . . . (Menacing music.)

"Grove Farm." Door, bucket on doorstep, dog on kennel, weed-grown wheel and barrows, tractors. Tracking back on each shot. Weeds in mist (backtrack). Tracking shot along brambles, etc. (Sad music.) "This is what happened after the last war . . ."

Discussion at War Agricultural Committee: . . . *doesn't look as though we could get a harvest before 1945 . . . get power from London to take possession* . . .

At the farm, interior with Christmas decorations. "The Sunday before Christ-

mas, Mr. Martin has gone to meet Ken's parents. Ken is now at least 90 percent country, and his hero is Bob, the tiller driver." Ken at table with Meccano model tiller. Bob helps him get it working. Ken's parents arrive. Father: *We don't know how to thank you, Mr. Martin . . . It's the first time I've been on a farm . . .* Ken shows the model tiller to parents. Martin says: *You'd be driving a real one if it weren't for the frost.*

(Music.) Snow. Icy furrows. "But don't think country folk are taking a holiday . . ." Tractor smoke against landscape. At the forge, new parts for tractors (conversation). *Just waiting for snow to clear, then we're going over . . .*

(Music.) "When the thaw comes, the attack on Grove Farm begins . . . First job—digging trenches for drains . . ." *It's wet, very wet . . .* Ken calls out: *Mr. Martin, look!* LS landscape. No sign at first, then tiller very slowly comes into view. Ken gets a chance to ride it. (Heavy mechanical sounds.) Low-angle shot of tiller retreating from camera. BCU earth. Low-angle, tiller comes toward camera. "After twenty years, the earth gets another chance to produce food instead of brambles . . ." Brambles crushed beneath tiller. Two pheasants escape from brush. Dog barks. Horses run.

(Music.) VLS horse ploughing. Scarecrow. Harvest. Pastoral rhythms of hay lifting.

"Remember . . . we've looked after the land properly only during periods of war . . . In September 1939 you asked the countryside to provide you with a safe refuge for your children and security against famine. Both these things it has given you. Now the countryside asks you to do something in return.

When peace comes, don't forget the land and its people again."
(Music to END.)

WELFARE OF THE WORKERS (1940)

GPO Film Unit, for the Ministry of Information

10 minutes

Producer: Harry Watt

Asst. Producer: J. B. Holmes

Directors: Humphrey Jennings, Pat Jackson

Photography: Jonah Jones

Editors: Jack Lee and Joe Mendoza

Commentary: Ritchie Calder

Sound: Ken Cameron

(Music: brass band as in *Spare Time*.) CU factory worker. "This man is a skilled worker . . . comes of generations of men as proud and jealous of their skill as he is, men who fought like him for trade union rights, better conditions, better wages . . . insurance . . ."
Wipe of brush blacking-out factory (see *Listen to Britain*). "Then war came . . . Factories had to be camouflaged. Sunlight was blacked out, workers were shut in . . ." Blackout scenes. ". . . workers left the factories depressed and tired out. But the alternative was the blackout of liberty . . . on the Continent, Hitler had destroyed the trade unions . . . To resist such tyranny, the British worker was asked to surrender some of his hard-won rights, to give up by choice what Hitler takes by force." Radio, with listener: . . . *We*

need plenty of arms for victory . . . goodnight, and go to it!
". . . June 1940, Bevin . . . began to redeploy labor, and adapt existing welfare arrangements . . ." Girl leaving home. "This girl is being asked to transfer from her job in one part of the country to war work in a distant factory . . ." WVS (Women's Voluntary Service) worker looks for billets for her. "The new job becomes an adventure . . . She's introduced to her new home and her hostess. Next morning she starts out for work . . ." Illustrative shots. "Why a factory in a cornfield? . . . compared with what she's been used to, it's like stepping from the nineteenth century into the twentieth . . ." Factories in country landscape.
". . . The Welfare officer—new opportunities of happiness for her . . . He looks after things like the Sunday opening of cinemas . . . cheap excursions to the country . . ." Illustrative shots. "She's going to have leisure. The Ministry of Labor insists upon that . . ." Very long descriptions of new regulations for workers, including workers in the farm industry. Illustrative shot from *Spring Offensive*.
Worker at canteen table (see *Listen to Britain*). Will Fyffe in "Workers' Playtime" sings. Shot of old man at table spitting, as in *Listen to Britain*. Bevin on platform, gives "work hard" speech. (Cheers.) Bevin: *We can not only work and fight, but we can be cheerful in doing it as well.* (Cheers to END.)

LONDON CAN TAKE IT!
(1940)

GPO Film Unit, for the Ministry
of Information

10 minutes

Directors: Humphrey Jennings and
Harry Watt

Photography: Henry Fowle, Jonah Jones

Music: Vaughan Williams's "A London
Symphony"

Commentary: Quentin Reynolds

Sound: Ken Cameron

Editors: Stewart McAllister and Jack Lee

The film was intended primarily for export to North and South America. A
five-minute version was prepared for
the domestic market, entitled *Britain
Can Take It.*

St. Paul's dome behind titles. (Music
begins, and continues under commentary for some time.)

High-angle vista of London, St. Paul's
discernible in the distance. "I'm speaking from London. It's late afternoon and
the people of London are preparing for
the night." LS of the perspective of a
London suburban street. Down the deserted roadway a family with two baby-
carriages walks toward camera. Shots of
bus queues outside Selfridge's, buses
and traffic passing L-R. "Everyone is anxious to get home before darkness falls,
before our nightly visitors arrive." (Music fades.)

LS Big Ben tower from across Westminster Bridge. Tram crosses it toward
camera. Picadilly Circus traffic. Entrance
to Underground. "This is the London
rush hour. Many of the people at whom
you are looking now . . . the greatest civilian army ever to be assembled . . .

now going home to change into the uniform of their particular service . . ."
Women defense workers with respirators pass sandbagged shelter entrance.
Dissolve to:

Night sky silhouette of listening apparatus swinging into position. Cut to its
crew moving with it. "The dusk is deep-
ening . . . listening crews are posted
. . . to pick up the drone of the German
planes . . ." Huge poster above store
says: CARRY ON LONDON AND KEEP
YOUR CHIN UP!

CU shelter sign: S Here. Pan/tilt down
to long queue waiting; prominent is a
woman with a white bandaged head. A
busker with accordion entertains them.
"This has been a quiet day for us, but it
won't be a quiet night . . . They'll be
over tonight; they'll destroy a few buildings and kill a few people, probably
some of the people you're watching
now . . ." LS of same queue. Closer
shot of its head as warden opens a door
and people begin to enter for the night.
". . . This is not a pleasant way to spend
a night, but the people accept it . . ." LS
A.A. gun rising against night sky. The
line of people shuffles past, R-L. A
child in its mother's arms gazes into
camera. ". . . These civilians are good
soldiers . . ."

LS Palace of Westminster. "Now it's
eight o'clock." (Big Ben chimes.) Observers' post outlined against sky.
"Jerry's a little bit late tonight." Searchlights. Guns rise. Firemen tend their
pumps. They look upward. Warden
looks up. Ambulance men mount car
with placard: *Stretcher Party No. 103,
Marylebone.* ". . . The people's army:
they are the ones who are really fighting
the war."

BCU siren switch. Hand moves it from

OFF to WARNING. "And there's the wail of the banshee!" Vista shot of London at dusk, horizon in distance. (Siren alert wails.) Deserted street. "The nightly siege of London has begun . . ." Very dark shot of a few people entering a shelter door, which then closes onto blackness.

Two wardens stand in street, looking up. "Here they come." Sky shot, one balloon visible. (Drone of bombers increases.) High-angle shot of empty baby carriages parked at curb. Sky behind buildings; dark, mackerel clouds. A searchlight facing us. It suddenly lights up. "Now the searchlights are poking long, white, inquisitive fingers into the blackness of the night."

Long-held shot of lighted clouds across horizon. Darkness broken by sudden gun flashes, which briefly illuminate guns and crew, searchlight crews, gun firing, two wardens outside shelter, S sign. (Gunfire, planes roar.) "These are not Hollywood sound effects . . . this is the music they play every night at London . . . the symphony of war . . ." (A bomb whooshes down, explodes.) "That was a bomb" (dryly).

Inside shelter, men play darts. An elderly couple sleep in a bed, their clothes on. Blackness interspersed with flashes, single-frame shots of guns. (Gunfire, explosions on soundtrack.) A sleeping man gently swings in a hammock. More blackness, flashes of an archway, a listening post, a searchlight, A.A. guns firing, a warden walking in a street (one over-exposed frame), St. Paul's silhouetted against sky (also one frame). Blackness. (Explosions, etc., continue.)

Panning CU across sleeping faces of a father, child, and mother. "The very young and the very old . . . sleep in the shelters. Do you see any signs of fear on these faces?"

A church on fire in the darkness. A house explodes. More fire and firefighting shots, with fire engines flash-illuminated. "Now the people's army swings into action. Bombs have started fires. When a bomber starts a fire, he immediately returns and uses it as a target and drops more bombs . . . Yet the people's army ignores the bombs . . . brokers, clerks, peddlers, and merchants by day, they are heroes by night . . ." (Blitz noises continue.) Darkness. "The night is long, but sooner or later the dawn will come . . ." The sky at dawn. Dissolve to:

LS Palace of Westminster. BCU hand turns siren switch to RAIDERS PAST. (Siren sounds the "all clear.") ". . . And there's the wail of the banshee again; this time a friendly wail." CU of water of the Thames, a buoy. "It's just six a.m. In its last hour of precious sleep, this strange new world finds peace." (Siren continues.) Elderly couple seen before turn over in bed. View along Millbank of Palace of Westminster. Couple in bed tuck up. Fade out. (Silence.)

VLS view of London. "London raises her head, shakes the debris of the night from her hair, and takes stock of the damage done." City alley with rubble in foreground. Tilt down facade of blitzed house to suburban street. Low-angle shot, a woman looks out through shattered panes of her window. Another woman comes to back door, collects milk from doorstep, kicks broken glass from steps, looks across, goes inside. Two women chat with official on rubble-strewn lawn. Dog roots around the rubble, while a boy watches and a woman walks past. "London doesn't look down upon the ruins of its houses . . . churches . . . hospitals . . . London looks upwards towards the dawn . . . with calmness and confidence." A gravestone stands upright in a blitzed churchyard. Blocks of workers' flats, bombed and derelict.

MS, man looks, puts pipe in mouth, moves off R. LS, same man walks L-R past damage, looking over his shoulder at it. High-angle shot of London street with tall blitzed buildings, trucks clearing rubble, pedestrians and traffic winding slowly through it. Another shot of workers walking past rubble L-R. "The people's army go to work as they did in that other comfortable world . . ." London bus up-ended against a ruined house. "Not all the services run as they did yesterday, but London manages to get to work on time—one way or another . . ." Low-angle shot, suburban train passes over partly bombed viaduct. Four well-dressed civilians ride through a London street on a flat horse-drawn cart (following shot, probably from a car).

"In the center of the city the shops are open as usual. Many of them are more open than usual . . ." Pedestrians walk past blitzed shops. A broom sweeps up broken glass from shop-front as people's feet walk past. A woman steps into shop window display through the place where glass would have been. She greets shop man who is clearing up, helps him by handing him display garments.

"Dr. Paul Josef Goebbels said recently that the nightly air raids had had a terrific effect upon the morale of the people of London . . ." Householders remove belongings from their home,

load them in baby carriage. Woman in bombed street folds and packs dress in suitcase. "The good doctor was absolutely right. Today the morale of the people is higher than ever before . . ." The Queen and the King walk through rubble, Her Majesty touching a broken concrete block lightly. Workers walk L-R, one man helping a woman with a heavy bucket. Viewed through a blitzed building, more people walk L-R. Civil Defense workers dig in rubble. "They know that thousands of them will die, but they would rather stand and face death than kneel down and face the kind of existence the conqueror would impose upon them."

The Queen talks to workers. Men shoveling at a huge pile of rubble at foot of the Monument. High-angle view of bombed store at Oxford Circus, bus moving past. Trafalgar Square, with statue of Charles I boarded up. Bombed house in Nash terrace at Regent's Park. Whitehall building shored up. St. Paul's from Ludgate Circus. Firemen hosing down a smouldering warehouse. Close view of rescue workers. Group of civilians in rubble. Trucks outside bombed houses.

High-angle shot of people in station yard, many buses in foreground. ". . . England is not taking its beating lying down. They are guarding the frontiers of freedom . . . London is fighting back. I am a neutral reporter. I have watched the people of London live and die . . . I can assure you, there is no panic, no fear, no despair in London Town . . ." Crowd of people (parents?), man with megaphone. Closer view of crowd of children being assembled for evacuation. Buses roll out of yard with evacuees.

"And they know that every night the RAF bombers fly deep into the heart of Germany . . ." News vendor writes in chalk on his board: BERLIN BOMBED. RAF men load bomber (shot from beneath bomb bay). News board: RAF SMASH INVASION PORTS. Three bombers in formation in sky.

"It is true that the Nazis will be over again tomorrow night, and . . . every night . . ." CU, hand brushes plaster debris off cooking grill. Man sweeps glass in street. Two Civil Defense men talk. Tram passes ruins. Bombed "Dutch Boy Laundry" with Union Jack at window. LS London street, rubble apparent. "They will drop thousand of bombs, and they'll destroy hundreds of buildings and they'll kill thousands of people." CU, cat is handed up from beneath rubble to another rescue worker. General view of bombed buildings. "But a bomb has its limitations: it can only destroy buildings and kill people. It cannot kill the unconquerable spirit and courage of the people of London." C.D. worker cadges light from taxi driver, walks gaily off from camera, steel helmet cockily askew. "London can take it." Statue of Richard I, sword raised, in front of bomb-damaged window of Palace of Westminster. Superimposed END title. (Music.)

HEART OF BRITAIN (1941) (U.S. title: THIS IS ENGLAND)

Crown Film Unit, for the Ministry of Information

9 minutes

Producer: Ian Dalrymple

Director: Humphrey Jennings

Photography: Henry Fowle

Editor: Stewart McAllister

Music: Beethoven and Handel, played by the Halle Orchestra conducted by Sir Malcolm Sargent, and the Huddersfield Choir

Commentary: Jack Holmes

Sound: Ken Cameron

(Opening music—Elgar.) Bleak moorside. "The winds of war blow across the hills and moorlands of Yorkshire and Derbyshire. They stir the grasses in the sheep valleys of Cumberland, ruffle the clear surface of Ullswater. They sing in the cathedral towers of Durham, in the tower of Liverpool (still building), in the spires of Coventry. But the heart of Britain remains unmoved and unchangeable." Shots of rocks.

Twilight factories (from *Spare Time*), Sheffield steel furnaces (also one shot from *Spare Time*, later used in *Listen to Britain*). "In the shadow of the hills live the great industrial people, thronging the valleys of power and the rivers of industry . . ." Almost imperceptible dissolve from stock shot of furnace operators to shot of George Good and his mates walking away from furnaces, wiping their faces. "At the end of a shift . . . George Good comes off hot and tired, but nowhere near beaten . . . he's an air-raid warden as well . . ." (This commentary more conversational in tone than the earlier declamation.)

Good talks self-consciously, mostly to the camera: *Well, I reckon I've had a rough shift today. Never mind, got a good dinner to go home to. After that, I'm going on the ARP bit.*

Wipe to Bolton cotton mills. "From Yorkshire to Lancashire; from steel to cotton . . ." Night sky, chimneys.

". . . All night now there must be men to watch for fire-bombs . . ." ARP men talking amongst themselves. "This used to be the playground of a school—one of the places where Liverpool trains her rescue squads . . ."

CU's women typing and working. "Behind this grim work lies an infinite number of patient everyday jobs for the women, dull jobs like typing lists of addresses. Unending ones . . . the simplest, most difficult task of all—just staying put, with the war round the corner." Shots of viaduct, houses, factory chimney.

"On a hazy day, Jerry comes droning over about three miles up . . . When the roof spotters think he means trouble, they send the millgirls down to shelter for a few minutes . . ." Girls entering shelter. "Just look at these Lancashire lassies cowering before the Luftwaffe . . ." Inside shelter, girls playing a ball game, with much hysterical laughter. "These are the folk whom Field Marshal Goering hopes to bomb into capitulation."

Poster for Halle Orchestra, in Manchester. "But in Manchester today they still respect the genius of Germany—the genius of the Germany that was . . ." Malcolm Sargent conducting Beethoven's Fifth Symphony. (Music continues over shots of, and a very long pan across ruined Coventry, and under the first part of the next sequence.)

Tea urn, WVS woman. "Here in Coventry, those everyday tasks of the women came right through the fire and became heroic . . ." (Music fades.) "Listen to Mrs. Patterson . . ." Woman speaks to camera: *Y'know, you feel such a fool standing there in a crater . . . handing cups of tea to the men bringing up the bodies, and to know that there's someone there—actually in that bombed house—who's alive, and you can give that tea to. Then to hear the praises of the men themselves—"that tea's jolly good—just washed the blood and dust out of my mouth." We feel that we really have done a job, and a decent job.*

Choral society sings "Hallelujah Chorus." Intercut with shots of Coventry and other ruins. Singing continues to triumphant conclusion at the end of the film, under the following commentary:

"People who sing like that in times like these cannot be beaten. These people are slow to anger, not easily roused. Now they and their mates, their wives and their children, have been subjected to the most savage ordeal ever inflicted upon human beings. But these people have the power to hit back." War factory, with details of bomber construction, Coventry cathedral, bomber taking off. "And they are going to hit back, with all the skill of their hands, the tradition of their crafts, and the fire in their hearts. Out of the valleys of power and the rivers of industry will come the answer to the German challenge." Moors, spires, moors, bomber, landscape, night bomber. "And the Nazis will learn—once and for all—that no one with impunity troubles the heart of Britain."

WORDS FOR BATTLE (1941)

Crown Film Unit, for the Ministry
  of Information

8 minutes

Producer: Ian Dalrymple

Director/Script: Humphrey Jennings

Editor: Stewart McAllister

Music: Beethoven and Handel played by the London Philharmonic Orchestra; conducted by Sir Malcolm Sargeant

Sound: Ken Cameron

Commentary: Laurence Olivier

(Handel's Water Music behind titles.) Moving, rolling clouds behind titles dissolve into page showing map of "Britannia" at beginning of Camden's book. Music fades as the page turns and we dissolve into spring trees against a clear sky (from *Britain at Bay*).

"For the air is most temperate and wholesome . . ." Rocky promontory with gulls. ". . . Walled and guarded with the ocean . . ." Landscape of wheatfields. ". . . The earth fertile with all kinds of grain . . ." Quarry side. ". . . Rich in minerals—coal, tin, lead . . ." Landscape, cattle in foreground. ". . . Abundant with pasture . . ." VLS landscape with copse of trees. ". . . Plentifully wooded . . ."

Castle on hill above town. ". . . beautified with many populous cities, fair boroughs, good towns, and well-built villages . . ."

Stained-glass rose window, from interior, tilt down to aisle. (Music begins.) MS busts of poets, including Milton. CU bust of Milton. BCU of Milton's bust, music fading as we dissolve to:

Aerial view of roads and buildings—probably an industrial estate. "Methinks I see a mighty and puissant nation rousing herself after sleep." High-angle shot of air cadets approaching a Spitfire on the ground. Low-angle shot of Spitfire taxiing R-L. MS cadets watching off-screen L. "Methinks I see her as an eagle, mewing her mighty youth . . ."

Spitfire propellor in background dominates shot of cadets shading eyes to look upward and left, off-screen. CU one cadet shading his eyes, looking up. He turns L-R. Spitfire flies L-R. ". . . Kindling her undazzled eyes at the full midday scene . . ."

As plane flies into distance, fade to black. Then fade-in shot of clouds fast receding (probably reversed shot), dissolving into Nazi flag waving in breeze. ". . . While the whole noise of timorous and flocking birds, with those also that love the twilight . . ." Dark shot through trees of Hitler and Goering conferring as they walk. ". . . flutter about . . ." Nazi soldier raises plumed standard. Another draws sword. ". . . amazed at what she means . . ." Pan R-L along ranks of Nazi leaders—Schacht, Goebbels, etc. Fade to black.

Children evacuees, mothers, teachers hasten along London street R-L. Pan L-R against this movement. Natural sounds of feet and chatter.

CU plaque on wall: "WILLIAM BLAKE 1757–1827/Poet and Painter/Born Here." "Bring me my bow of burning gold . . ." High-angle shot of evacuees at station, moving up the screen away from us. "Bring me my chariot of fire . . ." Locomotive steams up past camera L-R, dissolve to train-window view of London house backs passing R-L.

"I will not cease from mental fight . . . till we have built Jerusalem in England's green and pleasant land." Evacuee schoolboys in boat on water, laughing, larking about. LS children in boats and punts on sylvan river. (Pastoral music behind these and next few shots.) Children rush down wooded hillside. At bottom of slope, girls gather brushwood. Fade out.

Page of Robert Browning's verse strip-illuminated at "Home-thoughts from the Sea."

Porpoises leaping alongside in ship's wake. "Nobly, nobly Cape St. Vincent . . ." Pan L-R along warships at anchor at sunset (from *S.S. Ionian*). Ensign being raised at stern (*S.S. Ionian*), dissolve to sidelit statue of Nelson. Dissolve to pan L-R VLS of Gibraltar (*S.S. Ionian*). LS Gibraltar (*S.S. Ionian*). ". . . Dawned Gibraltar, grand and gray . . ." LS Malta harbor. MS Captain on bridge. MS ensign being raised (both from *S.S. Ionian*). ". . . How can I help England, say? . . . While Jove's planet rises yonder, silent over Africa . . ." VLS battleships at sunset (*S.S. Ionian*). Fade to black.

Fade in tombstone illumined: RUDYARD KIPLING/BORN 30 DEC. 1865/DIED 18 JAN. 1936. Fade out.

Pan L-R shot of bombed suburban street. Civil Defense at work. Church spire in background (from *Christmas under Fire*). "It was not part of their blood, it came to them very late . . . when the English began to hate . . ."

Similar scene, with Civil Defense workers and weeping women walking toward camera.

Another shot of blitz damage, C.D. at work in dust. ". . . It will not swiftly abate through the chill years ahead . . ." Reprise of shot before last. "When time shall count from the date when the English began to hate . . ." Funeral, with black-plumed horses, followed by C.D. workers, passes bombed building crazily tilted. Fade out.

Faint notes of trumpet overlap: "We shall go on to the end . . ." MS Churchill inspecting troops, moves L-R toward camera. Trumpet continues. Low-angle shot of soldier with Sten gun at ready. ". . . We shall defend our island whatever the cost . . ."

Rolling surf on beach, with natural sound. ". . . We shall fight on the beaches . . ." Traffic sounds. Workmen rebuilding wall in London street; bus passes R-L. LS Edinburgh castle in mist. ". . . We shall never surrender . . ." Traffic sound ceases and trumpet call begins, increasing in intensity.

Dissolve to VLS troops marching against skyline. Masses of ANZAC (Australia and New Zealand Army Corps) troops fill screen, order arms. ANZAC troops march L-R up hill. ". . . And even if this island were subjugated and starving, then our Empire beyond the seas . . . would carry on the struggle until . . . the New World . . . steps forth . . ." Trumpet ends.

Dissolve to CU statue of Lincoln. CU his name on pedestal. CU head of statue. "It is for us, the living . . ." Big Ben begins to strike, lost later in sound of tanks and traffic. LS Lincoln's statue in Parliament Square, London. Tank passes it. " . . .We here highly resolve . . ." Big Ben tower, tanks enter shot from R. Tilt down to pick them up as they pass to L. ". . . That the government of the people, by the people . . ." Tanks pass Lincoln statue L-R. Tracking shot behind tanks as they move through Parliament Square. Tanks move L-R past Lincoln statue in background, traffic on other side moves R-L, occasionally obscuring our view. (Handel's Water Music begins, mingled with traffic sound, then takes over soundtrack to end of film.)

As bus passes camera, we cut to several shots of pedestrians moving L-R, interrupted by passing traffic as "wipes": A sailor and a civilian, three army officers, four soldiers and a civilian, and three WRENS (Women's Royal Naval Service). We pan with them. A civilian girl between an army corporal and an airman. (Music to END.)

LISTEN TO BRITAIN (1942)

Crown Film Unit, for Ministry
  of Information

20 minutes

Producer: Ian Dalrymple

Director/Script/Editor: Humphrey Jennings and Stewart McAllister

Production Manager: Dora Wright

Asst. Director: Joe Mendoza

Photography: Henry Fowle

Foreword spoken by Leonard Brockington

Sound: Ken Cameron

Behind the titles, which show an antiaircraft gun, a violin, and a stave of music, we hear a trumpet call, a babble of voices, a dog bark, then a roll of drums.

Fade-in shot of springtime trees against the sky, blowing in the wind. A faint roar of planes increases in volume, and continues over:

Wheat blowing in the wind. Two Spitfires cross the sky L-R. The wheat blows wildly. A farmer and two landgirls collecting potatoes look up briefly. Two official observers watch through binoculars. LS the observers' post, built up like a mound in the field. One observer points up. Four Spitfires cross the clouds L-R. VLS shows observation post,

then a tractor crosses R-L close to camera, pulling a baler.

VLS several planes in formation cross the clouds in the sky. (Plane drone mixes to BBC's time signal, six electronic pips.) Exterior of a cottage, with white paling fence. Outside a window; a woman inside places a lighted oil lamp in it. Dissolve to a dark ocean rolling in on beach. (During these shots we hear *This is the BBC Home and Forces Programs. Here is the news, and this is Joseph McLeod reading it . . .* The sound mixes with that of the ocean beach.)

Two servicemen are silhouetted sitting on a bench overlooking the evening ocean. (Faintly, we begin to hear the strains of "Roll Out the Barrel.") Another soldier, in MCU, on "stand-to" at the seaside, dons his greatcoat.

CU Poster: *Members of H.M. Forces in Uniform ½ Price.* Shadows pass it. (The dance music, "Beer Barrel Polka," is now very loud.) LS inside Tower Ballroom, Blackpool, filled with dancers, moving L-R. Many are in uniform.

MS, a girl walks R-L past an airman and a girl "sitting out." She is looking at a snapshot, and will not show it to him. (Mixed with the music we hear her giggles.) Another couple on her left join in the banter.

CMS, the original couple. The girl giggles. CMS, the young man from the left, looking at a snapshot, smiling.

LS, the dancers as before. Many are now singing "Roll Out the Barrel." Now a VLS, including the band on stage, and showing the circular movement of dancers around the ballroom.

(The music continues faintly, then fades out.) The serviceman on "stand-to" has now been joined by another, who puts on his steel helmet. Fade out.

(Sounds of mine machinery.) In near darkness, a shift comes on duty at a pit, carrying their safety lamps. A second shot shows them moving along a tunnel away from camera. Then, they move toward us, their lamps shining in a row. Exterior shot shows mine works faintly in blackout, then pit head wheel immobile and silhouetted against night sky. (Sounds of shunting.)

Railway signalman in his box looks out of window, then retires inside. Signal, against the night sky, drops with a clang. Low-angle shot against night cumulus clouds shows locomotive moving L-R toward us, coming to a halt. (Train sounds.) Dissolve to:

Inside the train, a Canadian sergeant strums a guitar to accompany the singing of "Home on the Range." Two-shot, an older sergeant chatting to a companion: . . . *grandstand that night, the RSM pinched one of my dolls . . . a big electric lamp . . .* Intercut singers, from another angle. Return to sergeant and listener: *Remember Tommy and the Brandon Babe? Oh yes, do I? It was a great night. Took 'em all day to ditch us . . .* Return to singers, closer shot. Another soldier plays an accordion. MCU Canadian soldier singing. Return to original two soldiers. The guitar-player's companion lights a cigarette, yodels.

Signalman returns to his window, as we hear shunting sounds which replace singing. The locomotive whistles, then moves off in almost complete darkness, faint gleams passing the camera L-R. Insert shot of signal now raised. Another shot of train passing into the night. (We hear, rather than see, it. Then, in blackness, we hear the signal fall.)

Inside a plane factory (natural sound). Men are assembling a bomber. MCU technician at propellor. Another general view of operation. Then night shot of bomber as it taxis R-L, away from camera, to take off on mission.

From the ensuing blackness, we pan R-L across to a notice: AMBULANCE STATION 76. A contralto voice is singing "The Ash Grove." General view, low-lit basement of London's Old Bailey: flagstones, statue of Charles I, classic painting on wall above piano. An ambulance worker is at the piano, singing and entertaining her sister workers. MS the singer (part of statue is in foreground) and her audience behind her. Insert shot of steel helmets, marked "A" for "ambulance," and respirators hanging on wall hooks. MS five of the listeners. Back to shot of statue and pianist as we first saw them, but nearer. Fade out.

Fade in Big Ben at night. It strikes. Radio masts at night, pan R, dissolve to night shot of Thames, factory chimneys, etc. (Soundtrack: *This is London calling!* "British Grenadiers" march.)

Houses of Parliament at night: Victoria Tower is in scaffolding (it was under repair when war began.) (Soundtrack: *London calling at the beginning of tonight's broadcasting in the African Service . . .*; medley of radio voices in various languages.) Another LS silhouette view of Thames, dockside cranes, etc. The river at night, a buoy floating in the water. Dissolve to radio tubes on panel. CU ammeter, needle moving in rhythm with speech of announcer. Dissolve to clouds, dissolve to CU radio tube (as in *Speaking to America*). As we hear Big Ben strike the quarter hour, we see BCU of this radio tube, dissolving into shot of sea at night. (Female announcer: *This is the Pacific Ser-*

vice from London sending you all greetings, and wishing the best of luck to those of you listening who are serving in our armed forces on sea, land or in the air, and in the Merchant Navy.) Fade out.

Fade in leaves quivering on trees, pan L to dissolve to further silhouette shot of trees. (Birds' "dawn chorus" begins.) Fade out. Fade in long R-L pan across countryside horizon at dawn.

Sound of horses' hoofs precedes dissolve to industrial scene (factory chimneys) as man leads horses across cobbles. Factory workers enter gates at dawn. (Natural sound.)

Dissolve to high-angle pan across London, as we hear extract from BBC exercises program "Up in the Morning Early." (A man chants in waltz time *Right press, left press again, right and press— look well up!)* Dissolve to shot of a "little man" emerging from building, putting on his bowler hat. His respirator and steel helmet are dutifully slung over his shoulder. He walks steadily R-L and round a corner away from camera as "Up in the Morning Early" slowly fades out. (. . . *Lift your chest when you press there, now turn, press and swing! Press, and stop, drop your arms and look to the front . . .)*

(Steam sounds.) Shot from window of train approaching Victoria Station, showing Battersea Power Station behind tall apartment blocks (moving L-R). Steam from factory siren. Another view of factory.

Sunlit tree against sky. (Piano begins a simple polka-type tune.) Interior: a woman is clearing a meal, the window open behind her. A framed photo is between the window and the radio. (A child's voice calls *Mummy!)* She turns to look out. Probably from her POV,

school playground behind railings across the street, where young primary school children are dancing in a circle to the piano tune. CU woman looking out of window. Closer shot of children dancing. They pause to engage in hand-clapping movement with their partners. Back to woman as in previous shot. She turns to look indoors, at the photo, which we now see in CU. It is a soldier in field service uniform. Closer again to the children, concentrating on two couples. The girls move past their partners to the center, then return, while the boys remain in place clapping out the beat. One little girl mistimes her move, then corrects her error. (Sound mix from piano tune to roar of tanks.)

Troop carriers come down a sunlit country village street (Alfriston, Sussex) toward camera. CU a driver, cocky in his steel helmet. He drives past L-R. Low-angle shot of timbered gable of an old house, curtains blowing at the open window. From inside a window we see an armored car pass R-L down the sunlit street, with half-timbered houses opposite. Exterior, a sign hanging above a door says "Guests—Teas." (Sounds of vehicles roaring and spluttering.) Troop carrier roars L-R down street, half-timbered houses in background. CU its tracks and wheels as it passes. CU a little girl in bathing suit looking off camera R and smiling in the sunshine. Convoy passes L-R past the camera, past a row of cottages. In the doorway of one stand a woman and child peering out, behind a child gate. Pan R to see vehicles disappearing down street.

(Fanfare on soundtrack—*Calling All Workers!*—signature tune, a lively march, of "Music While You Work" begins.) Dissolve into aerial shot of small industrial estate (as in *Words for Battle).*

Fast mix into traveling shot along road behind a truck, approaching a railway bridge that crosses the road. At this point, a steam freight train crosses the bridge R-L. We go under the bridge, and an imperceptible dissolve takes us into a fast-moving railway-window shot L-R past backs of houses and a water tower. Dissolve into CU of a spinning flywheel.

(We hear the rest of the BBC announcement: *Music While You Work will be played to you this morning on rhythmic records.* Music of "Yes, My Darling Daughter" begins, its rhythm underlined by the sounds of the machines.) Low-angle shot of Tannoy loudspeaker fixed near ceiling. CU machine pistons pulsing back and forth. General shot, girls at work. MCU one girl singing, checking razor blade packages. MCU another doing the same. Tannoy from another angle. Line of girls at work. MCU third girl smiling as she works. Machinery operating, as music fades, dissolve to:

Train window shot L-R, dissolve to Waterloo Station, soldiers and others moving around platforms. (Guards' whistles, station sounds.) Group of servicewomen sit on piled kitbags, etc., on station floor. Group of servicemen stand with mugs of tea.

Exterior: a tea van, with soldiers and firemen standing around. (Fade in sound of Flanagan and Allen song "Round the Back of the Arches," mixed with natural sounds of station, etc.)

LS man on ladder painting blackout on factory windows (as in *Welfare of the Workers*). Interior: factory canteen, girl workers collecting plates of food. Tilt down CU of a sign: "In the Canteen Today at 12.15./Flanagan and Allen." Dissolve to Flanagan and Allen singing

"Round the Back of the Arches" (one of a series of sequels to their most famous prewar song, "Underneath the Arches"). Intercut chalked handwritten menu board: "Menu: Scotch Broth/Fried Cod and Chips/Grilled Sausages/Greens/Boiled Potatoes/Lemon Pudding/Jam Sauce/Damson and Custard."

Back to Flanagan and Allen LS from back of hall, showing performers on stage, band and piano behind them. CU elderly worker. He spits (from *Welfare of the Workers*). Repeat shot of menu board. Worker passes it with plate. CU young worker sitting smoking (from *Welfare of the Workers*); he smiles. Different views of Flanagan and Allen on stage. Audience begins to join in song by whistling the tune. CMS two girl workers watching and smiling. LS from behind Flanagan and Allen, showing audience filling large hall. The two girls are seen sitting at front. High-angle shot of audience whistling and swaying to tune. Men standing at rear of seated audience, also involved singing and whistling. Jolly, rather plump girl worker standing in front of menu board, smiling. Flanagan and Allen on stage as before. LS from behind them, as before. Dissolve to:

Exterior, National Gallery in Trafalgar Square. (Music mixes to Mozart's Piano Concerto in G Major.) Dissolve to interior, orchestra and Myra Hess at piano on platform. MS violinists, in uniform. Sign: "Lunchtime Concerts." People pass it upstairs. MS woodwinds, in uniform. MS violins as before. CU notice: "Fri. June 13—1 o'clock/The Orchestra of the Central Band/H.M. Royal Air Force/Myra Hess—Pianoforte." MS woodwinds as before. Interior shot, entrance from top of steps inside. Two women Civil Defense workers sit on landing eating sandwiches. Low-angle shot of skylights, blackout cloths in position. Closer shot of same scene. Third shot of similar window lights. General shot of audience. MCU favoring two women in audience, one in C.D. uniform. She looks down. CU program of concert.

MS violinists. MLS revolving entrance doors; mostly servicemen enter. Low-angle shot of two C.D. workers on steps with sandwiches. Notice: "War Artists' Exhibition." Men in uniform pass it. C.D. worker and servicewoman approach railings of balcony. Woman passes two men looking at a picture. C.D. woman, FAP (First Aid Post) on helmet slung over shoulder, looks at a revolving rack of postcards. Another angle of the two women eating sandwiches. A sailor bends down to study detail of naval painting (probably Dunkirk evacuation). Detail of painting. LS concert hall from rear, showing audience and performers.

MCU: Myra Hess at piano, airman beside her to turn pages of music. She begins to play. Airman turns page. Three members of audience, one of whom is H.M. the Queen. Return to Myra Hess as before. LS concert hall as before. Interior of National Gallery showing sandbags piled against wall. Pan R-L to show an empty frame on wall. High angle of same scene. CU firebuckets and sand container (for incendiary bombs) in same location. Another view of part of audience. Two audience members. Myra Hess at piano. Several women in audience. Two women, one in uniform. CU soldier standing in audience (seen previously), leaning close to a Fragonard painting. Audience members, favoring a

man with bandaged head. MCU girl standing in front of a medieval painting. Myra Hess at piano. Previous shot of Queen, Sir Kenneth Clark and equerry. Hess at piano. Music continues over:

Outisde, girl on National Gallery balcony stands reading in sunshine. Plane tree leaves in sunshine. View from Trafalgar Square shows National Gallery balcony, leaves and girl. Closer view from street shows girl on sunlit balcony. Between pillars of National Gallery, a silvery barrage balloon in sky. High-angle shot of traffic in Trafalgar Square outside South Africa House. High-angle shot of bus stop outside National Gallery. Bus stops, passengers alight. Coat of arms on pediment of National Gallery. Another high-angle view of traffic in Trafalgar Square. From National Gallery roof, dome in foreground, Nelson Column in midground, Big Ben in background. Closer shot of Nelson on his column. MS, back of sailor on National Gallery. General shot, National Gallery.

(All these shots are cut to the beat of the music, which swells to a climax, and now modifies to factory sounds.)

Docks, cranes, balloon in sky. Inside factory, man operates a press. (Natural sounds now.) Tank turret is swung into position. Closer shot, turret lowered into place. MS, woman worker at lathe. MS, another woman operates a drill. MS, a male worker assembles a tank caterpillar track. Machinery and steam. General shot of factory interior, tanks on assembly line moving R-L in background. Cut to black.

Stirring military march ("A Life on the Ocean Wave") played by Royal Marines regimental band marching toward camera along a street in Chatham, followed by Marines in full field-service order.

(The march blends into steel-mill rhythmic sounds.)

In a steel mill, worker brings out molten ingot from furnace. Another shot of the ingot. CU molten mass being shaped. Heavy pounding. Workers bring out another ingot. CU ingot being placed on anvil. MS workers manipulating it. CU ingot. Back to workers. Ingot being shaped. Masked workers with welding equipment. (Mixed with the steel-mill sounds, a choir singing "Rule Britannia" begins to fade in, then takes over soundtrack.) Steelworkers on balcony above furnace. LS steelworkers at furnace (as in *Heart of Britain*).

Exterior, flat facade of factory surmounted by three smoking chimneys. Waving field of wheat, as at start of film. Cooling towers and factory chimneys. Clouds drift across aerial shot of countryside (as in *Words for Battle*). ("Rule Britannia" comes to triumphant end over these shots.)

FIRES WERE STARTED (1943) (Original title: I WAS A FIREMAN)

Crown Film Unit, with the cooperation of the Home Office, Ministry of Home Security and the National Fire Service

62 minutes

Producer: Ian Dalrymple

Asst. Producer: Nora Dawson (later Lee)

Director/Script: Humphrey Jennings

Story collaboration: Maurice Richardson

Photography: C. Pennington-Richards

Sets: Edward Carrick

Editor: Stewart McAllister

Music: William Alwyn, directed by Muir Matheson

Sound: Ken Cameron, Jock May

Cast:

Sub-Officer Dykes: C. Officer George Gravett
Fireman Walters: Lt. Fireman Philip Dickson
Johnny Daniels: Lt. Fireman Fred Griffiths
J. Rumbold ("Colonel"): Lt. Fireman Loris Rey
Sidney H. Jackson ("Jacko"): Fireman Johnny Houghton
B. A. Brown: Fireman T. P. Smith
Joe Vallance: Fireman John Barker
Barrett: Fireman William Sansom
Mrs. Townsend: Asst. Group Officer Green
Betty: Firewoman Betty Martin
Eileen: Firewoman Eileen White

Behind first titles, dolly in to bas-relief of firemen wearing traditional helmets operating hose: *When the Blitz first came to Britain its fires were fought by brigades of regular and auxiliary firemen, each independent of the rest, though linked by reinforcement. In the stress of battle, lessons were learned which led in August 1941, to the formation of a unified National Fire Service.*

Behind last title, horizontal R-L truck shot of oil blaze: *This is a picture of the earlier days—the bitter days of winter and spring 1940/41—played by the firemen and firewomen themselves.*

(Music throughout these titles and opening sequence of Heavy Unit One being returned through East End streets to Auxiliary Fire Station 14Y.) Inside the station, two firewomen receive the docket, report the return from "work done." Clock shows 8:50 a.m.

Mrs. Townsend tells Eileen to make out a disc for Barrett, "the new man." They add his disc to the roster of riders of Heavy Unit One—"the crazy gang." (Music begins.)

A sequence showing the various members of the "gang" arriving: "Sub" at dockside chatting to a civilian friend. Another fireman watches dockside loading, strokes carthorse. Johnny Daniels in his garden spars with his small son. His attention distracted by his wife's call, he allows his son to hit him, mock-falls, and kids his son as he puts on his uniform jacket, goes off.

Brown greets Vallance on street; they walk together.

Jacko, in his newsagent's shop, bids farewell to his wife. *Don't do nothing silly, will you, Sid?* He mounts and rides his bicycle to work.

Brown inspects a kipper at a street stall.

Walters comes out of his front door, reading the newspaper.

Vallance is seen bargaining for a statue of a woman.

Rumbold at the dockside, looks up at Limehouse Church clock; it chimes for 9:45 a.m. (Music ends.)

A truck drives up and the driver asks the way to Alderman's Wharf.

A man stands in a doorway playing a penny-whistle. (His music accompanies the sequence at the gate of 14y as the men arrive, and are greeted by the gateman on duty.) Two men going off duty greet the "Colonel" and "Sub," and point out that it's full moon that night. Brown says, as he enters, *Kippers tomorrow, Charlie!* The Sub greets the girls as he goes into his office. Johnny, Vallance, and Charlie shout at Jacko as he rides by them. He acknowledges

their shouts wryly. (Whistler's music fades.)

Firemen gather round a blackboard, reading out the roster of "riders." Someone points at the last name under H.U.1—Barrett. *Who's that then? New man.*

Barrett in street, carrying his duffle-bag, asks the way to the fire station (14y) from a Chinese civilian standing on a corner.

Jacko tells Vallance of an incident at his home, when a *big lump of coal fell out* of the grate. Vallance comments: *That's doing it all wrong, having a fire in your own home!*

The "gang" is shown working together preparing H.U.1. Barrett arrives, and is watched curiously by the other men as he crosses the yard. (Penny-whistle in background.) Vallance is washing down the steps, and sloshes the water down them just as Barrett arrives.

Sub greets Barrett, calls Johnny in, hands Barrett over to him to show him around. Johnny introduces him to the "gang." Two men peel potatoes. Johnny sings *Ah, sweet mystery of life, I've found you . . .* Johnny polishing H.U.1, singing *I would like to be beside the seaside . . .* Walters checks with him that all equipment is aboard.

(Music begins.) At 14 Local Control, girls start checking equipment available around the district. Intercut is a shot that tilts down from the school gateway inscribed "Girls and Infants" to where the fire engine is being tended in the playground, one man beneath it. A man cleans hoses with a wet broom. Montage of polishing, loading, etc. A receding shot of a map of the district, showing Trinidad Street bordering the docks, and Alderman's Wharf.

Drill sequence: *Right, fall in, lads! Hook-ladder drill* . . . One fireman climbs practice tower, using hook-ladder, and watched closely and commented upon by instructor. Washing-down fireboat: A water fireman answers a theoretical question, watched by his mates: *I would proceed with caution downstream . . . I would assure myself . . . I would moor a line ashore . . .* Intercut fireboat in water. Hose drill sequence—hoses unrolled, connected, etc. Ladders rise. Man folds hose in rhythm with music. At climax, two high ladders, with firemen on them, rise in the sky toward each other. (Music modifies after climax to fanfare: "Come to the cookhouse door!")

Clock shows 1 p.m. Cook (male) calls: *Come and get it!* B. A. Brown, passing garbage cans, lifts lid of one, looks inside, returns it. Inside lunchroom, Barrett sits between Rumbold and Johnny. Sub enters, says to Johnny: *When you go down to the local this afternoon, take Barrett with you and show him the station's ground* . . . As he goes off, someone comments: *What's the matter with the Sub this morning?* Answer: *It's a full moon.* Dissolve to:

(Music.) Johnny and Barrett at taxi (now used to pull trailer pumps). Johnny: *I used to drive one of these once* . . . Barrett: *I used to write . . . advertising.* Johnny: *. . . 'schoolgirl complexion' stuff, eh?* Barrett: *More like 'liver bile'!* In taxi, they visit docks, walk around. Insert map. Johnny points out high tide. Camera tilts from river water filling screen upward to Thames sailing barges. Johnny: *Funny thing, about these riverside fires—when it comes to*

it, there's never enough water . . . They drive farther on, walk to visit Trinidad Street and Alderman's Wharf. Ship being loaded with guns and ammunition boxes. Johnny: *Ain't she a smasher, cock, eh?* They arrive at the river wall. A sign says: "Sunken Barge." Johnny: *There's a sunk barge down there, holds about 10,000 gallons . . . pretty useful in a pinch, you know.* Shots of barges on the river holding barrage balloons, one flying. (Music ends.)

Back at the station: Jacko lies asleep snoring lightly; B. A. washes his feet; Walters lies reading; Vallance lies on his stomach. Johnny and Barrett enter. Johnny throws a piece of screwed-up paper at Jacko, waking him. *Hey, Jacko, . . . What about a cup of tea?* Johnny: *'Ow about getting that ol' samovar of yours out?* Jacko puts kettle on gas ring, lights it, grumbling: *. . . dangerous, waking up a man like that . . . 'ow d'you know I wasn't dreaming about Ginger Rogers?* General chat in room. One man is polishing his axe; another paints at an easel.

Chief Fire Officer in hs office. A phone call. He tells his aide: *That was Home Office Fire Control—they'll be raiding tonight.*

In the recreation room at 14Y, pool table, darts, table tennis. Johnny brings in Barrett, takes him to buy a beer . . . *no bitter, have some mild . . .* B. A. and others join them. Over the bar is a sign: YE HYDRANT HEAD, with entwined hoses around a "coat of arms" showing an axe, a tankard of beer, 14Y, etc. The motto is USE YER LOAF. (Cockney rhyming slang for "head"—"loaf of bread".) Two men start putting up blackout boards at the windows. Brown accosts Barrett: *'Ow you fixed for braces?* Barrett: *I've got a belt on today.* Brown: *Ah, but in this gaff you need belt and braces.* Johnny interrupts—he bought a pair from Brown two weeks ago—*all they're good for is 'anging yourself.* Man plays accordion.

Exterior, dusk, the ship. At control, message received about wind direction and force. *Wind strong, NW to SE, blowing strongly across the river . . .*

Back in the recreation room, Rumbold playing Sub at pool. Barrett sits at piano, strikes a few notes. Johnny joins him: *What about tickling up the old ivories then?* Barrett rambles on the notes for a moment, then strikes up a strong rhumba-style rhythm. We cut to a moving shot (R-L) of the ship at anchor, then the warehouses by the river. Back in the room, Jacko smiles. Brown and Johnny are doing a comic "Egyptian" dance to Barrett's music. They are interrupted by a firewoman, who looks round the door—*token up!*

Sitting on their beds, togging up, Walters says: *What's it like out, Jacko?* Jacko replies: *Smashin' moon.* Walters: *Ah! That'll be us, then.* Sub takes leave of the firewomen: *Have to hold the fort yourselves tonight, you know.*

Barrett, at piano, strikes up "One Man Went to Mow" as Johnny enters. He clowns to the music, then leans over the piano singing and instructing Barrett as to who enters next. Barrett plays suitable music for each, as they come and join in: "The Colonel" (Rumbold), Walters, Jacko, Joe Vallance, B. A. (*Make it snappy!* says Johnny.) B. A. bows, turns, says: *And here comes the headmaster!* Sub walks across to suitably ponderous music. (Siren warning begins as music ends.) Barrett says: *What about number eight?* Johnny replies, *That's you, mate!*

You're riding with us tonight! They conclude the song "Eight Men Went to Mow," the siren rising above their voices until it dominates the soundtrack.

Exterior shots of darkness, mud, the ship, A.A. guns rising.

Inside, Rumbold is reading Sir Walter Raleigh's: *O eloquent, just and mighty Death! whom none could advise, thou hast persuaded; what none hath dared, thou hast done; and whom all the world hath flattered, thou hast cast out of the world and despised. Thou hast drawn together all the far-stretched greatness, all the pride, cruelty, and ambition of man, and covered it over with these two narrow words, Hic jacet!*

To which the Sub comments: *Righto, Colonel, we'll set that to music—when we come back.* (Guns and bombs on soundtrack.)

At OP (Observer Post) Control, a message is received from 36 OP-*incendiary bombs falling . . .* This is plotted on wall map. Another telephone message: *Fire at docks beach, love.* Response: *Right, send TP (trailer pump) from Y.*

At 14Y, waiting firemen are singing "Please Don't Talk about Me When I'm Gone." Firewoman enters, rings bell, calls: *No. 1 TP, please.* Several men leave. At Control, new message is received—*incendiaries.* Response again, *send TP from Y.* More singing men leave for TP 2, leaving only eight from H.U.1, still singing. A bomb falls nearby and a picture falls. The men cringe slightly. *. . . That's a bit warm: I don't want 'em any nearer than that . . .* A further message, then the firewoman rings the alarm bell again. *Heavy Unit One to Trinidad Street!* They leave, singing.

On the headlamp blackout cover is the word FIRE. The vehicle moves into the night. From inside, we track along a row of blacked-out houses. Johnny drives, singing Cockney song—*out wiv me barrer and me moke all day* . . . Sub rings bell at intervals. As Johnny sings, we get CU's of: Walters, Barrett, Vallance, Jacko, Rumbold. The ship. H.U.1 arrives at the warehouse in the dark. There is a small blaze on the top floor.

Barrett searches the ground, calls: *Hydrant here!* (In London, hydrants are concealed beneath iron manhole covers.) Brown arrives: *No, that ain't a bleeding hydrant, it's a sewer. You'll have the rats after us!* Farther along, the true hydrant cover is removed, and a hydrant head screwed in. Comment: *That wall looks a bit dodgy. Hope when it goes, it goes the right way.* Reply: *Yeah, me too.*

Sub finds an entry. Followed by Jacko and Rumbold, he shines a flashlight on two doors—"Deliver Orders Here" and "General Office." He pulls a bolt from a steel door, and they all go up the stairs. LS of the fire on the roof. Walters below, instructs Barrett as he pays out the hose: *We want three lengths . . . Up top!* He calls to the roof. On the roof, from a skylight, come Sub, Rumbold, and Jacko. Shot of the ship, with flames in the foreground. A line is dropped to Walters below. Sub descends. A hose is hitched to the line, and hauled up to the roof. (Plane, guns, bomb noises.)

Sub on the phone: *Hello? Fourteen local? . . . Make the pumps up to ten. Additional message: Order the fireboats to Alderman's Wharf—explosives involved in the fire.* Rumbold and Jacko organize the hose nozzle on roof. Below, Sub instructs Walters: *Take the rest of the crew—take a ladder—and get your brass in as far as possible.* Walters

and the others set about organizing the second hose. (A bomb falls.) Brown, Vallance, and Walters drop to the ground. *What a windy lot of bastards we are—that's half a mile away!* They rise and continue.

Message relayed at Control to sub-officer in charge. *Ten! He's got a hope. We'll send him five to get on with, anyhow.* Firewoman at phone issues the necessary orders.

On the roof, Jacko and Rumbold wait for water. Johnny is at the pump: the water begins to flow. *Stand by!* A second hose is taken up by Barrett and Vallance, to a different position. Sub returns to roof. Second hose begins to jet.

At Control, a fireboat is ordered out to Alderman's Wharf. *It's low tide, so they're gonna have a devil of a job.*

Rumbold and Jacko on roof.

Water begins to run low. Johnny sends Barrett to look for further supplies. . . . *go down the road, see whether there's any local water supply* . . .

Observation Post observers watch fire in distance. *That looks like Trinidad Street.*

Barrett runs down road. He is passed by man leading frightened horse. The water for both hoses gives out. Barrett runs to the sunken barge. (Blitz sounds continue.)

At O.P., observer comments: *That fire seems to be getting worse! Better give them another ring* . . .

Jacko, Sub, and Rumbold watch fire morosely.

Woman at telephone at Control passes message: *Fire seems to be increasing rapidly* . . . Hangs up, rubs eyes tiredly.

Barrett runs back to Johnny at the pump: *I found some . . . that sunk* barge . . . Johnny: *OK, go down the road there, stop those pumps. Tell them to relay the water on to us* . . . Men on roof wait. Barrett stops oncoming fire engine, reports main broken, asks for link-up. Man, from leading horse, approaches new chief. *You the officer in charge?* Response: *I've got some more men coming on duty, sir—don't worry.*

(Music.) Fireboat (floating camera) passes buildings on dockside R-L. Blazing warehouse. Inside, ammunition boxes. Ship, with flames in foreground. Three men on roof. At sunken barge, hose brought down, inserted in water. Three on roof wait. Hoses and pumps linked up. Water turned on: flows. Sub instructs: *Put it down there!* Brown and Vallance direct their jet upward. Pump dial fluctuates. (Music ends.)

At 14 Control, girl on phone. (General blitz sounds.) *Can you hold on?* (Bomb falls.) At HQ, firewoman on phone says, *Hello? Can't hear you.* At 14, girl gets up, cut on forehead bleeding. *Control? Oh yes, I'm sorry for the interruption. We have a message for you . . . our T.P.U. is out at Trinidad Street . . .*

At Control, Sub comments: *That's not so good, is it? Go round the district, check pumps available* . . . Image and voice montage of firewomen at phones, checking pumps available. Firewoman at blackboard, Sub watches. Firewoman: *Sub, only 66 pumps available.* Sub: *Right, get onto Brigade Control, further help required, pumps available only 66.* Enter commanding officer, gets report: *C District very much distressed, sir* . . . C.O.: *Right, well, I'll go and have a look round, I'll let you know* . . .

LS's fire raging in warehouse. Johnny and Barrett at pump below. Three on roof: Sub sends Rumbold down with message. Rumbold runs down flaming staircase, to new chief arrived at pump. *Message from sub, sir. Things are getting very difficult* . . . Chief calls *Up top!* No reply. Sends Barrett: *Tell 'em to come down at once, we've got a turntable ladder coming along* . . . Barrett goes up flaming staircase, fiery timbers falling as he goes up. Gets to roof. *District officer says you've got to get off the roof, sir.* Response from Sub: *How the hell does he think we're going to get down there . . .?*

Bomb falls, Sub injured, falls in flames. Jacko: *Pull 'im out of the flames, there!* Turntable ladder arrives. Operation to raise ladder with rescue line. Timbers fall, aflame, on crew below. Barrett: *There's a man hurt up here!* Ladder slowly extends, with fireman at end. He arrives on roof, they hitch Sub to line, lower him over. Jacko to Barrett: *Give me that line, I know what to do with it. You get down!* Barrett hesitates, then goes. CU Jacko. He takes the line. D.O. calls from below: *Come down off that bloody roof!* Jacko pays out the line. Walters says: *There's another man up there, sir!* D.O.: *All right, let's get this one down first, then we'll go back after him.* CU line slipping through Jacko's hands. Sub dangles down to safety.

Jacko alone with jet. Other two with jet. Jacko's foot in flames. Hose falls, Jacko falls. Johnny watches, aghast. *Jacko!* (Music.) LS, enormous explosion from warehouse. (Silence, except for bomb explosions.)

Switchboard. Message from fire control: *One hundred pumps have been ordered . . . to stand by in your area* . . . Girls at 14Y, working by hurricane lamps. Girl dabs forehead, relays message. Sub says: *That's something, anyhow.*

New fireman arrives, representing standbys. *Is this 14Y?* Firewoman greets him at the door. *You seem to have a regular pasting down here tonight.* Answer: *Yes, our boys are down at the docks.*

(Music.) Fireboat arrives. More hoses, more men. Brown and Vallance move out across burning "bridge." (Music assumes march rhythm.) Walters, Rumbold, and Brown take new hose up to vantage point. At all points, fire slowly becomes subdued. (Music assumes hopeful modulations.) Dissolve to:

Sub in bed, nurse bandaging head. *Mucking about on the roof. I should have come down out of it.*

Back to fire, hosing-down continues. (March now truimphant.)

OP phones control: *36 OP—fire appears to be under control.* Sub removes pin from map. *Thank goodness for that.* VLS fires in distance. (End music, trumpet coda.)

Dawn. Firemen hear "all clear," look up. Barrett winks at Johnny, lowers head tiredly. Scenes of smoldering ruins. Mobile Canteen arrives; girl opens it up. Firemen gather round. Man greets Brown and Vallance: *What's the matter, can't you take it, chum?* Brown responds: *You 'eard? No, what? Jacko's copped it. Copped it bad? He's copped it, I tell you!* Girl hands out mugs of tea. *Bless you, my beautiful!*

Walters is met by new chief officer. *Who's in charge here? I'm in charge, sir—our Sub's injured. Tell 'em to knock off, make up, and get off home.*

Making up. Barrett wearily rolls up hoses through rubble; Johnny unhitches hoses from pumps. (Sad, weary music.) Long, tired scenes of making

up, rolling up hoses. Barrett under rubble, suddenly finds dented helmet. (Music underlines.)

Johnny at loading platform, rolling up hose. Workmen coming on duty greet him. *Bad night!* Johnny replies: *Bad night? You wanna go down the road. There's a boat down there, good as new. She ain't got a scratch on 'er—a sight for sore eyes!*

(Triumphant music.) The munitions ship. A cripple and another man walk past the smoldering ruins. Three women with a child in a baby carriage. The wheel of H.U.1, rolling over wooden chocks to protect hoses. (Bell clangs loosely.) 14Y H.U.1 goes off R-L. Passersby wave. *Well, we left you a bit this morning!*

In Jacko's shop. CU radio. CU his wife listening. BBC: *. . . it does not appear that casualties are likely to be heavy . . . in one district the attacks became concentrated and several large fires were started. These, however, were successfully prevented from spreading . . .* Jacko's widow adjusts a stray tendril of hair.

The ship is being loaded. Foreman on phone: *We'll make it all right.* (Music.) At 14Y, a tree is in full blossom. Dissolve to:

Firewoman brings in tea and mugs to the rest room. B. A. is removing his boots. Rumbold lies on his bed reading *Macbeth*:

Ay, in the catalogue ye go for men;
As hounds and greyhounds, mongrels, spaniels, curs
Shoughs, water-rugs, and demi-wolves, are clept
All by the name of dogs: the valu'd file
Distinguishes the swift, the slow, the subtle,

The housekeeper, the hunter, every one
According to the gift which bounteous
nature
Hath in him clos'd . . .

Firewoman pours out six mugs, takes
them round. Walters lies on bed.
Johnny sits stroking a kitten. Vallance
lights a cigarette. Barrett receives his
mug; woman claps him on the shoulder,
calls him "Bill." He says: *Thanks, mum.*
Woman passes Jacko's empty bed to
B. A. He says . . . *I never expected to*
see you any more . . . Then, after a
pause: *Come on, chums, snap out of it!*
(Trumpet "last post" begins.)

Rushing water of ship's wake. The
ship moves L-R. Whitechapel Church
tower through bare trees. The coffin
borne by six bearers, the surviving firemen. Widow and Mrs. Green watch.
The bearers, favoring Johnny. Widow
and firewoman. Trees in bare tracery.
The ship. (Music picks up from trumpet,
continues to end.) Wreathed dented
helmet on rear of H.U.1. Sub (head bandaged) stands at attention. Six firemen
stand at attention. Dissolve to:

Bows of ship moving L-R. Dissolve to
END.

THE SILENT VILLAGE (1943)

Crown Film Unit, for the Ministry
of Information

36 minutes

Producer, Director, Script: Humphrey
Jennings

Asst. Director: Diana Pine

Photography: Henry Fowle

Editor: Stewart McAllister

Sound: Jock May, Ken Cameron

Music: Title and incidental music composed by Beckitt Williams, orchestra
conducted by Muir Matheson. Welsh
songs sung by Morriston United Male
Choir, and hymns by Cwmgiedd
Chapel Congregation

(Fanfare opens film: trumpet and harp
predominate.) A stream purls behind
the credits. Two exterior shots of the village and chapel (sounds of hymn singing), then four interiors of the chapel
congregation singing. At the mine, coal
is being weighed. A miner (a key character) is introduced. In the school classroom, the teacher is talking (in Welsh)
about the planets; the children repeat
the lesson together.

VLS of the valley. Shots of washday,
collecting coal, gardening (birdsong on
track), the grocer in his shop.

At the mine, the shift ends, the men
in the showers start to sing ad lib.
School dismisses. VLS valley—men
coming home. "Men of Harlech" sung
over:

Miners at home bathe and have tea.
Night, in cinema: Donald Duck on
screen (laughter takes over on soundtrack). Pub scenes (natural sound).
Night shot—mine chimney. At a meeting, silicosis is discussed by the miners'
union men.

Singing on soundtrack continues
quietly over: night scenes of stream,
wedding-dress fitting, children, chapel.

Title: Such is life in Cwmgiedd . . .
until the coming of Fascism. LS: slow
approach of menacing black car with
loudspeaker on roof, swastika emblem.
(Wagnerian martial music playing from
speaker, then . . .

Achtung, Achtung! . . . attention,

attention! To the population of Cwmgiedd . . . Man with dog listens, woman washing steps stops for a moment, then continues. Another shakes out a rug. *Deputy Reich Protector S. S. Obergruppenfuehrer Heydrich calls upon all classes of the people to give their loyal cooperation in the rebirth of your homeland . . . put your trust in the Fuehrer . . .* Shot of geese. (Military music.)

School. CU loudspeaker: *Achtung . . . state of emergency . . .* Woman dusts a vase in her parlor. Speaker announces . . . *civil state of emergency . . . courtsmartial entitled to pronounce three alternative sentences . . . (1) confiscation of property, (2) handing over to secret state police, (3) the death sentence . . .* Woman with child in arms. A coal cellar door is closed. The car retreats (. . . *continue your work calmly . . . put your trust in the Fuehrer . . .*)

Miners' union meets to discuss the orders and the situation. They vote to strike. Cut to leader addressing miners at pit . . . *Strike!*

Grocer's shop at night. Dog barks frantically at car. . . . *still individuals who insist on disturbing public order . . .*

Miners meet in barn, chickens clucking among them. CU jackboots, rifle butt. Radio announces . . . *those who are against the Reich will be destroyed . . .* The village at night. (Sounds of machine-gunning.) Bodies in barn, cow looks on. Milking stool overturned. Body taken out on stretcher. Chapel. Miner dies. Chapel, singing. Leaves blow in the wind.

In school, teacher announces sadly *No more Welsh . . . promise me one thing . . . do not forget your Welsh lan-guage . . .* Children respond. *Yes, ma'am.*

(Music—harp and trumpet.) Night scene at ancient castle. Secret meetings in mountains. Secret press at work. In a home interior, man asks his wife: *Where did you get this?* She answers: *It was put under the door . . .* CU the underground paper: "Go back to work, work slow, use sabotage. Put sand in the machines, pour water in the oil . . ." (Soft singing.) Night scenes at pithead. In the pub, man takes bottle by the neck, spits.

Winter scenes. Sabotage activities. (Soundtrack: "All Through the Night.") A sentry at the mine is shot. Explosions.

In school, teacher tells of the conquest of Wales. *It started in the reign of William the First. Having conquered all England, he turned his attention to Wales. And that's where . . .* Cut to castle. (Trumpet music.)

Radio: Roll of drums—important announcement, attempt on life of Heydrich. Nazi soldier stands beside village war memorial. Radios are playing in night interiors. Exterior shots of empty village. *Further details available . . . lady's bicycle at scene of crime* (long detailed description of bicycle) . . . Man and his wife listen. *Achtung . . . all persons over 15 years of age will register . . . German subjects are exempt . . .*

In the chapel, long line of residents comes toward camera, addressing their names, ages, occupations briefly and quietly off screen. Car. *Who can give information . . .?* Registration continues. (Choir sings quietly on soundtrack in background.)

Interior: Radio speaks: *The following today were sentenced to death by shooting . . .* Names are read out. By their birthdates we know they were young, in their twenties. . . . *they publicly approved of the attempt on the life of* . . . In the grocer's shop, the grocer is going through his bills, reading names.

Interior: Radio drumroll: *Official announcement . . . Heydrich succumbed to serious injuries received* . . . Funeral music. Old man listening picks lint off trousers. Hand switches off radio. Cut to car speaker: *Achtung! You will produce the assassins into the hands of the secret state police by 12 o'clock midnight* . . .

Bibles being read. In one parlor, an old photograph on the wall, flanked by ornaments on shelf. Exterior, night leaves blowing. Interior, grandfather clock. (Marching feet and commands on soundtrack.)

Men are lined up. Singing begins ("Land of My Fathers"). Children and women evacuated. High-angle composition: men lined up against churchyard wall. (Command: *Fire!*) Cut to graves in churchyard.

(Wagner music.) Water in stream flows. (Voice continues in German.) Burning village. Burning easel from school. Sewing machine, picture we saw earlier.

Title: But that is not the end of the story . . . (Choir singing.) Peaceful scenes of Cwmgiedd. The people hear news of Lidice. Woman reads it out. Miner responds: *No, colleagues, the Nazis are wrong . . . The name of the community has not been obliterated: the name of the community lives on!* . . . *It lives in the hearts of miners the world over* . . . (Singing.) *Lidice shall live again!* General scenes of Cwmgiedd, chapel dominating.

V.1 (1944)

Crown Film Unit

10 minutes

Producer: Humphrey Jennings

Script/Direction/Commentary: Fletcher Markle

Asst. Directors: Nora Dawson (Lee) and Jack Kranz

Camera: Cyril Arapoff

Sound: Ken Cameron

Bomb in the sky. The engine stops and it falls. Explosion on the ground.

"London is doomed, said Dr. Goebbels, and Adolf Hitler's intuitive propaganda experts claimed that in its first few days of attack last June, V.1., the flying bomb, the robot bomb, the buzz-bomb, had almost entirely removed the city of London from the war-scarred face of the earth."(Shots of bomb damage.) "But soon even German propaganda changed its spots. Once again, the great, patient, enduring city of London was suffering—suffering but alive. You can sit back in your seat in this theater and see and hear V.1." Explosion. "But you cannot imagine how London suffered" (shots of V.1s and damage) "and worked—and fought. Find yourself as V.1 might have found you, coming at you from dawn to dusk, dusk to dawn—any day, all day, all night, for eighty days and eighty nights."

Shot of wrecked Rainbow Corner. "You're an office worker, coming home around six, and this is your house." Bus in bomb crater, from *London Can Take It.* "You're a passenger on a cross-town bus, and this is the end of your last journey." Child in playground of wrecked school. "You're a kid at school and this is your lesson for the day." Wrecked restaurant. "You're a diner in a restaurant, and this is where you had your last bite." Wrecked hospital. "You're a patient in a hospital, and this is your final treatment." Wrecked church. "You're a worshiper in a church, and this is where you kneeled and never got up again."

Many shots similar to those used in *The Eighty Days*. ". . . 23,000 buildings utterly destroyed, one million damaged. Over 5,000 lives lost, over 16,000 broken. But London worked. You're a member of the heavy rescue squad, and you dig with your hands to save a life. You're an attendant in a first-aid station, and you haven't slept for three days. You're a G.I. MP, you break patrol to help the London bobby. You're the man on the street, and you do what you can . . . London suffered and London worked. And London fought."

AA guns on coast. Commentary becomes more excited. "You're part of a crew of an AA battery on the South coast, and you can't close your eyes. In the eighty days of the V.1. blitz you bring down more than 1,500 bombs with AA." Pom-pom guns. "You work hard on the South coast, in the white sun, and gray mist, and in the nervous night . . ." Sky shot of V.1.

"You're a member of a unit of the balloon barrage. In the eighty days you bring down nearly 300 buzz-bombs with only steel cables stretched in the sky." Balloons, bomb, explosion heard.

"You're the pilot of a Tempest or a Mustang, or a new type of Spitfire swinging through space, and you bring down nearly 2,000 pilotless bombers in the eighty days." Shot from Spitfire, V.1. explodes. "And it isn't easy . . . some get through, they come droning, and

sputtering and roaring, and you don't know when they'll suddenly stop and drop (silence) on you."

"You're a farm laborer, and it's like sitting in a dentist's chair when they come over—only worse." Potato pickers. "You're a hairdresser in for a swim on Sunday afternoon." Shot of girls in river. "It's like seeing snakes if you don't like snakes—only worse. You're a citizen of southern England, and it's a matter of life and death—*your* life and *your* death. You're a roof spotter, or any kind of spotter, and there's nothing you can do except watch out for them—and pray." VLS of explosion across London.

"London wasn't doomed, as Dr. Goebbels said, and London wasn't finished. But London *was* hurt . . . there was death . . . and pain . . . and chaos . . . schools . . . hospitals . . . churches . . . time-famed landmarks . . . Women and children headed the casualty lists . . ."

(Music begins.) "The city was hurt, but the city will heal . . . The people of London, of all England, are beginning the work of reconstruction now . . ." Shot of telephone disconnected on chair, while man shovels rubble in background. Various shots of reconstruction, re-roofing, etc. "150 million tiles and slates are on order for buildings like these, and 200 million square feet of ceiling and wallboard . . . 50 million square feet of glass . . ."

"Winter is here . . . tens of thousands haven't any homes in England . . . but home is where you hang your heart, and the people of a great city and a great land are at work, patient and enduring, knowing that their sons and their daughters are the future of a noble nation." Shot of children looking at the wreckage. (Music crescendo.)

THE EIGHTY DAYS (1944)

Crown Film Unit, for the Ministry
of Information

14 minutes

Producer/Director: Humphrey Jennings

Cameramen: Cyril Arapoff and Teddy Catford

Commentary: Edward R. Murrow

Editor: Stewart McAllister

Sound: Ken Cameron

Menacing Wagnerian-style music throughout first sequence.
CU Notice—Vergeltungswaffe/The Flying Bomb
Exhibition model V.1. "The doodlebug . . . for a time the basis of German strategy. For eighty days and eighty nights they came rumbling in over southern England . . . Londoners view the model with detachment . . ." British army officer in foreground with schoolboy points to it. Behind them looms a dummy German soldier with Iron Cross. Commentary explains intention of the strategy: "To batter the people of England to the point where they would demand a change in Allied strategy . . . But there was no public demand for a change in plan . . . The people were as calm and courageous as they were during that great battle four years ago. They were tested for the second time and they did not flinch. As Londoners examine the model of the flying bomb, another salvo was being prepared across the gray waters of the English Channel . . ." (Music fades to silence.)

The sea, from the beach. Bowling green, men playing. Statue of Queen Victoria on the seafront. Barbed wire protects the beach. Soldiers. A schoolboy. ATS girls. Binoculars. A.A. guns manned. An elderly woman peers out from doorway. A notice on the wall beside her:
"Evacuation—Official Parties/Mothers with Children under 5/may take with them/All Children up to 14 years old/ Register at 2 High Street, Rye."
(Natural sound now.) A.A. gundrill commands. Sound of buzz-bomb. Hooter alarms. Bomb in sky. Children in field put on tin hats. Potato pickers do the same. Guns fire at bomb. Mother takes a watching child in to safety. We follow the shellbursts in the sky around the bomb. ARP worker watches the sky, stroking a kitten in his arms. The bomb comes down, explodes.
Another passes on, past observers' post. Girls sunbathing, put on tin hats as they leap into river for shelter. Spitfires take off. Observers on ground. Shot taken from Spitfire, with the bomb in its gunsights. Barrage balloons. Bomb passes, drops, explodes in distance behind an air-raid shelter in foreground.
Another. Children come to gate to watch. Telegraph boy and schoolboy smoking in long grass, look up.
London, Trafalgar Square. People look up, women, men. VLS long-held shot of bomb exploding, smoke rising and drifting, not far from Big Ben.
Ambulance station. (Sad, mourning music from *Fires Were Started* begins quietly, continues under commentary.) CU burned arm. Wreckage. A victim is led out. Bodies. Wreckage, including twisted remains of bomb. "And that's all that is left of the weapon that was to

prevent the liberation of France. The Battle of London was part of the Battle of France . . . the people of southern England shared the battle as surely as if they had fought on French soil."

(Music changes to the Marseillaise.) De Gaulle visiting Rye. Bomb damage. "The German plan failed. Once again the enemy underestimated the courage of common men and women—the price they were willing to pay in defense of a common cause. For the second time in this war, London paid a heavy price. The grim and gay defiance of the old blitz days was gone. People were tired, but their strength was great, for they knew that the long battle was being won and that their sacrifices were speeding the victory." Rescue worker amid the wreckage hitches up his trousers; men dig in the wreckage with picks. A Union Jack hangs on a line, defiant in the dusty ruins. (Music.)

THE TRUE STORY OF LILLI MARLENE (1944)

Crown Film Unit

30 minutes

Producer: J. B. Holmes

Director: Humphrey Jennings

Asst. Director: Graham Wallace

Script: Humphrey Jennings

Photography: Henry Fowle

Sets: Edward Carrick

Editor: Sid Stone

Music: Denis Blood, directed by Muir Matheson

Sound: Ken Cameron

(Music, variations on the theme of "Lilli Marlene".) Title: "A reconstruction."

Track into Marius Goring sitting before the camera. Goring: "*Lilli Marlene* is the name of a song . . . The story of Lilli Marlene is a fairy story really. Only it's a true story as well . . ."

An ex-soldier setting up souvenirs on the wall of his home. "When the fighting men come home, they'll have trophies and souvenirs of the war . . . (German helmet, ration book, gramophone record) . . . But there's one trophy which you will find only in the homes of the Eighth Army: the disc of a German song, 'Lilli Marlene.'"

Record plays. "This trophy was captured in the Libyan desert in the autumn of 1942. But the history of Lilli Marlene takes us back to the year 1923, to the time when the men of the Eighth Army were still children . . ." Shot from *The First Days* of children playing on W.W.I. cannon outside War Museum. Goring describes German inflation and postwar history. Newsreel shots, and fragments from Ruttman's *Berlin*. "In 1923, out of this chaos Hitler made his first attempt to gain power, out in the streets of Munich . . . In the North, and particularly Hamburg, they stuck to democracy . . . Hamburg was the last German stronghold to fall before Hitler's attack . . . And it was in Hamburg, then the largest port in the world, that Lilli Marlene was born . . ." Set depicts a garret, with Humphrey Jennings at a typewriter, writing the lyrics for the song. He rises, reads them in German, then in English, over drawings of the lantern, the sentry, Lilli Marlene.

CU hands at piano. "The music for Lilli Marlene was written in 1938. The first person to sing of Lilli Marlene was a little Swedish girl—Lalli Andersen . . ." Scene of nightclub in Berlin, with Andersen at piano rehearsing. In foreground, a cleaner is washing the floor. Cleaner watches as Andersen sings.

Song is interrupted by "Heils"— newsreel shots of Hitler triumphant. "At that time nobody paid any attention either to Lalli Andersen or to the song . . . It was the first period of the war, and the Germans were given purely military music . . ." German marches play over newsreel shots of Germans in Paris, etc. Nazi flag. "In the autumn of 1940, after the fall of France, the Germans formed their famous Afrika Korps. They went into battle with their own special song— "Panzers Advance in Africa." Song sung by soldiers marching. "Lilli Marlene and Lalli Andersen were still unknown. Their first real appearance was in spring 1941 . . ."

Long dramatization of invasion of Yugoslavia, the bombing of Belgrade, the take-over of Belgrade radio station by "so-called Propagandakompanie— war correspondents, newsreel cameramen, and, particularly, radio engineers . . . They had with them a suitcase of gramophone records . . ." In the Belgrade studio, the German announcer, by candlelight, says: *Here is Radio Belgrade . . .*, gives announcements, concludes by announcing and playing Andersen's singing of Lilli Marlene, in English.

Dissolve to Afrika Korps troops in desert, U-boat sailors, listening. Return to Belgrade studio, now organized, water bottle, tumbler, etc.

Goring: "In Berlin they built a program around the song—a 'messages from home' program . . . In the same month, June 1941, they'd opened up a new front—the Russian front . . ." Tanks in Russia, newsreel shots. In Belgrade studio, the announcer speaks of . . . *new radio program, The Young Sentry of Belgrade . . . we call Uberfeldleber Karl Hoffman, #419276F— tender greetings from Mummy and Dad, and a big kiss from Liselot . . .*

Goring: "And the singer, what had become of her?" Nightclub set, Wehrmacht at tables. Andersen sings song in English. Intercut Belgrade studio: *Young Sentry program . . . Lalli Andersen winter relief fund . . .* Nightclub, intercut shots of Lilli Marlene "sets" and "flats." Another announcer: . . . *statue of Lilli Marlene erected on the Smolensk road . . .!* Cutout figure at roadside; passing tank obscures it with dust. Belgrade studio again: . . . *Italian allies have accepted Lilli Marlene as their battle hymn . . .* (highly operatic men's chorus). Studio announcement: . . . *This evening . . . Frau Emmy Goering will sing at Berlin State Opera House . . . will include Lilli Marlene in her program . . .* Fat contralto on stage sings, cheers from audience.

Goring: "1942, the Eighth Army, El Alemein . . ." Map, sand. "Here Denis Johnston of the BBC found our men also listening . . ."

Johnston in battledress: ". . . We used to turn on the news every night, and we'd sit there, with nothing to be seen except the radio . . ." Pan along men's faces in CU. "Chaps would come in . . . like birds coming in round a lighthouse . . . after the news was over, we'd turn over to this 'messages from home' program from Germany . . ." (Song on radio.) "Home, home, home. It's a funny thing the way the Germans, of all people, are sentimental about home. But they seem to forget that other people have homes too . . . We will see whose home thoughts serve them best . . ."

Gunflashes. Newsreel footage of Battle of Alemein, tanks against dawn sky. (Denis Johnston's excited BBC radio commentary on Alemein.) German prisoners. (Lilli Marlene played as sad march song.) Johnston: "The Eighth Army swept on to Agheila, capturing on its way 800 miles of desert, 75,000 prisoners . . . and a famous enemy song . . ."

BBC studio. Goring: "The German radio continued to broadcast the song, but . . . other listeners . . . in Britain, analyzed it in sober quiet." BBC monitors at work. "Then came Stalingrad." Newsreel shots, surrendering Germans. Belgrade announcer: *The struggle for Stalingrad is ended* . . . Shots of von Paulus surrendering. The nightclub sets and flats are stored away. "The tune of Lilli Marlene was stilled into silence . . ."

CU hand on barbed wire. Tilt down to Lalli Andersen. "From a neutral country came word that Lalli Andersen was in a concentration camp. *She* had been sending messages home—to Sweden— 'all I want is to get out of this terrible country.'"

Belgrade studio announcer mournfully: *There is not time for singing* . . .

Big Ben at night. Goring: "Now it was our chance, the BBC's turn, to send a message from Lalli Andersen to the German troops . . . same tune, different words . . . Lucie Mannheim . . ." In BBC studio, Lucie Mannheim sings "sad and weary" version, intercut with bodies of German troops in snow, empty sentry box drawing, drawing of lantern now a

mere broken shell. "Hang Hitler from the lantern of Lilli Marlene!"

Goring: "But that is not the end of the story." Soldier in pub: *Well, Lilli Marlene had followed us all the way up . . . at the Mareth Line . . . we had our own words written . . . Italian girls . . .* Cockney voice sings Lilli Marlene chirpily to a march beat, as we see shots of: sea, troop transports, invasion troops fix bayonets on deck. Troops whistle song.

Goring: "Lilli Marlene was born in the docks of Hamburg, and then she went to Berlin, and then flew to Belgrade. She was sent to the desert, and was captured. And then she was tranformed, and marched with the armies of liberation into the heart of Europe." (Mouth organ introduces male chorus of song.)

"Now look into the future. Peace. Come to the London docks on a Saturday night in peacetime. Here you will find the scene set for the last appearance of Lilli Marlene." Tune played on barrel organ on soundtrack while we see along railway arches, a line of street market stalls with naphtha flares. There is plenty of fruit, although artificial bunches of bananas hang from one stall. A children's carousel on a horse-drawn cart appears. At the corner is a tobacconist's shop with the blinds drawn over the windows, but lights on inside. In the open door stands the proprietor (ex-Army). He looks inside to his family.

Inside, a child is looking at a picture of dad in uniform. Mum takes it away from him, hangs it up. A candle is lit beside a Union Jack. Goring: "The lights of London are relit. The shining domes of Stalingrad have been rebuilt. Then the true people and the real joys of life will come together again, and the famous tune of Lilli Marlene will linger in the hearts of the Eighth Army as a trophy of victory and as a memory of the last war. To remind us all to sweep fascism off the face of the earth, and to make it really—the *last war*."

Shot of tomb of Unknown Soldier in Westminster Abbey.

A DIARY FOR TIMOTHY (1944–45)

Crown Film Unit

39 minutes

Producer: Basil Wright

Director/Script: Humphrey Jennings

Asst. Director: Richard Warren

Unit Manager: Diana Pine

Commentary written by: E. M. Forster

Commentary spoken by: Michael Redgrave

Photography: Fred Gamage

Editors: Alan Osbiston, Jenny Hutt

Music: Richard Addinsell, played by the London Symphony Orchestra conducted by Muir Matheson

Sound: Ken Cameron, Jock May

Introduction

Music under titles, which are on broadcasting studio's "on-off" lights. As light flashes on, music leads to haunting theme on solo violin. BBC announcer reads *the first news for today, Sunday September the 3rd . . . more news of German defeats . . .* Dissolve to countryside scene (baby sounds, babies crying): rows of baby cribs, pan and dolly

to Tim's. CU Tim. "And it was on the 3rd of September 1944 that you were born . . . in a nursing home near Oxford, England. Very comfortable . . ." Intercut shots of mother and Tim (CU's) "You've got parents who will take care of you. If you had been born in wartime Holland, or Poland, or a Liverpool or Glasgow slum, this would be a very different picture. All the same, you're in danger . . . around you is being fought the worst war ever known." Dissolve to soldiers marching in street as in *Listen to Britain*. (Marching music.) Three children walk through massive blitz damage. ". . . We were fighting for you—for you and all the other babies." (Music ends.) Tim being weighed. "You didn't know anything about this . . . but you were part of the war even before you were born." Coal-mine conveyer, pithead shaft against hills. "You see, this was total war. Everyone was in it. It was everywhere . . . in the valleys where Goronwy the coal miner carries his own weapons . . . in scenery which isn't exactly pretty . . ." Goronwy brushes his hair at home. Miners exiting from cage. Dissolve to farmer (Alan) walking in field, examining hay. He looks up. Plane passes overhead. ". . . Alan, the farmer . . . has spent the past five years of war reclaiming the land . . ." Dissolve to smoke stacks, silhouette of engine yard. Engine-driver (Bill) in his cab as locomotive moves on turntable. "In London, Bill the engine driver . . . no longer taking holidaymakers to the sea . . ." Dissolve to countryside, then to hospital ward, camera moves to Peter Roper's bed. (Sound of bomber in flight.) ". . . Peter Roper, who crashed in France and has his leg in plaster . . . All these people, Tim, were fighting for you . . . (fade to black) . . . though they didn't exactly know it."

September

Tim brought to his mother. "And now, Tim, we'll show you a little of the history of your first days on earth, the start of your life, the end of our war in Europe . . ." Picture of Normandy invasion, three ATS girls walk in line, mines are cleared from beaches. Commentator describes this as we see and hear it. "We were hopeful that the whole thing would be over by Christmas . . ." Tim brought home in car. ". . . your first adventure . . . September 17th, to be precise, the very Sunday that our bombers were towing the gliders to Arnhem. This, we thought, was the final stroke of victory . . ." Observer watching through binoculars (drone of heavy bombers). Tim being bathed. ". . . There's one very important member absent—your father . . ." Military photograph of him on wall. "Then, just at your bedtime, we heard what we'd been hoping to hear . . ." Radio: *Strong forces of the 1st Allied Airborne Army were landed in Holland this afternoon* . . . Plants blow violently in the wind outside. "For five years, Tim, we have had the blackout . . ." Men outside St. Paul's walk with dark lanterns. Lamp-lighters light street lamp. ". . . but this evening for the first time we have only to dim the streets . . ." Bill and his wife at their window, draw light curtains. (Locomotive sounds.) "That's Bill the engine-driver's home." Alan and his family watch home movies. Alan: *We spent this evening showing the children an old film . . . taken when we were clearing the farm . . . five years back . . . Had*

to get the engineers to blow the old tree trunks out of the ground . . . (We see the film he describes.) London at dusk, sirens wail. "I hope you'll never have to hear that sound, Tim." Bill's wife pulls blackout shade down. (Sound of V.1. approaching.) Dog looks up. Bill and his wife rise apprehensively. V.1. cuts off suddenly, and they all dive under the table. (Explosion.) Back to Alan's family watching film, where a tractor crawls across the land. Alan: *One thing, if it hadn't been for the war, I don't suppose we should have done it.* Fade to black.

October

(Music.) Shadow of fast-moving train on tracks. Bill in cab. Track from his POV. "Well, people get on with their jobs: Bill on his engine, Alan on his land . . ." Shot of Alan watching tractor. ". . . and Peter Roper at his job of getting better to go on fighting." Peter and his nurse exchange bantering dialogue about pills. Mrs. Jenkins studies demobilization tables in newspaper, brief dialogue with her mother, asking for details of husband's call-up. Tim outside in his pram. ". . . and you didn't know, and didn't care, safe in your pram." Strong wind blows. "But listen, Tim. Listen to this . . ." Shots of Goronwy and other miners reading paper; headlines show "Arnhem: Germans Advancing." Dolly into Goronwy's radio as he and family listen. Stanley Maxted (Canadian war correspondent at Arnhem) gives commentary on the siege of the airborne forces, while we cut to Bill's radio and family, the Jenkins radio and family, and Alan's radio as he sits listening. Maxted concludes: *Luckily, or unluckily, it rained, and they caught the water in capes and drank that . . . all right, water and rations didn't matter; give them some Germans to kill and even one chance in ten and they'd get along somehow.* (Overlap sound of Beethoven's Appassionata Sonata.) Dolly back from Myra Hess's hands at piano to full shots of her playing at the National Gallery. Poster: "Fifth Birthday Concert—Myra Hess . . ." As we watch her and some of the audience, we hear behind the music a repeat of Maxted's final sentences. The music continues as we see shots of rain falling on a static water tank in the streets, rows of roofs being repaired, dissolve to Hess's hands. ". . . the war certainly won't be over by Christmas, and the weather doesn't suit us . . . one-third of all our houses have been damaged by enemy action. Did you like the music that lady was playing? Some of us think it is the greatest music in the world, yet it's German music, and we're fighting the Germans. There's something we'll have to think over later on." (Music fades into mine sounds.) Feet of man and horse walk on wet street. "Rain. Too much rain." Miners underground, including Goronwy. "It's even wet under the earth. Look at the place where Goronwy has to cut coal." Tim in his cot, while his mother writes a Christmas card. ". . . she has to post it now, for he's out East . . ." Montage of waves on rocks, gulls, waves against barbed wire on beach, Bill driving his engine, railway tracks, heavy machinery, rain-soaked field, Alan studying his accounts, flywheel, water sluicing over small dam, turbulent water in reservoir, church steeple, minister baptizing Tim. Small children's choir sings hymn. Wheat reflected in water lying in field. "Rain. Rain all through October, rain on your baptism. A choral baptism—not

many babies run to that. Hmm. You're one of the lucky ones. Let's hope the luck lasts." Feet of Peter Roper, flanked by nurse and doctor. Dolly back to show him on crutches, learning to walk with them. (Sync. dialogue between the three.) Cut to mine cage coming up with wounded miner (Goronwy). "Oh, there's bad luck in the world, Tim, as well as good. It's a chancy world. People get hurt in peacetime, same as in war—although that shouldn't be." (Dialogue sequence showing Goronwy's removal to hospital, his wife being told. Forbidding brass orchestral motif mixes with baptism hymn repeated during part of this sequence.) "It's pretty shocking that this sort of thing should be happening every day, though we've been cutting coal for 500 years . . . Something else for you to think over . . ." As Goronwy's sister calls to her mother, dissolve to black.

November

Dissolve to soldier clearing beach mines. "Now it's November, and there's still danger on the beaches." Soldier's voice: *Trouble with these mines is, they lie in the sand for four or five years, get mixed up with the wire, and rusted up with the wet, and the only thing to do with them is blow 'em up.* Loud explosion, dissolve to bonfire of leaves in the park. Men digging in allotment (victory garden) with St. Paul's in background. (Jazz piano plays softly.) ". . . London in November looks a nice quiet place. But you'd find things are chancy here, too. And the bad so mixed up with the good you never know what's coming." Haymarket Theatre from outside, advertising *Hamlet*. On stage, Gielgud as Hamlet talks to gravedigger . . . *why was he sent to England? . . . Why, because he was mad; he shall recover his wits there, or, if he do not, 'tis no great matter there.* (Audience laughter.) Cut to canteen: ARP worker talking to his friends at a table. *Well, if this is the launching site, and that's the objective . . . it travels at 3000 miles an hour. How long does it take to reach the objective? Do you know?* Back to Hamlet: *Nay, I know not . . . Alas, poor Yorick!* Cut to canteen as explosion upsets the men at the table. They wipe tea off themselves, return to seats with rueful smiles. Hamlet addressing skull: *Here hung those lips . . . get you to my lady's chamber, and tell her, let her paint an inch thick, to this favor she must come; make her laugh at that.* Cut to men working in rubble, including two of the ARP men we have seen. *There's someone down here . . . quiet, please . . . quiet! . . . quiet!* (Silence.) *OK, carry on . . .* London Underground station entrance. Tracking shot along bunks of sleeping people on platform. Train enters and stops. (Attendant's voice echoes eerily: *All change!*) Dissolve to black.

December

Wind blows outside. CU Tim sleeping. "So it goes on . . . The war won't be over by Christmas, but we feel safe from invasion at least . . . and there's a stand-down parade of the Home Guard." Men removing barricades from beach. Home Guard parade. Home Guard in pub. ("Old Soldiers Never Die" on muted trumpet.) From radio we pan to face of Peter Roper being massaged. (Radio plays dance music.) Brief discussion among Peter, nurse, and doctor. . . . *the swelling's gone down a bit . . .* Tim's mother at home, and sol-

diers in barracks, erecting and decorating Christmas trees, etc. "Your first Christmas is coming, Tim . . . and here, Tim, comes the postman with a big surprise." Postman delivers letter to Mrs. Jenkins outside the house with Tim in his pram. (Gentle orchestral theme on oboe.) Mother: *Oh, look, Tim, this is for you!* She shows him the letter. ATS girls with accordion sing "Good King Wenceslas" in their barracks. Before we see them, their voices form a background for shots of soldiers and ATS window shopping, including slow pan along dummy heads modeling feminine hats in window. Explosions and battle sounds, and shot of Wellington statue in London fog introduce fog sequence during which we hear BBC announcement of major counterattack by Germans against American First Army. "In those days before Christmas, the news was bad and the weather was foul." We see two men, cold, standing by an open flare, reading newspaper (headlines: Major German Attack), foggy shots of water and trees, then train sounds and Bill peers through his cab window in fog. "Death and darkness, death and fog, death across those few miles of water . . . and death came by telegram to many of us on Christmas Eve . . . until, out of the fog, dawned loveliness, whiteness, Christmas Day . . ." Starting on an exquisite CU of frost-covered grass and plants beside still water, we pan up left to frost-covered trees and landscapes. (A boy's treble voice: *Come and behold Him . . .* full choir joins in: *Christ the Lord . . .*) As the carol continues, a montage of toasts to "absent friends"—Alan's family, soldier at a bar, Bill and wife, Tim's family. CU envelope addressed to Master Timothy Jenkins and Mrs. Jenkins reading the letter. Man's voice reads the contents of the letter: *My dear son, a very merry Christmas to you . . . I'm looking forward to being with mother and you again . . . may you always be happy and truly content with this life you have been given.* Organ plays violent, baroque piece as we see children sliding, skating, playing with new presents, etc. Cut to services' New Year's party, dollying back through dancers' feet to Peter Roper walking with two canes. Big Ben striking midnight. Everyone joins in singing "Auld Lang Syne." Dissolve to black.

The New Year

"And that's the end of 1944, and you're four months old, Tim, and here's the New Year . . ." Sunrise over tops of huge smelters at foundry. Bill approaches with lantern, passes train scheduling board to engine yard on smoky morning. (Train sounds.) "What's going to happen in 1945 and the years to follow, when we're not here and you are?" Woman walks past snow-covered barbed-wire fence. "During that awful autumn and winter, Tim, we'd been in the dark almost as much as you . . ." People shopping in street market. "But about the middle of January, we began to see something was coming . . . perhaps something tremendous . . ." (Fade-in BBC announcer: *Here's the news . . . Marshal Stalin . . .*) Cut to announcer in BBC studio: *. . . has announced a great offensive . . .* As the news reports continue, we see women at work inking in drawings, Alan walking in snowy field with a spade and starting to dig, CU spade entering soil, Goronwy in hospital having arm massaged, balers stacking winter hay, moon through tree branches. (The musical theme from opening swells up.) Announcer tells of Moscow radio broadcasting the Polish national anthem and Chopin's "Polonaise Militaire," which now occupies the soundtrack as we see buses in London passing newspaper sign, "Our Men Smashing the Enemy," a Ministry of Fuel sign on a fence, "Coal on Sale Here," and a line of women and men collecting baskets of coal. A new announcement tells of further victory salvos in Moscow, and from Chopin we go to a few bars of the Soviet national anthem. This continues under scenes of train rushing by, with Bill in the cab pulling the whistle, Goronwy and other patients exercising their arms (a woman calls instructions). Musical chords bridge a cut from Goronwy (CU) to army truck carrying howitzers passing over a snowy bridge. BBC reports: *The Russians are 20 miles inside Germany across the Silesian border on a 55 mile front . . .* Now Peter Roper and other patients are standing doing their exercises, as a male voice gives instructions. (The opening theme is played, first on a solo violin, then with all the violins in unison, to synchronize with the rhythm of the exercises.) A train crosses the horizon passing L-R through a village landscape. Another BBC announcement: *The Russians have today broken through to the Baltic coast . . .* As Peter continues his exercises, the full orchestra joins in little by little, with mounting intensity. Cut to yet another BBC announcer. Backed now by music, "Glory, glory, hallelujah," he says: *United States fighter pilots from England today saw the Germans defending their Oder front against the advancing Red Army. The Americans were escorting over 1000 Fortresses for*

*the heaviest attack yet made upon . . .
Berlin.* We see men rebuilding on a
housing estate, replacing a window, and
Tim being weighed in the doctor's office, while the BBC continues: *The
heart of Berlin had its heaviest bombing
of the war at midday today . . .* (Music
fades.) CU Tim on the scales. "Now that
the danger's over for us, V.1s and V.2s
and the rest of it . . ." More shots of reconstruction intercut with Tim being
weighed. ". . . Life is going to become
more dangerous than before, oddly
enough . . . because now we have the
power to choose and the right to crit-
icize . . . We're free men. We have to
decide for ourselves, and part of your
bother, Tim, will be learning to grow up
free." Another BBC announcer: *The
conference of the Big Three is over . . .
decisions were agreed on final victory . . .* Cut to Goronwy in emergency
hospital, sitting in big chair looking up
at ornate baroque painted ceiling, listening to broadcast. Goronwy's voice:
*That afternoon I was sitting thinking
about the past . . . the last war . . .* Feet
shuffling along, hand picks up coal, tilt
up to face of boy about fifteen. He
looks over rows of miners' cottages.
*The unemployed, broken homes, scat-
tered families. And then I thought, has
all this really got to happen again?* Cut
to children's choir in school hall, singing a bouncy song. Russian flag behind
them, banner overhead: "Greetings to
the Red Army and the glorious fighting
forces of the U.N." Intercut in time with
their songs are shots of Alan pointing
over fence with stick, planning; Goronwy
talking to wife, looking at clothes ration-
ing book, shots of wife's reaction. (Music fades.) Goronwy: *Look at the position after the last war . . . I remember

*people going to hospital on flat carts
. . . now we've got our own ambulance
. . . nursing service . . . hospitals . . .
canteens, private baths . . . Surely, if we
can do that thing during that period,
nothing at all will stop us after this war.*
Peter Roper talks to girl at dance, then
they rise to join the dancing. Peter: *I
think beachcombing's more in my line
. . . out in the Pacific, where I can sit in
the sun and do absolutely nothing.* "So
Peter goes back to his plane and Goronwy
back to his mine—back to everyday life
and everyday danger . . ." Shots of
them doing this, plus one of Bill moving
off with his locomotive. Peter in cock-
pit, plane takes off. "This doesn't look
like beachcombing." Goronwy's radio:
*The British Second Army and the Ameri-
can Ninth, under the command of Field
Marshal Montgomery, are crossing the
Rhine . . .* Bombs fall and explode, with
loud music, intercut with Tim being fed
from a bottle in his mother's arms (solo
violin with baby crying), then more
bombs, music, explosions, oily fires raging among trees on ground. Dissolve to
Tim lying in cot. He looks up right.
"Well, dear Tim, that's what's been happening around you . . . and you see it's
only chance that you're safe and sound.
Up to now, we've done the talking, but
before long you'll sit up and take notice. What are you going to say about it
and what are you going to do? You
heard what Goronwy was thinking . . ."
Picture of Tim's father on wall. Back to
Tim looking right. ". . . unemployment
after the war, and then another war and
then more unemployed. Will it be like
that again? Are you going to have greed
for money or power ousting decency
from the world as they have in the past?
Or are you going to make the world a

different place—you and all the other babies?" (Music has developed from a single violin theme to full orchestral mighty chord.) Dissolve to black, with solo violin theme returning, high and lonely, unresolved, as End and Crown Film Unit titles zoom forward, stop, dissolve to black.

MYRA HESS PLAYING THE FIRST MOVEMENT OF BEETHOVEN'S SONATA IN F MINOR, OP. 57 (APPASSIONATA) (1945)

Crown Film Unit

10 minutes

Producer: Humphrey Jennings (?)

Photography: Fred Gamage

Music: Beethoven

Sound: Ken Cameron

Myra Hess playing at a National Gallery lunch-time concert, on a Steinway piano, watched by an audience on either side. Shot mostly in MCU, with occasional CU's of her face and hands, and audience shots.

A DEFEATED PEOPLE (1946)

Crown Film Unit, for Directorate of Army Kinematography, with the cooperation of the Allied Control Commission of Germany, and of the Army Film Unit

19 minutes

Producer: Basil Wright

Director/Script: Humphrey Jennings

Photography: Fred Gamage and Army Film Unit cameramen

Music: Guy Warwick, played by London Symphony Orchestra, conducted by Muir Matheson

Commentary: William Hartnell

Sound: Ken Cameron

Map of British Zone of Germany behind titles. Title recedes into oblivion, accompanied by passionately violent music.

Shots of sea from the shore, wreckage, destroyed bridges, etc. Conversation on track: *Life in Germany must be terrible. Well, they asked for it, they got it. Yes, but we can't let them starve. I don't know about that, I've got a son out there; as far as I can see, it would be a good thing if some of them did die.* Hartnell commentary begins:

"Well, a lot of Germany *is* dead. Our last bombings were directed against their communications . . . (music) . . . At the finish, life in Germany just ran down, like a smashed clock." Image of smashed clock. "Place and time meant nothing, because the links between people were smashed, too. They were just left wandering, searching, looking for food, looking for their homes, looking for each other . . ." People sitting, standing, reading search notices. Notices on trees everywhere. (Various voices read them in German: *searching for* ——, *I seek* ——, etc.)

"There are 70 million people in Germany, and about 30 million of them are looking for someone, or are lost and lie looking without seeing, like the eyes of a dead rabbit." Shots of people and of dead bodies. "They are still stunned by what hit them . . . (music) . . . but the life force is beginning to stir again . . ." Man with barrel organ. ". . . Today, our powers of destruction are terrifying, but the will to live is still stronger . . ." Mother with child. "That's why we can't afford to wash our hands of the Germans because . . . we can't afford to let that new life flow in any direction it wants." Streams of people crossing bridges, flowing down streets. (Music.)

Shots of Control Commission interviews. "Our military government—that is, your husbands and sons—have to talk the Germans into putting their house in order. Why? We have an interest in Germany that is purely selfish. We cannot live next to a disease-ridden neighbor . . . Diseases of the mind, new brands of fascism, come springing up . . ." Shots of trench digging, rubble clearing. Bombed houses. "First of all, the material catching up . . ." (Music.) Very long tracking shot R-L along devastation. "But where in the meantime do they live?" (Music.) "Yes, all looks lifeless . . ." Smoke from pipe in rubble, interiors of rooms, German women. "But underneath the rubble there are people living, living in the cellars. The smoke from the cooking stove drifts up from the ruins to the open third stories where . . . people are living, too . . . Many in the big towns are living without light, without coal, without water, without soap, living in the stench of corpses and sewage, but still . . . with the will to live." (Music.) Statue of Alfred Krupp in ruined church.

(Trumpets.) "But the one thing on which all reconstruction depends is coal . . ." Mine, with British sentry at gate. "In Essen, . . . we organize the output and distribution of the whole Ruhr coalfields." Shot of meeting, inter-cut with trains, trucks, etc. (Music.) Commentary describes problems of distribution of coal to liberated countries . . . "The Germans themselves get no coal . . ." Germans sawing logs, cutting and carting brushwood, etc. (Music ends.)

"There are some seventeen newspapers published in the British Zone. They all carry advertisements asking for the whereabouts of relatives. In Hamburg, there is a British-run personal search station to which enquiries come in at a rate of 50,000 a day." Shot of station. "But when someone contacts his relatives, they must be cleared before they can travel by train . . ." Shots of train coming into station. People climb into open trucks. One man hanging on to buffers is removed by Tommies. "All this has to be supervised by *our* sergeants and *our* M.P.'s." (Sounds of loudspeaker . . . *Achtung!* . . . *Forbidden to ride on the buffers* . . . [music in background] *Absolutely forbidden to ride on the buffers* . . .) Shots of train, cyclists.

"We have to safeguard ourselves . . . military courts are set up by British judges . . ." Union Jack, tilt down to judge in court. Description of court procedure. "Then the German police force is being remade . . ." Shots of police training. (Music.) "The new German policeman has to understand that he is the servant of the public and not its master . . ." Comments on health checks; German ration is half ours—checks to ensure ration "is just sufficient to keep Germany at work." Shots of health checks, etc.

Children playing on cannons, lecturer, children at school. "But the greatest headache is education. Will we ever get Nazi ideas out of the heads of some of the adults, particularly those living away from the devastated areas? What about the children? For them, the desolated back street provides a dream playground. The derelict weapons of war might have been specially designed to have games with . . . Teachers must be found, and themselves taught to teach the children . . . The schools are in ruins, the teachers too few, the children too many. And as the months go by, the children are growing up . . ."

Ruins of Berlin. "Today, Berlin has still the aspect of a battlefield. The Reichstag, seat of past German governments, has been gutted . . . The Krupp family who, with the other German industrialists, first backed Hitler, and then produced the weapons for world domination, have been scattered and arrested." Pan along picture of the Krupps, dissolve to ruins. Long pan across the desolation. "They are just as responsible . . . as Hitler and Goering. By killing they grew rich. This time, their war plants have been left a mass of twisted girders . . . Look!" (Music.)

POW camps. Delousing. Demobilization scenes. ". . . the Wehrmacht . . . the master race of men are stumbling along . . . They are stripped of their insignias, deloused, numbered. But this mass of humanity has to be sorted out into something like order—not only their bodies but also their minds . . . Let one man or woman who still believes in the Nazi regime take office, and you have the beginnings of another war . . ."

Denazification center. "Note this meek little man who looks like a clerk or a grocer (CU man) . . . Here is his portrait in Luftwaffe uniform (CU his papers with photograph) . . . They are stripped and examined for the SS mark tattooed under the left armpit . . . then suspicious characters are examined by our intelligence officers. Every so often there appears one . . . whose answers are not good enough." Shots of interrogation, accompanied by musical themes (trombone British, violin German). "Rejected—back to the cage." (Trombone concludes.)

Night silhouette shots. "When night falls in Germany, the people must remember the curfew . . ." Women go into shelters. (Siren) "The the air-raid siren wails again, to remind them that they lost the war of their own making . . . to remind them . . . that, much as we hate it, we shall stay in Germany until we have real guarantees that the next generation will grow up sane and Christian again." Shadows of girls linking hands in dance in sunlight. "A Germany of light, life and freedom. A Germany that respects truth and tolerance and justice . . ."

Swearing in judges: *Now gentlemen, you'll raise your right hands and take the oath with me . . .* (Oath delivered in English, repeated by judges in German) *I swear by Almighty God—that I will at all times—apply and administer the law without fear or favor—*This soundtrack, accompanied by light violin tune, continues over shots of: Girls dancing in ring. LS: German memorial in background; doubledecker bus passes it. Blasted tree and cross with German helmet on it in foreground. LS: British flag flies outside untouched administration building. CU's of new German judges as they repeat the oath: *. . . to establish equal justice under the law for all persons—so help me God.* (Music to END.)

THE CUMBERLAND STORY (1947)

Crown Film Unit, for the Central Office of Information and the Ministry of Fuel and Power, with the cooperation of the United Steel Companies and the National Union of Mineworkers

39 minutes

Producer: Alexander Shaw

Director/Script: Humphrey Jennings

Photography: Henry Fowle

Art Directors: Scott MacGregor, John Cooper

Editor: Jocelyn Jackson

Music: Arthur Benjamin, played by The Philharmonic Orchestra, directed by Muir Matheson

Sound: Jock May

Research: Diana Pine

Camera Operator: Noel Rowland

Continuity: Jean Graham

Production Manager: Dusty Buck

Unit Manager: Richard Warren

(Machine-like, dramatic music.) Diagram of coal levels behind titles. Credits: "Actual people involved . . ."

The sea. A bay, a village. An expensive-looking car drives through the village streets. Nimmo in it. Nimmo: "I came to Cumberland just after the outbreak of the war. I was the general manager of a group of collieries lying along the sea coast . . . I knew [the job] wouldn't be easy . . ." From car's POV a one-legged man in the street in front. (Car horn blows.) Subjective shots from Nimmo's POV to the pithead.

"I began with a tour of all the pits . . ." Shots of hostile workers arguing about conditions. Pithead wheel against sky. Underground, Nimmo crawls along loading belt. Shots of underground workings.

In the office, Nimmo studies charts. *As you can see, Mr. Nimmo, there's not much life on the landward side. No, it looks as if we've got to go out under the sea . . .* Nimmo tells us of John Buddle, who over a hundred years ago had a plan to work the Main Bend under the sea from Lady Pit. "We had a book of his notes in the office . . ." Picture of Buddle. Buddle's notes studied, while we hear his voice; outlining the plan.

Exterior, on cliffs, Nimmo looks out to sea. Old workings. (Music.) "What had happened to Lady Pit?" Overlap sound of singing over this shot, leading to scene in pub, where Nimmo sees memorial on wall: *Names of the Colliers drowned in Lady Pit, Workington/* (names conclude with: . . . *a boy not known*).

(Singing: "My Bonny Lies Over the Ocean.") Shot of the sea.

Voice with local accent gives contemporary account, while we see costume recreation of what's being read. *The coal was worked . . . 150 yards under the Irish Sea . . . the manager . . . proceeded in a reckless and unguarded manner . . . warning was given of approaching danger by heavy falls of roof accompanied by currents of salt water . . . On 28 July 1837, the whole neighborhood was appalled by the breaking in of the sea . . . 36 men and boys, with as many horses . . . and machinery . . . irrecoverably destroyed . . .* Scene shows inundation, concluding with shot of water lapping silently in pit. (Music.)

"It was in 1940 and 1941, during nights of fire watching, that I began to make a plan . . ." Shots of tin hat, thermos. Nimmo studying charts. Studies fingers while thinking. The sea at night. Nimmo's commentary now explains about "faults," stone breaking through coal, and diagram illustrates this. "Suppose we were to tunnel . . . under the Lady Pit workings . . ." (Music.) "Here you are . . ." Diagram again to illustrate his explanation.

Nimmo dictating a letter in his office (boys' football game goes on outside). *. . . We have decided to reorganize production . . . develop seaward area . . . really go-ahead lines.* Nimmo talks to Cyril (Robinson), his assistant, reads Buddle's notes with him.

"I still had to get the confidence of the men . . ." Miners Association office: *Now, Mr. Stephenson, I'm not satisfied . . . the miners are obsessed with the past . . .* Long response from Stephenson, who sounds somewhat artificial. After Stephenson tells of past problems of miners, intercut with him shots of hunger march in 1934, "Abolition of Means Test" banners, and some other stock shots. (Sad music and marching feet with these.) Further discussion between the two.

In the office, Nimmo and Cyril discuss charts. . . . *gradient 1 in 50, right? . . .* "In May 1941 we began to go for Buddle's Main Band . . ." Surveying, drilling underground. "Next thing . . . a wages agreement . . . I decided to call a meeting . . ." Meeting scene, intercut with a few explanatory cutaways. Nimmo passes round photos of new machines. Very dull set-ups here, head-on. Very long, very dull scene. Slow dolly-in to Stephenson's face, dissolve to reminder shots of Means Test march, music in background.

Another meeting, at the Miners Association, to discuss "day wage." *. . . You fellows are still thinking about the past . . .* At pithead, Stephenson explains to men: *This is a fair wage . . .*

"In the autumn of '42 . . ." Machines are demonstrated at colliery. Intercut CU's of colliers receiving instructions about their handling. Surveying underground. In the office, more discussion with Cyril, underground shots, diagrams again, animated to explain their decision to gamble on direction of shaft drive.

Drilling, blasting, collecting, and chuting coal. CU's of colliers. In the office, studying charts again. Underground drilling and blasting. Office at pithead, call to Nimmo on phone: *They've just struck a fault . . . you're coming over in the morning . . . right . . .*

Underground drilling and blasting. Shaft bottom calls pithead office: *no Main Band . . .* Nimmo told. *What have you got? Sandstone. Tell them to put a hole up . . . I'm sure it's somewhere up there . . .*

Drilling into roof, two men hold the drill. Dust falls on them, gray (sandstone). They change bits twice. Gradually the dust becomes black.

In the office, Nimmo on phone. *Cyril, we've got the Main Band! I think we can give ourselves a pat on the back . . . give Buddle one too!* (Music.)

". . . We were lucky . . . we went straight ahead into the new seam . . ." Underground shots. . . . *It's champion! . . .* Shot of sea. (Music.) Underground working shots.

In the office. ". . . After a few months, production began to drop . . ." Explanation is made that the supply system is too slow for their fast production. Decisions made.

Underground, fast cutting proceeds. A fault is struck. An exploratory blast is fired. Water drips. Men prop up roof. Steady dripping from roof.

In the office. . . . *It's a mussel band . . . we've got through the fault and that's what we found. That means the coal's been thrown up about fifty feet. I'll let Cyril know . . .*

Union meeting. Stephenson makes a speech. *In the past, battles with coal owners tended to divide the miner from the mining engineer . . . now, the miner himself can become a modern craftsman . . . now our battle with the coal owners is ended, and the pits belong to us all . . .*

Underground, coal-cutting and CU's of colliers. Final shot shows dust rolling after blast, obscuring miners. (Soundtrack carries final exhortation of Stephenson, with music . . . *This can be done in every coalfield in the country . . .*)

Fire! Blast explosion. (Music to END.)

DIM LITTLE ISLAND (1949)

Wessex Films for Central Office of Information

11 minutes

Producer/Director: Humphrey Jennings

Asst. Director: Harley Usill

Photography: Martin Curtis

Editor: Bill Megarry

Music: Ralph Vaughan Williams

Commentary: Osbert Lancaster, John Ormston, James Fisher, Ralph Vaughan Williams

Lancaster drawings, the artist reflected in mirror. *Lancaster:* "In ancient times, the licensed fool was allowed to speak while the others held their peace. So perhaps I, as an avowedly comic artist, may be allowed to speak first. The comic artist is the guardian of reality: it is his privilege to remind the public of what they really look like, and to destroy their happy illusions of dignity and beauty . . . There are many other illusions. For instance, the illusion that, compared to the romance and mystery of High Tibet, or the rolling prairies and limitless expanse of the Golden West, Great Britain is rather a dim little island." Men knocking down a factory chimney, outlined against the sky. Drawings. ". . . that, of course, now as always the country is going to the dogs . . ." Shot of rain falling on water, from *A Diary for Timothy.* "Ichabod, Ichabod, thy glory is departed . . ."

Picture: *The Last of England.* "Perhaps you may remember a Victorian painting of emigrants, called *The Last of England.* It was painted in 1852, to us, looking back, a time of optimism, of expansion and the Great Exhibition. But this was not, I fancy, the reality which the departing emigrants observed." Wrought-iron lace against steam-railway station. "To them, England was the land of the twelve-hour day . . . still suffering from the effects of the Hungry Forties . . . its faith undermined by Mr. Darwin . . . Many of these things were indeed realities: the illusion was that they would result in the collapse of Britain . . ."

Shipbuilding scenes. *Ormston:* "The first iron ship in the world was launched from the Tyne in 1852 . . . for nearly a century, British yards were building ships better than other people, cheaper and quicker . . . men were proud to call themselves craftsmen . . ." Unemployed on shore at shipyards. "Then we ran into trouble . . . the introduction of machinery began to take away the skill more and more and we . . . neglected in the altered circumstances to train the apprentices . . . most of our shipyards . . . only started to get busy again under the threat of approaching war." Lacy structures of girders in shipyard. Cut to lacy patterns of reeds and willows.

Fisher: "This is a secret place. Trespassers trespass at their peril. It's called Mindsmere, on the Suffolk coast, a bird reserve managed by the Royal Society for the Protection of Birds." Weeds on assault course barriers. "During the war, it was a protected area of another kind, and where the assault course was laid out, shelducks now rear their broods in peace . . . Wild nature in Britain—what's the use of it? I'll tell you: it's interesting. We learn from it. It's beautiful, and you refresh your souls with it. It's fun—you can take pleasure in it." Man on rock with binoculars, overlooking the ocean. (Music.) "This chap's on the edge of Scotland, 600 miles from London, on the coast by Cape Wrath, the northwest tip of Britain." Tents, rubber boats. "You don't have to go to the Arctic or the tropics to explore. There's still plenty to do in Britain. Human life is withdrawing, receding into nature. The land is slipping back to nature, becoming a wild pleasure-ground, a wild treasure-ground for the enquiring naturalist." Industrial towns. "Here's a contrast: the industry that keeps us alive—it's all over the place. You can't get away from it? Nonsense, of course you can." Shots of Pennine Hills. "For five bob you can get from almost any in-

dustrial city of the North to country like this . . ." (Music ends.)

Panning shots of clouds and of reeds. (Man sings folk song on soundtrack.) *Vaughan Williams:* "Listen to that tune—it's one of our English folk tunes. I knew it first when I was quite a small boy, but I realized even then that here was something not only very beautiful, but which had a special appeal to me as an Englishman." (Tune now orchestrated into a Vaughan Williams orchestral piece, continues under his voice.) Elizabethan engraving, man and lute. "It dates from a time when people, of necessity, made their own music, and when—as has been well said—they made what they liked, and liked what they made. I like to think of our musical life as a great pyramid . . . at the apex our great virtuosi performers and composers of international renown." Shots of organ and Malcolm Sargent with the Halle Choir ". . . then those devoted musical practitioners . . . true artists . . . spreading love of music in our schools . . . our musical festivals . . ." Shots of choir practice. ". . . Next layer, a great mass of musical amateurs . . . As a foundation, we have our great tunes . . ." Music swells and continues under shots of field of corn—panning, shipbuilding—panning, chimneys—photographic still life of mandolin and peaches—four chimneys. "So perhaps we are not so unmusical after all. Nevertheless, our music has lain dormant—a candle that shines like a good deed in a naughty world? Byrd, Purcell, or Arne?" Pictures of them. "And lately the candles have become more numerous . . ." Title pages of works by Elgar, Vaughan Williams, Bax and Britten. "People have come to find . . . a special message in our music which that of other nations cannot give them . . ."

Seashore shot. (Quiet music now continues under commentaries.) *Fisher:* "But it's not all that easy . . . nature's hard to manage . . . We'll sometimes have to ration the fun we can get out of it . . ." Reeds, bird's nest. ". . . If we don't go on learning about it, we'll hurt it . . ."

Shipbuilding. *Ormston:* "But today we can no longer build ships better than Sweden or quicker than the Americans." Quick insert of rain on water again, and *Lancaster* murmurs "Ichabod, Ichabod, our glory is departed." CU shipbuilding operative. *Ormston:* "Have we really lost our touch as shipbuilders? No, I don't think we really have. There's one very big thing in our favor—that we are good sailors, we always have been and we are still." Shots of boys playing on shipbuilding yards. "But we need more work from below and more drive from the top. If we can get supplies, if we don't take things too easily (two very big if's) we can still compete." (Music fades.)

Panning shots of ships in docks, culminating in the discovery of one named *British Genius. Lancaster:* Doubtless, were we a rational race, the spectacle of our present position would overwhelm us . . . We remain deaf to appeals to reason. We're convinced that the experts are invariably wrong. And at Dunkirk, which was the illusion and which the reality?"

Shots of fire ablaze, firemen, from *Fires Were Started. Vaughan Williams:* "So—the fire is ready. Does it require a match to relight it? To set the whole ablaze? Some great upheaval of national consciousness and emotion?" Eliz-

abethan engravings intercut with blitz shots. "The Elizabethans experienced this, and as a result they produced poetry and music that has never been surpassed. Have we not also experienced lately such a national upheaval? And is this not the reason why, during the late war, those who had never taken music seriously before began to crowd our concert halls from Kensington to Harringay to hear the symphony concerts?" Shots of the Promenade Concerts, the Albert Hall, and Harringay Arena. "Today our music, which so long had seemed without life, is being born again." (Organ music.) Beachy Head lighthouse seen from the cliffs.

Lancaster: "Who can talk of an end, when we're scarcely at the beginning?" *The Last of England* under END title.

A FAMILY PORTRAIT (1950)

Wessex Films

25 minutes

Producer: Ian Dalrymple

Director/Script: Humphrey Jennings

Asst. Director: Harley Usill

Photography: Martin Curtis, Bill Pollard

Editor: Stewart McAllister

Music: John Greenwood orchestra conducted by Muir Matheson

Commentary: Michael Goodliffe

Sound Recording: Ken Cameron

Festival of Britain symbol behind titles. Snapshots: a beach crowded with people, Santa Claus at a Christmas tree, a christening (Timothy Jenkins?), blitz damage, crowded beach again.

"We live on a small island. We like to think of ourselves as a family . . . so the Festival of Britain is a kind of family reunion . . . to let the young and the old, the past and the future, meet and discuss . . . to pat ourselves on the back, to give thanks that we still are a family, to voice our hopes and fears, our faith in our children."

Beachy Head, looking down on lighthouse (as in *Dim Little Island*). "Where to begin? Here. This is Beachy Head. There's the Channel, joining and dividing." Old radar station. "That's the remains of a radar station here during the war . . . 'Air Ministry property—Keep Out'."

Drake, engravings of Armada. "When Drake was fighting the Armada—this is part of family history—the Spaniards said he had a magic mirror in his cabin which revealed enemy ships to him. What we should call, marine radar . . ."

Beach. "You could have seen the Armada from here—and the Normans too, over there, the other side of Eastbourne—and the Romans. The fact is, our ancestors nearly all came as invaders. They had to be enterprising chaps and good sailors to do it." Monoliths, probably Avebury Ring. "Early Bronze Age, late Bronze Age, different layers of Celts, shiploads of Jutes, Vikings, and Saxons." Long Man of Wilmington. "Remember Kipling? 'Where the Long Man of Wilmington looks naked to the shires.' Saxon, probably . . ."

Shots of rocks, plains, windmill, mining shots from *The Cumberland Story*. "A very mixed family, as you see. But who, together, have resisted further invasion for nearly a thousand years . . . (music) . . . Then the extraordinary diversity of nature in this small space—

the variety of land structure, the local variation of soil and climate, the wrack of exchanges on the weather front, the jumble of coal and rock underground. It all somehow matches the diversity of Englishmen."

Docks . . . street sign "Bankside." "You can see it in Shakespeare. Today, it's all wharves, warehouses, imports, exports. But the place is still called Bankside. It was here that Shakespeare created Hamlet, Lady Macbeth, and Falstaff." Pub: fat man viewed from window outside, behind word A L E. "'To hold as 't'were a mirror up to nature . . .' Not to catch those gods or heroic figures, but individual people with souls of their own." (Barrel organ music.) Inside pub, man mimes a cello and a flute with a stick and a hatstand. "And the small parts—the comics and hangers-on, all different from each other. As we feel ourselves to be." Falstaffian figure. (Fade out barrel organ.) Docks, Tower Bridge, barges. "As for the wharves and warehouses—we have to eat, don't we? 'Sweet Thames, run softly till I end my song.' You see, for centuries the family has mixed poetry and prose together." (Music, minuet version of The Lambeth Walk.)

Greenwich Observatory, LS London in twilight. "Stand up above the Thames, by the Observatory at Greenwich. There's the great city of trade. Down the river, the sails everywhere of her merchants." MS sailor on deck at night. CU ship's compass as it gently swings. (Music swells up in rhythm.) "We had to learn—we had almost to create—the art and science of navigation. Study the magnetism of the earth, the path of the moon, the position of the stars. We began in a matter-of-fact way, keeping our eyes on the object . . ." Astronomer at eyepiece of telescope. ". . . but at the same time that we were making these observations to help ships find the longitude at sea, we produced Newton . . ." Statue of Newton. ". . . whose genius saw that they in fact described the structure of the universe itself . . ." (Music comes to a climax.) "Today, Greenwich gives a longitude to the world, and her telescope still checks the time on the meridian—if the weather and the smoke permit." Docks, clouds, twilight, St. Paul's in twilight, in silhouette. Chimneys smoking. Woman cleaning mirror. Coal mine.

"The air that blinds the modern astronomer is also the emblem of invention, because something like a quarter of the family live right on top of coal. (Brass band plays faintly.) James Watt statue. "Power for the winning . . ." Coal mine yard. "And again, we needed two sides of the family to meet. James Watt crossing Glasgow Common one Sunday morning suddenly to see a separate condenser in his mind's eye . . ." (Brass band now playing against shot of iron foundry.) "And the skill of a John Wilkinson and the ironmasters of the time, to get a steam-engine made at all. The meeting of scientific imagination and engineering skill—a new kind of poetry and a new kind of prose." Steelmaster in foundry now "conducting" the brass band music on soundtrack, as he makes his working gestures. "In work and play alike, we began to hear the march of the machine." (Music swells.)

Trevethick—drawing of racehorses on track. "And then came Trevethick, building the first locomotive in the world in a Welsh iron foundry, to take the place of horses, and calling one of them 'Catch Me Who Can' and backing it to run against any horse at Newmarket." (Music develops a new "racing" theme from Handel.) "And then Stephenson . . ." Stephenson picture, modern train, horses racing, train, horse-track crowd. Train crosses Forth Bridge. ". . . from Newcastle, saying he could drive a railway straight across Chat Moss, which won't bear the weight of a man . . ." (Music.) "Local lads who used their wits and had a good laugh, and then, like Shakespeare and Newton and Watt, started something at home that went right round the globe."

Viaduct, polluted river, slums, boys playing cricket in the street. "But to be honest, our matter-of-fact way can get the better of us. Problem: as the towns and population grew, the practical gifts never met the imaginative ones, and one part of us lost sight of the other. Rifts in the family we're still having to repair. (Music.) We can only thank heaven we produced a Blake, a Shaftesbury, a Dickens to proclaim love, and health, and life." Modern school—cricket at the Oval under the gasholders. (Music.) "What a mixture of muddle and orderliness, dinginess and open air!"

Oak tree in foreground. Rothamsted. "How to reconcile the farm with the factory? Stand here by the oak. That is the most celebrated strip of farmland in the world—Rawbrook Field, Rothamsted, known in the outback and the mid-west, where we first began to bring the land and the laboratory together. This was in 1843—the hungry forties . . ." Dickens engraving—Oliver Twist. ". . . they were called, and they were the reason for Rothamsted. Every day we had more and more mouths to feed."

BCU picture of Darwin. "And it was now that the mind of Darwin began turning over what the eye had seen in the forests of Brazil and the hedgerows at home . . ." Dolly along row of blossoming trees, dissolve to workers crossing London Bridge. "The minute variations of nature, the hunger of all living things—and began to imagine, to deduce from them the laws of our own origin and being in the struggle for existence."

Shot of garden in Devon, quaint wooden figures. "And in this struggle we are helped—saved, perhaps—by our very paradoxes. So the most eccentric among us can discipline life itself (remember Lewis Carroll and Edward Lear)." TV aerial perched on thatched roof. "So we admire innovations, need and produce them, and also love tradition." Garden. "So we like sitting quietly at home . . ." Trooping the Colour on Horse Guards Parade. (Elgar's "Pomp and Circumstance" on soundtrack.) ". . . and we like pageantry. But then, pageantry in Britain, believe it or not, isn't put on by a sinister power to impress anyone, nor just to have fun. It's part of the pattern of life." Rowers at Cambridge, the Cup Final at Wembley. "The year itself swings round in a pattern of events." (Music swells up.) "The secret is that we created these things ourselves—gradually but, as Milton warned us, not without dust and heat." Durham Miners' Gala. National Union of Mineworkers banner and trophy carried. Banner blows upwards to reveal slagheaps behind it. (An almost indis-

cernible cut seems to have been used.)

Runnymede Memorial, Edinburgh Castle, Houses of Parliament. "The banks of Runnymede, the heights of Edinburgh, the Palace of Westminster itself, were once battlegrounds where the burning ideas of our civilizations were bitterly adapted to the climate at home." Miners, students, local council meeting where the mayor presides, ceremonial mace below him. "We were lucky to learn the trick of voluntary discipline, of dining with the opposition, of calling meetings which would end purposely in compromise." ("Pomp and Circumstance" continues.)

Woman in her rose garden. "But for the most paradoxical thing, compare Britain herself with the rest of the world. No eternal snow, no unending forest or drenching jungle—small and varied and restrained." Shipping and shipbuilding—long dolly shot L-R. (Natural sounds of yards.) "And yet our history has taken us precisely into the vast and violent areas of the globe. Captain Cook going to the South Seas with a new chronometer for guidance, Livingstone taking the Bible from the Falls of Clyde to the Falls of the Zambesi—'the earth is the Lords' and the fullness thereof.' The skill of Sheffield and Swansea and Belfast going the road to Mandalay and Cape Town and Cairo [sound overlap of bagpipes] . . . the crack of the bat heard on the Australian plains . . ." Pipers march R-L. ". . . the skirl of the pipes in Canadian snows—the idea of Parliament itself spreading from the Thames to the Indus and the Ganges." (Pipes crescendo.)

Ocean shot, shipping, Elizabeth I. "Four hundred years ago, Gilbert told the Queen that the earth itself was a great magnet." Memorial to Captain Scott. "We know it's true now. We have been to the poles of the magnet." (Big Ben chimes.) "And all the time the return voyage has brought us back food—and food for machines . . ." Docks, Westminster. ". . . brought us back genius (Rutherford from New Zealand to Manchester and Cambridge) . . . brought us experience and responsibility on a world scale." (Music.) "All this we inherit and celebrate, but we know that the times have changed." Smoke. "Great men have been among us. When we admire a sunset, we are using the eyes of Turner." Picture of Faraday. "When we switch on a light, we are tapping the mind of Faraday . . . But the very genius of Clark Maxwell, Thomson and Rutherford shook the foundations of matter itself . . ."

Viaduct, water, radar screen. "The Elizabethan journey ended with the Battle of Britain. And then, as the battle raged, out of the fragments and tracks of matter, we made the magic mirror that the Spaniards dreaded—radar." Deck of ship, radar. "Using the fundamental research of radio engineers, new navigation. Prose and poetry again were put together in a new way." Nelson's "Victory"—seagull soaring in sky. (Music.)

"At the time of Nelson, Australia was five months' sail from home, but already in 1800 a Yorkshire squire called Caley had written down the laws by which the airplane flies." Shot of Caley's notebooks. Planes, planebuilding, seagull soaring. "And now we, with the turbo-jet and the propellor-turbine, we are talking about making it to Sydney in thirty-six hours, Cape Town in eighteen,

New York nonstop in six. A lot of wealth of family brain and eye and hands are helping us change the world. This is the new Britain. So, in the making of penicillin, biologists, biochemists, crystallographers working together did it. Solitary shade of Caley, look at the teams of designers and draftsmen doing your job today!" Steel press, turbine blades. "Shades of the ironmasters of old, listen to your hammers stamping the steel discs of the jet! The skill that put the first steam-engines together now fits the delicate feathered blades of this . . ." Turbine fitting. Testing an engine, dials, etc. "How eagerly the eyes of Stephenson and Watt would have followed the test of an aero-engine! 14,000 revolutions a minute!" Shot of workman. "Science that spies into the inside of things, the industry that gives them shape: which is the poetry, which is the prose?" "Comet" plane flies over a harrow in the field—Comet—harrow. "The earth is the Lord's and the fullness thereof."

Huge crowd fills screen. "But at the end of all this, no less than half the family are living on food from abroad. At the Norman invasion there were about two million of us. By the defeat of the Armada, five; and by Trafalgar, fifteen. But today there are more than fifty million of us, on the same stretch of land. So we must try and plan the use of the small space we have . . ." Building activities. ". . . where to live, where to work, where to draw power from water as well as coal . . ." Forestry. ". . . where and how to plant new forests, what to preserve, what to exploit." Power lines. Shot of mace. "And learn to compromise again, between one use and another." Horse sale, cows.

"And how does the individual fit into all this? The countryman, for example . . ." Two men walk beneath the Long Man of Wilmington—a farmer and a scientist testing soil. ". . . with his local wisdom, his human doubts of scientists, his sense of the living thing . . ." (Music.) "Can you really treat John Barleycorn as you do the blades of a turbine? Two sides of the family here—farmer and scientist. The farmer learning to trust, the scientist learning to accept, accept the fact that the land varies from yard to yard. Accept the richness and subtlety of nature—not as errors to be corrected, but as part of the truth to be understood. We should pray for these two to agree—our bread and butter depend on it." (Music.)

Avebury Rings, radar telescope at twilight, trees against night sky, radar against half-moon in sky. "But it goes deeper than that. Under the surface of the practical world lies the insatiable curiosity of the human spirit. Tonight, there are new shapes on the skylines of home—the fantastic antennae of modern science, reaching out into the unknown." Interior of observatory, girl picks up film record of radarscope track of meteor, holds it and checks it. "Peacetime versions of radar, picking up radio waves coming in from the blank space of the void, or plotting the tracks of meteors as they rush through the sky. That's a meteor, there." (Music.) Royal Society—mace at Royal Society meeting—radarscope. "But this in turn depends on the exchange of knowledge begun in the days of Newton and Pepys at the meetings of the Royal Society.

And this exchange itself is in danger, for it's not science that tyrannizes, but the pride of man. Tolerance in Britain is linked to the Royal Society's defense of free enquiry. Remember Newton, saying that he felt like a little boy playing on the shore of the great ocean of truth? 'Canst thou bind the sweet influences of the Pleiades, or loose the bands of Orion?' (Music swells.) 'Knowest thou the ordinances of heaven? Canst thou set the dominion thereof in the earth?'" (Music.)

"We were lucky again . . ." Bible, radar, Bible, landscape. "Science began here at the very time of the great translation of the Bible into English." (Music.) Beachy Head. "In the end, most of the family faces look back to Scandinavia, to German, to France. Our ideas, our faith, have their roots in Italy, Greece, Israel. (Music.) Avebury, Bodleian Library in Oxford, girl with radarscope record. "We have just had the knack of putting prose and poetry together."

Beach. The sea. "And now we also belong to a communion across the Atlantic, the South Seas. We are too small, too crowded to stand alone." Liner sails—Parliament, the Speaker's opening procession. "We have become both inside the family of Europe, and the pattern overseas. We are the link between them. For all we have received from them, and from our native land, what can we return? Perhaps the very things that make the family, a pattern, possible—tolerance, courage, faith. A world to be different in—and free—together. (Music.) Blitz snapshot, beach snapshot.

APPENDIX B

SOME OF JENNING'S THEATRICAL ACTIVITIES

At the Perse School, Cambridge

1923 (27 March) — *In the Cellar*—a farce, adapted by F. A. Aldworth. Jennings played "Lady Kidderminster."

The Sultan's Moustachios—a farce by Aldworth and Jennings. Jennings played "Peper-Popp, wife of Ali Baba." (H.J. was one of five people—two masters, three pupils—responsible for the entire concert of plays, skits, and songs.)

1923 (Christmas) — *Chester Miracle Play*—designed costumes, played Noah's wife.

1924 (?) — Designed set for play about St. Simon Stylites.

1925 — Designed *Trial by Jury*.

1926 (?) — (?) Played "Bottom" in Mummery production of *A Midsummer Night's Dream*.

1926 (Christmas) — *Le Théatre des Souris Blanches*—divertissement. (H.J. responsible, with two other pupils.)

1927 (16–17 Dec.) — *The Finding of the King*, a nativity play. H.J. (who had left the Perse) returned to design costumes and décor, and played "The Innkeeper of Bethlehem." Stage manager was his friend Marius Goring.

1928 — H.J., now at Pembroke College, designed a Persean revue, a tribute to the retiring headmaster, W. H. D. Rouse.

At Cambridge

1926 — ADC, *The Christmas Revue*, produced by Frank Birch. H.J. designed, acted, and danced in sketches.

1927 (Feb. 5)   Played in "A Man in a
                  Bowler Hat" in *Drag-
                  ons—A Symbolic Play
                  in Three Scenes,* writ-
                  ten and produced by
                  Basil Wright. Also
                  played "Jack Ketch,
                  the Hangman" in *The
                  Tragedy of Punch,* a
                  "fantastic play" by
                  Russell Thorndyke and
                  Reginald Arkell (ADC
                  Nursery Production).

1927   Marlowe Society,
                  Thomas Heywood's
                  *The Fair Maid of the
                  West,* directed by
                  Dennis Arundell. H.J.
                  designed costumes
                  and played female
                  lead opposite Michael
                  Redgrave.

1927   ADC, A. P. Herbert's
                  At the Same Time.
                  Played "Timothy
                  Spratt."

1928, Feb. 3   New Theatre, Purcell's
                  King Arthur, directed
                  by Dennis Arundell.
                  H.J. designed sets and
                  costumes.

1928, Nov.   ADC, Stravinsky's *The
                  Tale of a Soldier,* di-

rected by Arundell.
H.J. designed cos-
tumes and setting.

1929, May   Cambridge Guildhall,
10–11   Morax/Honegger's
                  King David, directed
                  by Arundell. (Basil
                  Wright played a
                  messenger.)

In London

1929–30,   New Scala Theatre,
Dec.–Jan.   Locke and Gibbons'
                  Cupid and Death, and
                  Purcell's *Dido and
                  Aeneas,* both directed
                  by Arundell. H.J. de-
                  signed sets and
                  costumes.

In Cambridge

1930, March   New Theatre, Euripi-
4–8   des' *The Bacchae.* H.J.
                  designed. (Music by
                  Handel arranged by
                  Arundell.)

1931   New Theatre, Purcell's
                  The Fairy Queen, di-
                  rected by Arundell.
                  H.J. played "Bottom."
                  (James Mason played
                  "Oberon" and stage-
                  managed.)

NOTES

CHAPTER 1

1. Humphrey Jennings, letter to Leonard Amey, n.d., c. 1926.

2. Peter King, conversation with Anthony W. Hodgkinson, 5 April 1979.

3. Mary-Lou Jennings, transcript of interview given to Robert Vas for BBC television program, "Heart of Britain," broadcast in 1970.

4. Ibid.

5. George Pitman (C. Allen Hutt), "Men of Our Time No. 8: Humphrey Jennings," *Our Time* (London, July 1944).

6. Jennings, interviewed by Vas.

7. Marius Goring, "Humphrey Jennings 1907–1950," unpublished essay, c. 1971, p. 2.

8. S. J. D. Mitchell, *Perse: A History of the Perse School 1615–1976* (Cambridge: The Oleander Press, 1976), p. 124. Chapter 2 contains a complete account of Caldwell Cook's work at the Perse.

9. Humphrey Jennings, ed., introduction to *William Shakespeare, "Venus and Adonis": The Quarto of 1593* (Cambridge: The Experiment Press, 1930).

10. Jennings, letter to Amey, n.d., c. 1927.

11. Leonard Amey, statement of 4 April 1979, pp. 1–2.

12. Goring, unpublished essay.

13. Dennis Arundell, conversation with Hodgkinson, 9 April 1979. The ensuing information about the Arundell/Jennings theatrical activities derives from this conversation and from subsequent letters from Arundell of 9 February and 25 April 1980.

14. Gerald Noxon, "How Humphrey Jennings Came to Film," *Film Quarterly* (Winter 1961–62), p. 19.

15. Goring, conversation with Hodgkinson, 13 May 1979.

16. Ibid.

17. Noxon, "How Jennings," p. 21.

18. Julian Trevelyan, *Indigo Days* (London: MacGibbon & Kee), 1957, pp. 17–18.

CHAPTER 2

1. Gerald Noxon, "How Humphrey Jennings Came to Film," *Film Quarterly* (Winter 1961–62), p. 23.

2. *The Motor* (London), 3rd show no., 16 October 1934, p. 551.

3. Noxon, "How Jennings," p. 24.

4. Pat Jackson, conversation with Hodgkinson, 22 April 1979.

5. Basil Wright, conversation with Hodgkinson, 21 March 1979.

6. Noxon, "How Jennings," p. 24.

7. See Alan Wood, *Mr. Rank: A Study of J. Arthur Rank and British Films* (London: Hodder & Stoughton, 1952), p. 77.

8. Ian Dalrymple, letter to Hodgkinson, 24 April 1979.

9. Stuart Legg, letter to James Merralls, 7 February 1957.

10. Alan Lovell and Jim Hillier, *Studies in Documentary* (New York: Viking Press, 1972), p. 66.

11. Sir William Coldstream, conversation with Hodgkinson, 7 March 1979.

12. Noxon, "How Jennings," p. 25.

13. Adrian Cornwell-Clyne, *Colour Cinematography*, 3rd ed. rev. (London: Chapman and Hall), 1951.

14. Ibid., p. 419.

15. Ibid., p. 313. See also Brian Coe, "The Development of Colour Cinematography," *International Encyclopedia of Film* (London: Michael Joseph, 1973), pp. 29–38.

16. Charles H. Dand, "Britain's Screen Poet: Humphrey Jennings's Documentaries Constitute a Unique Film Phenomenon," *Films In Review*, 6, 2 (February 1955), p. 73.

17. "Shell's Robot in Colour," *World Film News* 1, 2 (1936), p. 25.

18. Obituary of Alex Strasser, *Film and Television Technician* (January 1975), p. 10.

19. C. H. Dand, "Colour Film: 'Lubrication by Shell,'" n.d., c. 1936. Copy in Information Department of British Film Institute, London.

20. Humphrey Jennings, "Note on Production," addendum to Dand, "Colour Film."

21. Sleeve notes for Holst's *The Planets*, Los Angeles Philharmonic Orchestra (London: Music for Pleasure Ltd., LP Recording MFP 2014, n.d.).

22. Humphrey Jennings, "Colour Won't Stand Dignity," *World Film News* 3 (June 1936), p. 13.

23. Review of "Dufay Shorts: Beethoven's 'Pastoral' Illustrated: Last of the Schooners," *Today's Cinema*, 5 October 1937, p. 20.

24. Review of "The Farm," *Today's Cinema*, 4 August 1938, p. 6.

25. "Onlooker," "Up and Down the Street," *Today's Cinema*, 19 February 1938, p. 2.

26. Coe, "The Development of Colour Cinematography."

27. Humphrey Jennings, "As I Look," *Poems by Humphrey Jennings* (New York: The Weekend Press, 1951), p. 9.

28. Marius Goring, conversation with Hodgkinson, 13 May 1979.

29. Russell Ferguson, "Dial G.P.O.," *Sight and Sound* (Winter 1938–39), pp. 170–71.

30. Rachael Low, letter to Hodgkinson, 3 April 1979.

CHAPTER 3

1. André Breton, *Les Manifestes du Surréalisme* (Paris: Le Sagittaire, 1955).

2. Ibid.

3. James T. Soby, *Joan Miró* (New York: Museum of Modern Art, 1959).

4. David Sylvester, *Francis Bacon* (New York: Pantheon, 1975), p. 18.

5. Rudolf Arnheim, *Film as Art* (Berkeley: University of California Press, 1957).

6. Source now unknown, but noted by Hodgkinson at the British Film Institute, c. 1954.

7. Marcel Jean and Arpad Mezzei, *The History of Surrealist Painting*, trans. Simon Watson Taylor (New York: Grove Press, 1959), p. 272.

8. William S. Rubin, *Dada, Surrealism, and Their Heritage* (New York: Museum of Modern Art, 1968), p. 216.

9. Paul C. Ray, *The Surrealist Movement in England* (Ithaca, N.Y.: Cornell University Press, 1971), p. 258.

10. Julian Trevelyan, *Indigo Days* (London: MacGibbon & Kee, 1957), p. 25.

11. Jill Craigie, "Humphrey Jennings," *The Tribune* (London) 20 October 1950.

12. Humphrey Jennings, "Who Does That Remind You Of?" *The London Gallery Bulletin* 6, October 1938, p. 22.

13. Jennings, "In Magritte's Paintings," *London Gallery Bulletin*, April 1938, p. 15.

14. Jennings and Gerald Noxon, "Rock Painting and 'La Jeune Peinture,'" *Experiment 7*, Spring 1931, p. 89.

15. Foreword to *Catalogue, Humphrey Jennings, 1907–1950, Memorial Exhibition* (London: Institute of Contemporary Arts, n.d., c. 1951).

16. Kathleen Raine, as quoted in *Catalogue, Humphrey Jennings, 1907–1950*.

17. Ibid.

18. R. Q. McNaughton, interviewed in "Humphrey Jennings—*Berichte über einen englischen Filmmacher*," broadcast by Westdeutsches Fernsehen, Cologne, West Germany, 3 November 1976.

19. Edgar Anstey, interviewed in "Humphrey Jennings," West German television, 3 November 1976.

20. Charles Madge, transcript of interview given to Robert Vas for BBC television in 1970.

21. Humphrey Jennings, *Poems of Humphrey Jennings* (New York: The Weekend Press, 1951), p. 7.

22. Jenny Stein, letter to James Merralls, 28 August 1958.

23. Jennings, *Poems*, p. 9.

24. Ibid., p. 5.

25. Ibid., p. 7.

CHAPTER 4

1. Anthony W. Hodgkinson, "Humphrey Jennings and Mass-Observation: A Conversation with Tom Harrisson," *University Film Association Journal* 27, 4 (1976), p. 33.

2. Compton Mackenzie, *The Windsor Tapestry* (London: The Book Club, 1939), pp. 458–59.

3. David Lampe, *Pyke, The Unknown Genius* (London: Evans Bros., 1959).

4. Geoffrey Pyke, letter ("King and Country") in *The New Statesman and Nation*, 12 December 1936, p. 974.

5. Charles Madge, letter ("Anthropology at Home") in *The New Statesman and Nation*, 2 January 1937, p. 12.

6. Hodgkinson, "Humphrey Jennings."

7. David Gascoyne, conversation with Hodgkinson, June 1978.

8. Tom Harrisson et al., letter ("Anthropology at Home") in *The New Statesman and Nation*, 30 January 1937, p. 155.

9. Madge, "The Birth of Mass-Observation," *The Times Literary Supplement*, 5 November 1976, p. 1395.

10. Mass-Observation, *First Year's Work, 1937–38* (London: Lindsay Drummond, 1938), back cover.

11. Jennings and Madge, eds., *May the Twelfth: Mass-Observation Day Surveys 1937* (London: Faber & Faber, 1937).

12. Ibid., p. x.

13. Ibid., pp. 16–25.

14. Ibid., p. 44.

15. Ibid., p. 46.

16. Ibid., p. 67.

17. Ibid., p. 16.

18. Ibid., p. 85.

19. Ibid., p. 205.

20. Ibid., p. 204.

21. Ibid., p. 349.

22. E. C. Large, "The Coronation Mass-Observed," *The New English Weekly*, 30 December 1937, p. 231.

23. Jennings and Madge, *May the Twelfth*, pp. 413–14. (Emphasis added.)

24. Hodgkinson, "Humphrey Jennings," p. 33.

25. James Agee and Walker Evans, *Let Us Now Praise Famous Men* (Boston: Houghton Mifflin Co.), 1941.

26. Agee and Evans, *Let Us Now Praise*, p. viii.

27. Ibid.

28. See Humphrey Spender, *Worktown: Photographs of Bolton and Blackpool Taken for Mass-Observation 1937–38* (Falmer, Brighton: University of Sussex Press, 1977).

29. Agee and Evans, *Let Us Now Praise*, p. ix.

30. Ibid., p. 13.

31. Harry Watt, *Don't Look at the Camera* (New York: St. Martin's Press, 1974).

32. "E. V. W.," review in *Monthly Film Bulletin* 6, 7 (British Film Institute, July 1939), p. 153.

33. Lindsay Anderson, "Only Connect: Some Aspects of the Work of Humphrey Jennings," *Sight and Sound* (April/May 1954), p. 181 et seq.

34. Alan Lovell and Jim Hillier, *Studies in Documentary* (New York: Viking Press, 1972), p. 71.

35. Basil Wright in John Grierson et al., *Humphrey Jennings 1907–1950: A Tribute* (London: British Film Institute, n.d., c. 1950).

36. Ibid.

37. Richard Kelly, "Tin Whistle Soldiers," *The Guardian*, 2 May 1979, p. 10.

38. Basil Wright, "Humphrey Jennings," *Sight and Sound* (December 1950), p. 311.

39. Elizabeth Sussex, *The Rise and Fall of British Documentary: The Story of the Film Movement Founded by John Grierson* (Berkeley: University of California Press, 1975), p. 159.

CHAPTER 5

1. "British Documentary Activity," *Documentary News Letter* (February 1940), p. 7.

2. Pat Jackson, conversation with Hodgkinson, 21 April 1979.

3. See John Snagge and Michael Barsley, *Those Vintage Years of Radio* (London: Pitman, 1972), p. 179.

4. Harry Watt, *Don't Look at the Camera* (New York: St. Martin's Press, 1974), pp. 128–29.

5. Review in *Documentary News Letter* (January 1940), p. 6.

6. Basil Wright, conversation with Hodgkinson, 21 March 1979.

7. Review in *Documentary News Letter* (December 1940), p. 7.

8. Gerald Noxon, "How Humphrey Jennings Came to Film," *Film Quarterly* (Winter 1961–62), p. 25.

9. Alan Lovell and Jim Hillier, *Studies in Documentary* (New York: Viking Press, 1972), p. 75.

10. Hugh Gray, letter to Hodgkinson, 15 November 1978.

11. Laurie Lee, letter to Hodgkinson, 26 February 1979.

12. Joe Mendoza, conversation with Hodgkinson, 27 February 1979, and subsequent letter of 18 January 1980.

13. Gray, letter to Hodgkinson.

14. Review in *Documentary News Letter* (November 1940), p. 15.

15. Mendoza, conversation with Hodgkinson.

16. See Mass-Observation, *War Factory* (London: Mass-Observation, 1941).

17. Roy Armes, *A Critical History of British Cinema* (New York: Oxford University Press, 1978), p. 153.

18. Watt, *Don't Look*, pp. 138–39. See also Elizabeth Sussex, *The Rise and Fall of British Documentary: The Story of the Film Movement Founded by John Grierson* (Berkeley: University of California Press, 1975), pp. 125–26.

19. Watt, *Don't Look*, p. 141.

20. Sussex, *The Rise and Fall*, p. 128.

21. Ian Dalrymple, letter to James Merralls, 25 January 1957.

22. Tom Harrisson, *Living through the Blitz* (London: Collins, 1976), p. 86.

23. Review in *Documentary News Letter* (November 1940), p. 14.

24. Norman Longmate, *How We Lived Then: A History of Everyday Life during the Second World War* (London: Arrow Books, 1973), p. 432.

25. Watt, *Don't Look*, p. 140.

26. Quentin Reynolds, *Britain Can Take It: The Book of the Film* (London: John Murray, 1941).

27. Watt, *Don't Look*, p. 140.

28. Sussex, *The Rise and Fall*, p. 128.

29. Review in *Documentary News Letter* (March 1941), p. 48.

30. Ken Cameron, conversation with Hodgkinson, 7 March 1979.

31. Mendoza, conversation with Hodgkinson. (Most of the subsequent information about *Words for Battle* and *Listen to Britain* comes from this source.)

32. Humphrey Jennings, "National Gallery 1941," treatment, Crown Film Unit, 28 April 1941.

33. Jennings, "The Music of War," treatment, Crown Film Unit, 23 May 1941.

34. Mendoza, conversation with Hodgkinson.

35. Sussex, *The Rise and Fall*, p. 146.

36. "Film of the Month: *Fires Were Started*," *Documentary News Letter* 4 (1943), p. 200.

37. Daniel Millar, "Fires Were Started," *Sight and Sound* (Spring 1969), p. 100.

38. Nora Lee, transcript of interview given to Robert Vas for BBC television program in 1970.

39. William Sansom, "The Making of *Fires Were Started*," *Film Quarterly* (Winter 1961/62), p. 27.

40. Ibid., p. 28.

41. Ibid., p. 29.

42. Fred Griffiths, recording of speech made at National Film Theatre, London, 5 May 1954. (Original with National Film Archive, England).

43. Millar, "Fires Were Started," p. 102.

44. Lovell and Hillier, *Studies in Documentary*, pp. 90−98.

45. Eric Rhode, *Tower of Babel: Speculations on the Cinema* (London: Weidenfeld & Nicolson, 1966), p. 77.

46. Sansom, "The Making of *Fires*," p. 28.

47. Griffiths, interview with Vas.

48. Lee, interview with Vas.

49. Sansom, "The Making of *Fires*," pp. 28−29.

50. Gavin Lambert, "Jennings' Britain," *Sight and Sound* (May 1951), p. 25.

51. Erik Barnouw, *Documentary: A History of the Non-Fiction Film* (New York: Oxford University Press, 1974), p. 147.

52. Millar, "Fires Were Started," pp. 102, 104.

53. Noel Joseph, *The Silent Village: A Story of Wales—and Lidice* (London: The Pilot Press, 1943), p. 2.

54. Diana Pine, conversation with Hodgkinson, 24 April 1979.

55. Lovell and Hillier, *Studies in Documentary*, p. 102.
56. Nora Lee and Pat Jackson, conversation with Hodgkinson, 21 April 1979.
57. Ibid.
58. Lee, letter to Hodgkinson, 27 February 1980.
59. Adrian de Potier, letter to Hodgkinson, 8 April 1980.
60. de Potier, conversation with Hodgkinson, 26 January 1979.
61. Lovell and Hillier, *Studies in Documentary*, p. 104.
62. Pine, interview with Vas.
63. Betty Jenkins, interview with Vas.
64. Wright, conversation with Hodgkinson.
65. Basil Wright, *The Long View* (London: Secker & Warburg, 1974), p. 202.
66. Wright, conversation with Hodgkinson.
67. Wright, *The Long View*, fn. to p. 202.
68. Lindsay Anderson, "Only Connect: Some Aspects of the Work of Humphrey Jennings," *Sight and Sound* (April/May 1954), p. 181 *et seq.*
69. Lambert, "Jennings' Britain," p. 26.
70. Rhode, *Tower of Babel*, p. 80.
71. Evan Cameron, *An Analysis of "A Diary for Timothy": Cinema Studies No. 1* (Bridgewater, Mass.: The Experiment Press, Spring 1967).
72. Introduction to *King's College Chapel: A Festival of Nine Lessons and Carols on Christmas Eve MCMLXXVIII* (Cambridge: Cambridge University Press 1978), p. 2.

CHAPTER 6

1. Basil Wright, conversation with Anthony W. Hodgkinson, 21 March 1979.
2. Alan Lovell and Jim Hillier, *Studies in Documentary* (New York: Viking Press, 1972), p. 112.
3. See Elizabeth Sussex, *The Rise and Fall of British Documentary: The Story of the Film Movement Founded by John Grierson* (Berkeley: University of California Press, 1975), p. 169.
4. Wright, conversation with Hodgkinson, 21 March 1979.
5. Transcript of interview given to Robert Vas for television program "Heart of Britain," broadcast in 1970 by the BBC.
6. Eric Rhode, *Tower of Babel: Speculations on the Cinema* (London: Weidenfeld & Nicolson, 1966), pp. 71–72.
7. Edgar Anstey, telephone conversation with Hodgkinson, 21 April 1979, and subsequent letter of 29 January 1980.
8. Ian Dalrymple, letter to James Merralls, 18 July 1959.
9. Diana Pine, conversation with Hodgkinson, 23 April 1979.
10. Stephen Watts, review of *The Purple Plain*, *Sunday Chronicle* (London, 19 September 1954).
11. Television program, "Humphrey Jennings—*Berichte über einen englischen Filmmacher*," produced by Westdeutsches Fernsehen, Cologne, W. Germany, 3 November 1976.

12. Dalrymple, conversation with Hodgkinson, 20 March 1979.

13. Julian Trevelyan, conversation with Hodgkinson, 14 June 1978.

14. Dalrymple, conversation with Hodgkinson, 20 March 1979.

15. Lovell and Hillier, *Studies in Documentary*, p. 110.

16. Ibid., p. 115.

17. Dalrymple, conversation with Hodgkinson, 20 March 1979.

CHAPTER 7

1. Humphrey Jennings, "Working Sketches of an Orchestra," in Hubert Foss and Noel Goodwin, *London Symphony Orchestra: Portrait of an Orchestra* (London: The Naldrett Press, 1954), pp. 210–52. (This book is long out-of-print; an abridged version of the Jennings material can be found in *Film Quarterly* (Winter 1961–62), pp. 12–18.

2. Geoffrey Keynes, ed., *Blake, Complete Writings with Variant Readings* (London: Oxford University Press, 1969), p. 457.

3. Ibid., p. 149.

4. Hannah Arendt, introduction to Walter Benjamin, *Illuminations* (New York: Harcourt Brace and World, 1968), p. 47.

5. Ibid., p. 4.

6. Christopher Harvie et al., eds., *Industrialization and Culture 1830–1914* (London: Macmillan, for the Open University, 1970).

7. W. H. D. Rouse, *Machines or Mind? An Introduction to the Loeb Classical Library* (London: Wm. Heinemann, n.d., c. 1920).

8. Ibid.

9. Ibid.

10. Ibid.

11. Ibid.

12. Ian Dalrymple, conversation with Hodgkinson, 20 March 1979.

13. See James Merralls, ""Humphrey Jennings: A Biographical Sketch," *Film Quarterly* (Winter 1961–62), p. 34.

14. Dalrymple, "Humphrey Jennings, O.B.E.: A Tribute," *British Film Academy Quarterly* 11 (January 1951), p. 3.

CHAPTER 8

1. S. J. D. Mitchell, *Perse: A History of the Perse School 1615–1975* (Cambridge: The Oleander Press, 1976), p. 89.

2. Kathleen Raine, quoted in *Catalogue, Humphrey Jennings 1907–1950, Memorial Exhibition* (London: Institute of Contemporary Arts, n.d., c. 1951).

3. Transcript of television program "Timothy's Second Diary," broadcast 7 September 1960 by Granada Television Ltd.

4. Jennifer Selway, "The Week in View," *The Observer* (London), 21 June 1981, p. 44.

5. See Eric Rickman, "Gladiateur and the Jennings [sic]," *The British Racehorse*, July 1965, pp. 176–83.

6. "Notes on Contributors," *Contemporary Poetry and Prose* 2 (June 1936).

7. Stuart Legg, transcript of interview given to Robert Vas for BBC television program "Heart of Britain," broadcast in 1970.

8. Bernard Coulson, conversation with Hodgkinson, 21 April 1979.

9. Joe Mendoza, conversation with Hodgkinson, 27 February 1979.

10. See Alan Lovell and Jim Hillier, *Studies in Documentary* (New York: Viking Press, 1972), p. 116.

11. Philip Strick, "Great Films of the Century No. 11—*Fires Were Started*," *Films and Filming* 7, 8 (May 1961), p. 16.

12. Lindsay Anderson, "Only Connect: Some Aspects of the Work of Humphrey Jennings," *Sight and Sound* (April/May 1954), p. 181 et seq.

13. Anderson, transcript of interview given to Vas.

14. Anderson, letter to Hodgkinson, 25 January 1980.

15. Julian Trevelyan, conversation with Hodgkinson, 14 June 1978.

16. Gerald Noxon, "How Humphrey Jennings Came to Film," *Film Quarterly* (Winter 1961–62), p. 25.

17. David Gascoyne, conversation with Hodgkinson, 19 June 1978.

18. See Humphrey Spender, *Worktown: Photographs of Bolton and Blackpool Taken for Mass-Observation 1937–38* (Brighton: University of Sussex Press), 1977.

19. Richard Sennett, *The Fall of Public Man* (New York: Alfred A. Knopf, 1977), p. 222.

20. Anderson, interview given to Vas.

21. See Arthur Unger, "American TV—through a British Critic's Eyes," *The Christian Science Monitor*, 27 March 1981, p. 19.

22. Marius Goring, interview given to Vas.

23. Anderson, "Only Connect."

24. Richard M. Barsam, *Non-Fiction Film: A Critical History* (London: George Allen & Unwin, 1974), p. 68.

25. Fred Griffiths, interview given to Vas.

26. Nora Lee, conversation with Hodgkinson, 21 April 1979.

27. Bill Megarry, conversation with Hodgkinson, 11 April 1979.

28. Lee, conversation with Hodgkinson.

29. J. Bronowski, "Recollections of Humphrey Jennings," *The Twentieth Century* (January 1959), p. 48.

30. Diana Pine, conversation with Hodgkinson, 23 April 1979.

31. Pat Jackson, conversation with Hodgkinson, 21 April 1979.

32. Bronowski, letter in *The Twentieth Century*, February 1959.

33. Lee, conversation with Hodgkinson.

34. W. B. Pollard, conversation with Hodgkinson, 17 April 1979.

35. Betty Jenkins, transcript of interview with Vas.

36. Fred Griffiths, recording of speech at National Film Theatre, London, 5 May 1954.

37. See Lovell and Hillier, *Studies in Documentary*, p. 115.

38. Diana Pine, transcript of interview with Vas.

39. Adrian de Potier, conversation with Hodgkinson.

40. Edgar Anstey, interviewed in "Humphrey Jennings—*Berichte über einen englischen Filmmacher*," television program broadcast by Westdeutsches Fernsehen, Cologne, West Germany, 3 November 1976.

41. Humphrey Jennings, "The Theatre Today," *The Arts Today* (1935), p. 213.

42. Kathleen Raine, introduction to *Poems of Humphrey Jennings* (New York: The Weekend Press, 1951).

43. Lovell and Hillier, *Studies in Documentary*, pp. 65–66.

44. Eric Rhode, *Tower of Babel: Speculations on the Cinema* (London: Weidenfeld & Nicolson, 1966), p. 77.

45. Charles Madge, letter to James Merralls, 26 September 1957.

46. Howard Ferguson, conversation with Hodgkinson, 28 March 1979.

47. Goring, interview with Vas.

48. Charlotte Arnell, interviewed for West German TV program "Humphrey Jennings."

49. George Steiner, *On Difficulty and Other Essays* (New York: Oxford University Press, 1978), p. 21.

BIBLIOGRAPHY

BOOKS

Agee, James, and Evans, Walker. *Let Us Now Praise Famous Men*. Boston: Houghton Mifflin, 1941.

Armes, Roy. *A Critical History of British Cinema*. New York: Oxford University Press, 1978.

Arnheim, Rudolf. *Film as Art*. Berkeley: University of California Press, 1957.

Barnouw, Erik. *Documentary: A History of the Non-Fiction Film*. New York: Oxford University Press, 1974.

Barsam, Richard M. *Non-Fiction Film: A Critical History*. London: George Allen & Unwin, 1974.

Beacock, Derrick. *Play Way English for Today*. London: Nelson, 1943.

Belmans, Jacques. *Humphrey Jennings*. Paris: Anthologie du Cinema, 1970.

Breton, André. *Les Manifestes du Surréalisme*. Paris: Le Sagittaire, 1955.

Cornwall-Clyne, Adrian. *Colour Cinematography*. 3rd ed., rev. London: Chapman and Hall, 1951.

Erben, Walter. *Joan Miró*. Translated by Michael Bullock. New York: George Braziller, 1959.

Haftmann, Werner. *Painting in the Twentieth Century*. New York: Frederick A. Praeger, 1965.

Harrisson, Tom. *Living through the Blitz*. London: Collins, 1976.

Jean, Marcel, and Mezzei, Arpad. *The History of Surrealist Painting*. Translated by Simon Watson Taylor. New York: Grove Press, 1959.

Jennings, Humphrey, and Madge, Charles, eds. *May the Twelfth: Mass-Observation Day Surveys 1937*. London: Faber & Faber, 1937.

Jennings, Mary-Lou, ed. *Humphrey Jennings: Film-Maker, Painter, Poet*. London: British Film Institute in association with Riverside Studios, 1982.

Keynes, Geoffrey, ed. *Blake, Complete Writings with Variant Readings*. London: Oxford University Press, 1969.

Lampe, David. *Pyke, The Unknown Genius*. London: Evans Bros., 1959.

Longmate, Norman. *How We Lived Then: A History of Everyday Life during the Second World War*. London: Arrow Books, 1973.

Lovell, Alan, and Hillier, Jim. *Studies in Documentary*. New York: Viking Press, 1972.

Mackenzie, Compton. *The Windsor Tapestry*. London: The Book Club, 1939.

Manvell, Roger, ed. *International Encyclopaedia of Film*. London: Michael Joseph, 1973.

Mass-Observation. *First Year's Work 1937–38*. London: Lindsay Drummond, 1938.

———. *War Factory*. London: Mass-Observation, 1941.

Matthews, J. H. *Surrealism and Film*. Ann Arbor: University of Michigan Press, 1971.

Mitchell, S. J. D. *Perse: A History of the Perse School 1615–1976*. Cambridge: The Oleander Press, 1976.

Raine, Kathleen. *Defending Ancient Springs*. London: Oxford University Press, 1967.

———. *The Land Unknown*. London: Hamish Hamilton, 1975.

Ray, Paul C. *The Surrealist Movement in England*. Ithaca: Cornell University Press, 1971.

Read, Herbert, ed. *Surrealism*. London: Faber & Faber, 1936.

Rhode, Eric. *Tower of Babel: Speculations on the Cinema*. London: Weidenfeld & Nicolson, 1966.

Rubin, William S. *Dada, Surrealism, and Their Heritage*. New York: Museum of Modern Art, 1968.

Sennett, Richard. *The Fall of Public Man*. New York: Alfred A. Knopf, 1977.

Snagge, John, and Barsley, Michael. *Those Vintage Years of Radio*. London: Pitman, 1972.

Soby, James T. *Joan Miró*. New York: Museum of Modern Art, 1959.

Steiner, George. *On Difficulty and Other Essays*. New York: Oxford University Press, 1978.

Sussex, Elizabeth. *The Rise and Fall of British Documentary: The Story of the Film Movement Founded by John Grierson*. Berkeley: University of California Press, 1975.

Sylvester, David. *Francis Bacon*. New York: Pantheon Books, 1975.

Trevelyan, Julian. *Indigo Days*. London: MacGibbon & Kee, 1957.

Watt, Harry. *Don't Look at The Camera*. New York: St. Martin's Press, 1974.

Wood, Alan. *Mr. Rank: A Study of J. Arthur Rank and British Films*. London: Hodder & Stoughton, 1952.

Wright, Basil. *The Long View*. London: Secker & Warburg, 1974.

BOOKLETS AND PAMPHLETS

Cambridge University. *Cambridge Colleges*. Sevenoaks, Kent: J. Salmon, n.d.

———. *King's College Chapel: A Festival of Nine Lessons and Carols on Christmas Eve MCMLXXVIII*. Cambridge: Cambridge University Press, 1978.

Cameron, Evan. *An Analysis of "A Diary for Timothy": Cinema Studies No. 1.* Bridgewater, Mass.: The Experiment Press, 1967.

Cook, Caldwell. *Littleman's Book of Courtesy.* Cambridge: The Perse School, 1914.

Grierson, John et al. *Humphrey Jennings 1907–1950: A Tribute.* London: British Film Institute, n.d., c. 1951.

Harvie, Christopher et al., eds. *Industrialization and Culture 1830–1914.* London: Macmillan, for The Open University, 1970.

Jennings, Humphrey, ed. *William Shakespeare, "Venus and Adonis": The Quarto of 1593.* Cambridge: Experiment Press, 1930.

Jennings, Humphrey, and Gascoyne, David, trans. *Remove Your Hat: Twenty Poems by B. Peret (With a Note by Paul Eluard).* London: Contemporary Poetry and Prose Editions No. 1, 1936.

———. *Poems by Humphrey Jennings.* New York: The Weekend Press, 1951.

Joseph, Noel. *The Silent Village: A Story of Wales—and Lidice.* London: Pilot Press, 1943.

Lovell, Alan. *Study Unit 11—Humphrey Jennings.* London: British Film Institute, 1969.

Madge, Charles et al. *Catalogue of Paintings by Humphrey Jennings: Memorial Exhibition.* London: Institute of Contemporary Art, n.d., c. 1951.

Overbury, Sir Thomas. *A Fair and Happy Milkmaid.* Illustrated by Humphrey Jennings. London: The Glebe Press, 1927.

The Perse Players. *Programme for "The Finding of the King."* Cambridge: The Perse School, 1927.

Reynolds, Quentin. *Britain Can Take It: The Book of the Film.* London: John Murray, 1941.

Rouse, W. H. D. *Machines or Mind? An Introduction to the Loeb Classical Library.* London: Wm. Heinemann, n.d., c. 1920.

Spender, Humphrey. *Worktown: Photographs of Bolton and Blackpool Taken for Mass Observation 1937–38.* Brighton: University of Sussex Press, 1977.

St. Andrew Church. *St. Andrew, Walberswick: History of the Church.* Walberswick, Suffolk: Twelfth Edition, 1978.

ARTICLES, REVIEWS, NEWS ITEMS, AND PUBLISHED LETTERS

Anderson, Lindsay. "Only Connect: Some Aspects of the Work of Humphrey Jennings." *Sight and Sound,* April/May 1954, p. 181 et seq.

British Film Institute. "Films and Scientific Research—A Report on the Paris Scientific Film Congress." *Sight and Sound,* Winter 1936, p. 164.

Bronowski, J. "Recollections of Humphrey Jennings." *The Twentieth Century,* January 1959, pp. 44–50.

———. Letter to the editor. *The Twentieth Century,* February 1959.

Coe, Brian. "The Development of Colour Cinematography." *International Encyclopaedia of Film,* 1973, pp. 29–38.

Contemporary Poetry and Prose. "Notes on Contributors." *Contemporary Poetry and Prose* 2, June 1936.

Craigie, Jill. "Humphrey Jennings." *The Tribune*, October 20, 1950.

Dalrymple, Ian. "Humphrey Jennings O.B.E.: A Tribute." *British Film Academy Quarterly* 11, January 1951, pp. 2–3.

Dand, C. H., and H. J., "Colour Film: 'Lubrication by Shell.'" n.d., c. 1936. Copy in Information Department, British Film Institute.

———. "Britain's Screen Poet." *Films in Review* 6, no. 2, February 1955, p. 73.

Documentary News Letter. "The First Days." *Documentary News Letter*, January 1940, p. 6.

———. "British Documentary Activity." *Documentary News Letter*, February 1940, p. 7.

———. "London Can Take It!" *Documentary News Letter*, November 1940, pp. 6–7, 14.

———. "Welfare of the Workers." *Documentary News Letter*, November 1940, p. 15.

———. "Spring Offensive." *Documentary News Letter*, December 1940, p. 7.

———. "Heart of Britain." *Documentary News Letter*, March 1941, p. 48.

———. "Words for Battle." *Documentary News Letter*, May 1941, p. 89.

———. "Film of the Month—*Fires Were Started*." *Documentary News Letter* 4, 1943, p. 200.

———. "The Silent Village." *Documentary News Letter* 5, 1943, p. 216.

———. "A Diary for Timothy." *Documentary News Letter* 6, 1946, p. 9.

"A.F." Review of *Listen to Britain*. *Motion Picture Herald*, September 14, 1942.

Ferguson, Russell. "Dial G.P.O." *Sight and Sound*, Winter 1938/9, pp. 170–72.

Film and Television Technician. Obituary of Alex Strasser. *Film and Television Technician*, January 1975, p. 10.

Harrisson, Tom et al. Letter to the editor, "Anthropology At Home." *The New Statesman and Nation*, January 30, 1937, p. 155.

Haworth-Booth, Mark. "E. McKnight Kauffer." *The Penrose Annual*, 1971, pp. 83–96.

Hodgkinson, Anthony W. "Humphrey Jennings and Mass-Observation: A Conversation with Tom Harrisson." *University Film Association Journal* 27, no. 4, 1976, pp. 31–34.

"F. H. J." "The First Day At Cambridge." *The Player Magazine* 2, no. 1, 1923, pp. 4–5.

———. "A Lament." *Player Magazine* 2, p. 17.

———. "Pugnastics: An Operetta." *Player Magazine* 2, pp. 7–8.

———. "The Scarecrow." *Player Magazine* 2, p. 16.

———. "The Tie-Pin: A Scholastic Tragedy." *Player Magazine* 2, pp. 11–13.

————. "Scholastic Stoicism: A Ballade." *The Player Magazine* 3, no. 1, 1924, pp. 4–5.

————. "Song from the Sick Room." *Player Magazine* 3, pp. 15–16.

————. "Walberswick." *The Pelican*, July 1924.

Jennings, Humphrey. "King Arthur." *The Cambridge Review* 49, no. 1206, February 10, 1928, pp. 233–34.

————. "Design and the Theatre." *Experiment* 1, November 1928, pp. 13–16.

————. "Odd Thoughts at the Fitzwilliam." *Experiment* 2, February 1929, pp. 13–15.

————. "Notes on Marvell 'To His Coy Mistress.'" *Experiment* 5, February 1930, pp. 14–19.

————. "The Theatre Today." *The Arts Today*, 1935, p. 213 et seq.

————. "Colour Won't Stand Dignity." *World Film News* 3, June 1936, p. 13.

————. "Three Reports." *Contemporary Poetry and Prose* 2, June 1936, pp. 39–41.

————. "Reports." *Contemporary Poetry and Prose* 4/5, August/September 1936, pp. 94–95.

————. "Study for a Long Report: 'The Boyhood of Byron,'" *Contemporary Poetry and Prose* 8, December 1936, pp. 146–47.

————. "Review of *Surrealism*, Herbert Read, ed." *Contemporary Poetry of Prose* 8, December 1936, pp. 167–68.

————. "In Magritte's Paintings." *London Gallery Bulletin*, April 1938, p. 15.

————. "Who Does That Remind You Of?" *The London Bulletin* 6, October 1938, pp. 21–22.

————. "Working Sketches of an Orchestra." *London Symphony Orchestra: Portrait of an Orchestra*. Hubert Foss and Noel Goodwin, eds. London: The Naldrett Press, 1954, pp. 210–52.

————, and Noxon, Gerald. "Rock Painting and 'La Jeune Peinture.'" *Experiment* 7, Spring 1931, pp. 34–40.

Kelly, Richard. "Tin Whistle Soldiers." *The Guardian*, May 2, 1979, pp. 24–26.

Kinematograph Weekly. "Naval Review at Spithead to be Shot in . . . Dufaycolour." *Kinematograph Weekly*, May 20, 1937, p. 3.

————. "Three Dufaycolour Shorts." *Kinematograph Weekly*, October 7, 1937, p. 38.

Lambert, Gavin. "Jennings' Britain." *Sight and Sound*, May 1951, pp. 24–26.

Large, E. C. "The Coronation Mass-Observed." *The New English Weekly*, December 30, 1937, p. 231.

Madge, Charles. Letter to the editor, "Anthropology at Home." *The New Statesman and Nation*, January 2, 1937, p. 12.

————. "The Birth of Mass-Observation." *The Times Literary Supplement*, November 5, 1976, p. 1395.

Merralls, James. "Humphrey Jennings: A Biographical Sketch." *Film Quarterly*, Winter 1961/62, p. 34 et seq.

Millar, Daniel. "Fires Were Started." *Sight and Sound*, Spring 1969, p. 100 et seq.

The Motor. News item. *The Motor*, Third Show Number, October 16, 1934, p. 551.

Noxon, Gerald. "How Humphrey Jennings Came to Film." *Film Quarterly*, Winter 1961/2, pp. 19–26.

"Onlooker." "Up and Down the Street." *Today's Cinema*, February 19, 1938, p. 2.

The Perse School. "Perse Players." *The Pelican*. March 1923.

———. Reference to Humphrey Jennings. *The Old Persean Society Chronicle*, October 1977, p. 17.

Pitman, George. "Men of Our Time No. 8: Humphrey Jennings." *Our Time*, July 1944.

Pyke, Geoffrey. Letter to the editor, "King and Country." *The New Statesman and Nation*, December 12, 1936, p. 974.

Rickman, Eric. "Gladiateur and the Jennings." *The British Racehorse*, July 1965, pp. 176–83.

Sansom, William. "The Making of *Fires Were Started*." *Film Quarterly*, Winter 1961/2, p. 27 et seq.

Selway, Jennifer. "The Week in View." *The Observer*, June 21, 1981, p. 44.

Sheratsky, Rodney. "Humphrey Jennings: Artist of the British Documentary." *Film Library Quarterly* 8, nos. 3/4, 1975, pp. 6–39, 49–64.

Strasser, Alex. "Must Colour Follow Nature." *World Film News* 1, April 1936, p. 5.

Strick, Philip. "Great Films of the Century No. 11—*Fires Were Started*." *Films and Filming* 7, no. 8, May 1961, pp. 14–16, 35, 39.

Today's Cinema. "Dufay Shorts: Beethoven's 'Pastoral' Illustrated: Last of the Schooners." *Today's Cinema*, October 5, 1937, p. 20.

———. Review of "The Farm." *Today's Cinema*, August 4, 1938, p. 6.

Unger, Arthur. "American TV—through a British Critic's Eyes." *The Christian Science Monitor*, March 27, 1981, p. 19.

Vedres, Nicole. "A Memoir." *Sight and Sound*, May 1951, p. 24.

"E.V.W." Review of *Spare Time*. *Monthly Film Bulletin*, July 1939, p. 153.

Watts, Stephen. Review of *The Purple Plain*. *Sunday Chronicle*, September 19, 1954.

World Film News. "Gasparcolour Experts at Work." *World Film News* 1, no. 2, 1936, p. 13.

———. "Shell's Robot in Colour." *World Film News* 1, no. 2, p. 25.

Wright, Basil. "Humphrey Jennings." *Sight and Sound*, December 1950, p. 311.

Wyeth, Peter, and Macpherson, Don. "The Third Front." *Sight and Sound*, Summer 1978, pp. 143–44.

UNPUBLISHED MANUSCRIPTS AND LETTERS

Amey, Leonard. Statement of April 4, 1979.

British Broadcasting Corp. Transcripts of interviews given to Robert Vas for television program "Heart of Britain," broadcast by the BBC in 1970. In Information Dept. of British Film Institute, London.

Goring, Marius. "Humphrey Jennings 1907–1950." Unpublished essay, c. 1971.

Granada Television Ltd. "Timothy's Second Diary." Unpublished script of program broadcast September 7, 1960.

Jennings, Humphrey. Letters to Leonard Amey. n.d., c. 1926–28.

———. "National Gallery 1941." Treatment, Crown Film Unit, April 28, 1941.

———. "The Music of War." Treatment, with annotations by Stewart Mac-Allister, Crown Film Unit, May 23, 1941.

MISCELLANEOUS

Griffiths, Fred. Recording of speech made at National Film Theatre, May 1954. Original with National Film Archive, Berkhamsted, England.

Music for Pleasure, Ltd. Sleeve Notes for Holst's *The Planets*. Los Angeles Philharmonic Orchestra, LP recording MFP 2014.

Westdeutsches Fernsehen. "Humphrey Jennings—*Berichte über einen englischen Filmmacher*." Videotape of program broadcast Nov. 3, 1976, Cologne, West Germany.

INDEX